Deidre Sanders was [...]
Harrow County Grammar School and Sheffield
University. She first worked for *Medical News*,
the *Sun* newspaper and *Nova* magazine. After
travelling for a year in the West Indies and South
America with her husband, she worked on the
Sunday Times and *Woman's Own*, where she
edited the 'At Your Service' column, was
Consumer Journalist of the Year and was
awarded a Jubilee Medal.

Deidre Sanders is now the problem-page editor
for the *Sun*, and appears regularly on radio and
television. She is a member of the British
Association for Counselling and the British
Society for Research on Sex Education. After the
highly successful WOMAN REPORT ON LOVE AND
SEX she was commissioned by *Woman* to create a
survey of the sexual and emotional responses of
men.

Also by Deidre Sanders in Sphere Books

THE *WOMAN* BOOK OF LOVE AND SEX

The Woman Report on Men

Deidre Sanders

Research consultant: Anne Rigg

SPHERE BOOKS LIMITED

Sphere Books Limited, 27 Wrights Lane, London W8 5TZ
First published in Great Britain by Sphere Books Ltd 1987
Text copyright © 1987 Deidre Sanders
Survey copyright © 1985 IPC Magazines Ltd

Illustrations and diagrams by Isla Woiwod

TRADE
MARK

Set in 9/10½ pt Compugraphic English Times

Printed and bound in Great Britain by
Cox & Wyman Ltd, Reading

This book is dedicated to the 5,000 men who took part in the survey. Thank you.

Acknowledgements

Above all I thank Anne Rigg, research consultant for this survey and joint director of The Business Research Unit, whose expertise, advice and personal enthusiasm made the whole project feasible.

Thank you to Richard Barber, editor of *Woman*, whose interest and backing for the project made it possible.

I am very grateful to many others who made a valuable contribution: Anne–Marie Sapsted, of *Woman* magazine, who advised us through the early stages; psychologist Sue Martin who screened and coded all the questionnaires; Anne Dickson who originally shook up some of my preconceptions; Margaret Eaton, Yvonne Hammond, Cathy Aird (in Australia) and Janet Gunns (in Canada) who all helped with research; and Simone Waldock whose fingers flew typing out the volumes of research and manuscript. Thanks to Kaye Wellings, research officer of the Family Planning Association, Dr John Bancroft of the Medical Research Council Reproductive Biology Unit, Stephen Sanders, then Information Officer of the National Marriage Guidance Council, and Peter Watsen, who all kindly found time to read and comment on the completed manuscript.

Thank you to the man in my life for putting up with me, to my daughter for putting up with this rival for my attention, and to Jeannie Sperry, my domestic life-support system.

Contents

1 Introduction:
Love and sex – the man's view

T his is the first time that there has been a large-scale, carefully conducted survey of British men and their feelings
about and experiences of sex and relationships. Five thousand
men took part in this survey: labourers and lorry drivers, teachers and telephone operators, clerks and construction workers.
This survey does not just represent the views of a narrow section
of the articulate, but of men in all walks of life, from all over the
country, who hold all sorts of differing opinions.

It is supposed to be a man's world, but that is not true of public
discussions of emotional and sexual relationships. Here women
have generally held the floor. That is not because they have
necessarily wanted to, but because such subjects are often seen as
'women's subjects'. Suggest an article connected with 'relationships' at a newspaper editoral conference and it will be assigned
to the women's page. Where are any men's magazines covering
those areas of life rather than work, politics, cars and pornography – the answer is they are inserts in women's magazines.
Television researchers comb the country for men willing to talk
on programmes covering subjects such as infertility – equally a
male problem – but often in vain, so we usually end up hearing
what women feel.

This does not mean that men do not care about the quality of
their emotional and sexual relationships, do not feel hurt as
deeply as women do. Men are raised, by and large, to keep their
feelings more carefully screened from the public gaze than
women, to see such discussions as being ones which should be
kept private between a couple – but this does not make their
emotions any the less intense.

We had detected more and more impatience from men about
the way they felt they were becoming labelled; as unemotional,
unable to talk about their feelings, not caring enough about their
personal relationships and family life, as insensitive sexually, as

1

being in the wrong. 'It's about time that someone did something to let man speak for himself rather than always assuming that "such and such" is the case,' wrote a 24-year-old electrical contractor when he posted in his completed questionnaire. 'I thank you for giving me the opportunity to say my piece.'

When *The Woman Book of Love and Sex* was published, based on a survey of thousands of women, it was men who kept saying to us, 'Aren't you going to do a survey on men, and give us a chance to tell our side of the story?' Men do not want to be named in interviews, appear on television screens for all their mates to learn of their problems, but felt quite differently about an anonymous survey form to be filled in privately away from any curious gaze.

It was then that Richard Barber took over as editor of *Woman*, believed the project was worthwhile, and provided the considerable funding a survey of this scale and depth entails.

Our first worry was how we should conduct the survey. We considered traditional interviewing, and realised that few men are going to tell all to an interviewer face-to-face – we knew of other projects which had run into problems that way. We thought of inserting questionnaires into newspapers, trade and hobby magazines but realised how difficult it was going to be to make sure they were seriously presented and completed, and that even all those differing readerships put together might not have the real breadth of the *Woman* readership. The six million readers of *Woman* are a very good cross-section of the population. They are mainly women but they have men in their lives, and it was men's feelings about and experiences of relationships with women that we were mainly interested in discovering.

Before proceeding with the survey proper, we also conducted a small pilot survey of fifty men. We were very conscious that, though we had Richard to give a male viewpoint, the detailed work was being done by women and we wanted to eliminate any line of questioning that men might think tendentious or biased against them. We also wanted to see if we were asking them questions which they found relevant, or whether there were any gaps from their point of view. For example, several of the men taking part in this mini-survey pointed out that we had not asked whether they had ever visited a prostitute. It turned out that just over half of men have at least wondered about it, and 15 per cent have done so, so clearly it is an area of men's interest that women tend (defensively?) to under-estimate.

After all this groundwork a very detailed and time-consuming questionnaire – more than 120 questions – was published in *Woman* as a special pull-out central section in the magazine. We asked women to pass it on to the men in their lives – husbands and boyfriends, brothers and sons, friends and lovers. We also asked them to give the men privacy to fill in the questionnaire and not to ask to see their replies. Judging by the responses from the men, very few women got so much as a glimpse.

We were astounded when we received replies from five thousand men. This meant that we could select a sample to reflect men in the UK in the right proportions for age and region. We could be sure that our final statistics painted a true picture of the love-lives and opinions of men aged sixteen to sixty (see Note on Methodology, page 241).

While we heard from men in all the social-economic groupings and from all over the country, there were no significant differences according to region and class, though age was an important factor. Where the findings overlap with our surveys of women on matters of fact, such as how often couples make love, they tally remarkably exactly, supporting our confidence in their accuracy.

So many men welcomed the survey. 'Thank you for printing this questionnaire. It's about time men were asked their feelings on relationships and sex,' said a bankclerk. 'How good it is to have a survey like this and bring things into the open, to discover how men think and react in a relationship,' wrote a civil servant. 'The way men react with their male friends and the sex they talk about is, I feel, very far removed from the truth. This survey should show how men really feel.'

A probation officer wrote: 'No one ever asks men how they feel. The mythology of the strong, silent man is clung to all through society as though it is dangerous to question it. As a man of 43, I can tell you that men do have feelings, and strong ones. Women are permitted to show directly how they feel. Men feel just as much, but their feelings are supposed to be expressed indirectly through art, war, crime and, these days, drug abuse. In my business, social work, lip service is paid all the time to sexual equality and self-expression, but in practice behaviour is still expected to conform to the old social norms.'

Some sounded almost puzzled that they had found the whole exercise interesting enough to have devoted so much time to it. 'I'm not sure why I've answered all this. Perhaps it's a desire to express yourself in a normally taboo area.' Many pointed out

3

they had never been so frank before in their lives. 'My answers contain parts of my life never before revealed,' said a postman. For many it was the first time they had ever revealed their feelings and experiences. 'I have welcomed the chance to unburden myself of the guilt of past sexual experiences. I have often wanted to disclose these but have never been able to for fear of rejection. It's good to have some of the weight taken from my shoulders. Thank you.'

Some found that working through the questionnaire not only relieved feelings but in itself helped sort out difficulties. 'Thank you for the questionnaire. It has helped me sort out many problems.' Some men did decide to share their answers with their partner (obviously those who felt it was safe) and found it increased understanding. 'It was only after I had answered the questions that we discussed them in depth,' wrote a farmer. 'We found this both enlightening and constructive. We found many points raised in the form that we had not previously thought to discuss or mention. We have always tried to be as open and honest as possible with each other and found that we reached a new understanding of ourselves and our relationship. Although I know that not everyone could complete this questionnaire together as we have, for us it was a very beneficial exercise and one which we thoroughly enjoyed!'

Some had read *The Woman Book of Love and Sex*, containing the reports on our surveys on women, which spurred them into action. A civil servant wrote: 'Normally I don't bother with surveys. The questions often irritate me because the answer options do not fit any of my feelings or opinions and there is no chance for clarification. However, having read the results of the previous survey in your book, which I found fascinating and revealing, I am completing this questionnaire with notes on many of my answers.'

Throughout the questionnaire we were careful to leave space for men to insert their own alternative where none of our suggestions fitted, and encouraged them to add notes whenever they wanted to expand on their views or experiences. This makes the analysis harder work but the answers much more telling.

Hundreds of men attached lengthy life-histories, personal experiences and comments to their completed forms. Even if they found it a struggle, they obviously thought it was worth it. 'Please excuse the grammar,' wrote a 24-year-old joiner, 'but I didn't get this until a few days ago and I am trying to complete it in privacy in my mother-in-law's two-up two-down cottage. Thank you for the opportunity of letting men express themselves (as best as you can on paper). I think it's a tremendous thing you're doing.' It's what men say rather than bare statistics that fills most of this book. In every case we have given those quoted fictitious names in order to protect their identity.

We heard from single, married, separated, divorced and widowed men. We acknowledge that men who, either through choice or circumstances, are very much loners and have little do with women at all, even as family members let alone in emotional and sexual relationships, are under-represented in this survey. Men in exclusively homosexual relationships are excluded from the statistical analysis, since they could have distorted our findings about men's relationships with women – gay men's partners usually being subjected to differing pressures from those of heterosexual men. However, we received enough personal accounts from gay men to include some of their views, as we wanted to be able to do, in the hope of increasing mutual understanding. (See Chapter Eleven).

The core of this survey paints a picture of the mainstream – of men who, by and large, are interested in relationships with women. A minority of the men we heard from are very unhappy and had some telling points to make, but the majority of the men are at least reasonably happy, whether married or not. This makes their feelings and experiences all the more significant for those of us, men and women, who want our own relationships with the opposite sex to flourish.

Right at the heart of the survey's findings like a few key facts.

Men are twice as likely to be satisfied with the rest of their relationship as they are with their sex life.
The average British couple make love once or twice a week.
Three out of four British men want to improve their sex life.
Above all they want to be more skilful lovers themselves, and for their partners to be keener to make love more often, more experimental, more responsive and more willing to talk about how it feels.

Men are at the receiving end of some devastating blows to their confidence. (See Chapter Four). 'After an enjoyable romantic evening out,' said Leonard, 44, a teacher, 'my wife has often commented when we have returned home and I am showing amorous intentions, "It's been a wonderful evening. Let's not spoil it." '

Alan, 39, a works officer with the National Health Service: 'For me the most despairing thing is when I see my wife with her eyes shut and a look on her face saying, "I wish he'd hurry up and finish." '

Women, who generally regard themselves as the 'caring' sex, surprisingly often seem prepared to be cruelly wounding and unprepared to make an effort to improve their sexual relationship. (See Chapter Six).

Mike, 35, a teacher: 'We enjoy the same outlook in life and bringing up the children. This keeps us together despite my dissatisfaction with our sex life. Although my wife enjoys a kiss and a cuddle, anything more sexual than that and she tenses up and won't enjoy it. She wants to make love immediately then go to sleep. I feel the need for more time, more experimentation, more variety and more pleasure, both given and received. I have tried to raise the subject but she says she is just not a very good lover and not interested in sex. If I press the point she gets upset.'

Stephen, 27, a catering manager: 'I think my wife feels that sex is dirty, or parts of it are. We must have been married at least three years before my wife would touch my penis. I have suggested bathing together or massage but she does not think it's "nice". She allows me to take great time to arouse her with oral sex, but she does not do the same for me. When I mention the subject she just sulks for days and makes me feel bad for mentioning the subject. I think it's a way to stop me talking about it and ensure that I don't mention it again for a long time.'

Only two out of five couples (41 per cent) do talk really frankly about sex, and those who do not talk to one another openly are far more likely to have an unhappy sexual relationship. It seems ridiculous that a couple can share an intimate act like intercourse, yet not manage to talk to one another about it.

One important block to communication among adult couples is that as children they were never shown how to talk comfortably about such subjects. We found in our survey of women that only 12 per cent of mothers talk openly with their daughters about sex. This survey (see Chapter Two) shows that boys are left virtually to their own devices as far as sex education is concerned. *Only 6 per cent of mothers and even fewer fathers talk openly with their sons.*

Adolescent boys can be left in appalling ignorance. We have heard how frightened girls have been when they started their first period without having been told about menstruation. Peter was terrified the first time he masturbated to climax. 'I thought my penis had burst like a balloon. I actually thought I had broken my penis.' Peter is only 24 now, so we are not talking about a hangover from the days before sex education was commonplace in schools. In fact, *eight out of ten men believe that the sex education they received at school was inadequate.*

Young men's developing interest in sex and growing sexual urges are shut out from family life and values. They learn through comparing 'theories' in the playground and, these days particularly, from pornography. Robert, 21, a student: 'At school so much rubbish is talked among the lads concerning sex. Normally it related to how many times in a night a person could manage it and that a large penis was better than a smaller one when it came to sex. Few seemed to know what a clitoris was or its function.'

Most men gain such important information later on, but while young often see sex in terms of gaining experience rather than as part of a developing relationship. (See Chapter Three). *More than half of those who had intercourse by the age of 18 say that the first time was out of pure curiosity, rather than connected with any feelings for the girl concerned.*

When young men reach the stage where they start to worry about their partner's enjoyment and to feel that they should be skilful lovers rather than just out for their own pleasure, they often find that sex is not quite as straight-forward as they had been led to believe.

They may believe that their partner should reach orgasm during intercourse, but half of them have difficulty delaying a climax as long as they want to. (See Chapter Five). One in four is not happy with the frequency with which his partner climaxes, and it would probably be more if many of them had rumbled how common it is for their girlfriends to fake it. *While half of single men believe that their girlfriend usually reaches orgasm through intercourse, from our survey of unmarried women we know that only 24 per cent of single women say that this is true for them.* Two out of five fake at least sometimes, but only 3 per cent of single men have realised.

The problem is that both partners are pressured by an image of what adult love-making should be like: The Big Bang Theory of sex. This goes that foreplay is followed by intercourse followed by the Big Bang – climax for both partners. In fact only a minority of women do reach orgasm during intercourse, and to many

7

foreplay isn't an aperitif at all but the main course.

If their partner does not reach orgasm, men tend to see it as a criticism of their technique, though all sorts of other factors can affect a woman's ability to reach orgasm. A woman is not just a machine to be switched on Barbarella-style, and may not be able to respond fully to sexual stimulus because of inhibitions, tiredness, worries, resentments about other aspects of the relationship.

Even when they have fallen in love and are perhaps married, men tend to view their sex life as a separate strand of their relationship, rather than inextricably intertwined with and reflecting the whole.

Men place great emphasis on gaining 'experience' because they want to be 'skilful' lovers. They take the responsibility for the sexual success of their relationship – and their partners usually expect them to take the lead sexually, too. For all the talk of women being more sexually liberated, only 4 per cent of men would agree that women are too demanding sexually these days. Most want women to demand more!

What frustrates so many men is that, having become reasonably enlightened and skilful lovers – mostly gone are the days of 'Wham, bam, and thank you ma'am' – their partners are comparatively unresponsive and passive. Eddie, 35: 'Most men would agree to almost any suggestion a woman may make to improve love-making if only because it's nice to feel a woman has sexual preferences she wants to share.'

Only 3 per cent of men ever do refuse their partner's request to try something new, but more than ten times that many men say their partner refuses requests to experiment.

Sometimes men are distracted by their view that the quality of sex is mainly concerned with technique and exciting variety from realising that their partner may be clamming up not because of how they make love, but due to some resentment to do with other areas of their life. Many women find it hard to ask directly for what they want out of bed, let alone in it where they are affected by the 'nice girls don't' teaching of their teenage years.

This problem seems to come particularly into play, ironically, after marriage rather than before it. *Single men are more likely to rate their partner as an excellent lover than married men and nearly twice as likely to believe that that is how their partner rates them.* Generally this survey shows that marriage is bad for sex, though it is within marriage that most men expect to have the

8

most important and lasting sexual relationship of their lives, the one that all the others (if any others) have been building up to. Why is it such a disappointment?

While there should be no pressure on anyone, man or woman, to feel that good sex has to be frequent sex, we know from our survey of women that the most common change wives would like to make in their own love-making is to be keener to make love more often. The factor that often seems to turn various pressures into passion killers is the sexual guilt and ambivalence left within both partners since childhood. It is because women often connect the subject with guilt and anxiety that they so often tense up against sexual advances or experiments, are 'too tired' or 'don't feel like it'.

It is true that many women feel the need to receive more affection other than as a prelude to sex, and that husbands do less kissing and cuddling than single men, but husbands point out that even their tentative efforts to show affection may be shrugged off. It is this guilt and anxiety which also leads so many women to resist the idea of trying to change, of seeing that they are now sexual adults who can throw what 'Mother' said out of the window.

Time after time men said that their partners underestimate just how important sex is to them. 'She doesn't take the strength of my feelings seriously. If women want to be treated with consideration then they should be prepared to treat men with consideration.'

However, what men sometimes overlook is how much sexual guilt and ambivalence is left within themselves, and whether they are giving their partners conflicting messages.

It is a cliché that a man wants a wife in the home and a mistress between the sheets. In fact, he often wants a woman in the home looking after him just like mother used to do, maintaining the same standards of cleanliness, putting him and the children first. It can be a tall order for this same woman then to turn into a mistress between the sheets, a sexually assertive woman who can live up to his wildest dreams. He equally may need to throw 'Mother' out of the window, with the ideas she gave him of what a 'nice, marriageable' girl should be like.

He may also need to reevaluate some of 'Father's' standards about being strong, silent and a good breadwinner. *One in three married men says that what gets in the way of his making love more often is that he himself is too tired.* Many wrote about resenting the time that making a good living forces them to spend away from their wife and family. Some are beginning to wonder whether these are the right priorities. Barry, 48: 'I love all my children deeply and have tried to be a good father to them. I've worked hard to give them a good education and standard of living, but I wonder now whether it wouldn't have been more valuable to spend more time with them.'

It is the sort of change that women are supposed to have been wanting for at least a couple of decades. Yet Scott, 28, a van driver, who is very close to his young sons, said: 'I have shared the looking after with my wife but she gets very upset when either cry or are sad that they want me to cuddle them. She thinks it is not normal for boys to like their Dad and that they should go to her. Usually it causes a row and a few days of silence.'

It sounds as if some women want to share the work but not the emotional rewards that go with it.

Similarly, we continually hear that women want men to talk more about their feelings. Yet David, 25, a bank steward, pointed out: 'I have found not all girls like guys to be so open. My basic view on women is that they like guys with feelings, but not to show their softness and sensitivity.' In other words some women in effect give the message: 'Show me your feelings but only the ones I can cope with easily!'

Men do tell their wives time and time again how strongly they feel about lacklustre sex lives, but are they listened to? Mike, the teacher I quoted earlier, ended by saying: 'I have tried a variety of games, techniques and approaches. I have tried being patient and I have tried being demanding. I really don't think she wants to change. I know it would come as a complete shock to my wife but I think I could put all thirteen years of our happy relationship on the line for just one night of genuine, satisfying pleasure.'

And this is just what some men do (Chapter Eight). *One in four husbands has an affair – or affairs, since one in five of them has anything from five to more than twenty sexual relationships outside his marriage.*

Bill, 39, 'I've had many affairs. The main reason is a poor sexual relationship with my wife, and as a transcontinental HGV driver I have much opportunity.'

In fact 64 per cent of the men who have had affairs say it was because the opportunity presented itself and only 24 per cent that it resulted from a poor sexual relationship with their wife.

Men love the excitement – more than three out of five say

that's the main advantage of an affair over marriage. Phil, 43, a centre lathe turner: 'It was so exciting because I knew that she always wanted me. She used to wear stockings and suspenders and lovely bras, or often she would go braless and leave two or three buttons undone to excite me. We never needed much.'

Being a mistress is so much more exciting a role than being a wife. In fact, once women escape the expectations that being a wife make on them and husbands put on them, they discover a far more sexually adventurous side of themselves – which may later benefit their marriages. Greg, 48, said: 'One result of my wife's affair, surprisingly, is that we now have a more adventurous and satisfying sex life. She admitted she had done things with him she had always refused me. Gradually she seems to have overcome her inhibitions with me and admits now she enjoys our more varied and adventurous love-making.'

The safe way in which some couples introduce extra excitement into their relationship and loosen inhibitions is through fantasy. In Chapter Seven we discover the types of fantasy men keep private and those that they are eager to share. This is the realm where a man can be sure of being so skilful a lover that his partner is powerless to resist. Iain, 38, a clergyman: 'I am a slave and my wife is an empress. I am lined up with a number of other male slaves and she inspects us all intimately. She chooses me and leads me to her private quarters. She wants to do exciting things to me but, green or not, I can be in control and be masterful, and do what I want to her.'

The idea that all men should be sexually in control and masterful is one which men and women find hard to discard. In fact, some men feel that women's liberation has not opened the way for men to show their vulnerable side more, but rather set even higher standards. Tom, 28, 'Most women, feminist or not, are increasingly self-reliant, independent and confident. This is entirely good, but my impression is that women are still attracted to men more dominant than themselves – high-powered, self-confident men. This has actually raised the threshold of men's attractiveness so that quiet, perhaps more sensitive men have less chance than ever of forming relationships. Certainly this is true of my less aggressive male friends.'

Like many points raised by this survey, this one will take some perhaps uncomfortable self-examination by men and women during this time of flux in the relationships between the sexes. The stresses of being macho male were often mentioned by the men who took part in our survey, and either have relationships with men as well as women, or else find release by wearing women's clothes occasionally (Chapters Eleven and Twelve). 'I like the idea of having a protector-like figure, a strong man to hold me and make me feel safe,' explained a 20-year-old, wondering whether he is bisexual.

Jeff, 33, a labourer who is a transvestite, explains, 'On the very rare occasions I get to indulge these days I find it gives me the most relaxing feeling possible. Like a sort of escapism. I work in a dirty, noisy, smelly factory doing a hard, dirty job. I feel I have to keep a manly front up for the kids' sake and my wife's sake, even for my own sake. As a husband and father a man has a lot of responsibilities and is under a lot of pressure. As far as I am concerned, giving way to the feminine urges I have inside me acts like a safety valve. Most of you women don't realise how lucky you are – you can have the best of both worlds.'

Even though it is now accepted as normal for a woman to wear trousers, transvestite men are regarded with scorn even by gay men – which seems ironic, since you would think they, more than most, would understand that we cannot choose our sexual needs and identities. However, the most despised of men are those who sexually abuse children. Though we see in Chapter Seven, which covers men's use of pornography, that four out of five men see some form of pornographic material at least occasionally, and very few think it harmful, they are virtually unanimous in condemning pornography involving children.

Men suffer from sexual harassment and assault themselves as children to a far greater extent than is commonly realised (Chapter Ten). *One in ten men has been sexually harassed and one in twenty assaulted – usually while young by another male.* Though only 14 per cent of such incidents are reported to the police, many tell their friends. What a discomforting picture of male sexuality many boys must have as they move through adolsecence. Strange men who hang around waste ground and shift their seats in the cinema wanting to touch them; a resounding silence at home on the urgent desires they are experiencing and their desires to touch themselves; challenging talk among their friends about how to touch as much of a girl as possible. Yet adults think, 'The boys are all right. It's our daughters we have to worry about.'

Whatever their roles in life, we hope this survey helps those who want to reassess their relationships and understand what a straitjacket stereotyped expectations can be. Though I cannot speak for others who worked on the project, for me it has been challenging and often uncomfortable, but I hope it has increased my understanding.

2 'I took technical drawing instead'
An education for life?

W e want the best for our children. We want them to grow up at ease with the written word and with figures, to have a working knowledge of the world around them and to develop any special talents they may have for languages, science, music, business, crafts. We try to urge them on through the years of detailed study and hard work needed to fit them to take their place confidently in the adult world.

We also want them to grow up to have happy relationships, probably to marry and enjoy a sex life as satisfying or more so than our own. Our own experience tells us this is an important aspect of life, yet how much time is devoted to making sure that young men grow up into sensitive and fulfilled sexual partners?

Eight out of ten (81 per cent) of men say that they did not receive enough sex education at school.

Dominic, 24, an electrician, remembered: 'Sex was always treated as a big joke at school and everyone used to brag about their experiences, which were in fact non-existent. You were taught about sex and contraception if you chose to take biology. I took technical drawing instead (more useful for job prospects) and thus did not get to know about the facts of life.'

Yet as many men pointed out, the 'biology lesson' approach is not much of a preparation for human relationships. It teaches you the facts but gives little chance to talk about the feelings.

Nigel, now a married civil servant, commented: 'It would have been useful to have had a broader sex education in school. Ours was very much rabbits and frogs based. We did have one lesson related to human sexuality when the biology master tried to get on our wavelength by talking about the balls and the carrot (phraseology from *his* schooldays). Amusing but not particularly informative for fifth form boys. Contraception was never even mentioned.'

14

Nearly nine out of ten (88 per cent) of married men say that they did not receive enough information at school about sex and related subjects such as contraception. An even higher proportion – 95 per cent – of those in unhappy relationships now believe that their sex education was inadequate.

They want increased sex education, both at school and in the home. They agree with those who believe the facts of sex should be taught in the context of caring relationships and responsibility, but they do not want this to be at the expense of making sure that young men understand female as well as male sexual responses and how to prevent unwanted pregnancies.

They do not see withholding sex education as a way of preventing early sexual experiment, but as a cause of lasting relationship problems for men.

Brendan, 33, who works as a labourer, had discovered that his wife now has a lover. She can reach orgasm with him, whereas this has always been a problem with her husband. Brendan said, 'I never received any sex education from school or my parents. Maybe if I'd known more about female responses when I was younger, I'd be a better lover now.'

All the emphasis on the mechanics of reproduction, viewed as dispassionately as a pair of frogs playing piggy-back beside the school pond, can make the whole subject seem entirely separate from the urges and sensations being personally experienced by the young men in the classroom. It virtually teaches them to distance such discussions from what they are actually feeling, and does little to enlighten them and relieve their anxieties.

Malcolm: 33, now a teacher himself: 'When I was 14 or 15, I masturbated for the first time. It amazed me that I was capable of so much inner feeling.'

Pete, an unemployed 24-year-old, first experienced a climax with ejaculation when he was 14. 'I'd never had a climax before and I didn't even know it was a climax. I thought my penis had burst like a balloon. I actually thought I had broken my penis.' It is the sort of experience an adult can look back on and laugh about, but which must have been terrifying to that teenage boy.

There has, of course, been some increase in sex education. Henry, a ship's captain in his fifties, explained: 'During my years at school, 1939 to 1948, there was no sex education. Yet at home these matters were not talked about and any query would produce an answer like, "When you get older, you will find out about that." '

Nowadays sex education is often more sensitively called 'education for life' or 'health and relationships', partly to get away from the 'all plumbing and no morals' image flung in the face of sex education by those who are very anxious about young people and talk of sexuality being in the same room at the same time. (As if they don't talk about it when no adult is there to raise the topic!) For simplicity, since it is still known as sex education to the public at large, that is the term we will continue to use here.

While a very high proportion – nine out of ten (92 per cent of the over-40s) – say their sex education was inadequate at school, there is a majority (just – 52 per cent) among 16 to 18 year olds who believe that they were taught enough. However, this drops rapidly to one in three of 19 to 25 year olds, and just one in four of 26 to 30 year olds.

There has not been a sudden and dramatic increase in the quality of sex education in schools in very recent years so the figures suggest that as young men start to form deeper and more lasting relationships in their late teens and twenties, they run into gaps in their sex education they had not realised were there.

Bradley, an unemployed 20-year-old, pointed out, 'Even now I ask my girlfriend about her periods and what causes them. We were told about sex at school at the age of thirteen. It's OK looking at pictures and films and so on, but it really doesn't tell you what you want to know. Most kids are too embarrassed to ask questions at that age, so they just sit there pretending they understand.'

Who would want to ask a question about sex in front of 30 or 40 of their peers? Small groups where individuals could discuss the feelings involved and the implications of different attitudes, rather than simple exposition of the mechanics, would save the efforts being made in schools from being dismissed as contemptuously as, in different ways, they were by Bill and Sandy.

Bill, a bus garage foreman of 36, remembered, 'The embarrassed attempts of our pompous headmaster to tell us "the facts" at school were pathetic and largely irrelevant. I well recall his attempt to describe intercourse . . . "The male places his penis in the female's vagina and if he is excited sperm will flow." I wondered why he would do it if he were not excited. What was to excite him – the news that he had won the pools perhaps? It was all rather ridiculous and I already knew more than he told us.'

Sandy, a 22-year-old roofer/tiler who's single, commented: 'My school was always on about sex education and contraception.

It was really rammed down our throats. I never took any real notice. Contraception doesn't really bother me. I would never use condoms, they take away all feeling.'

The small groups that would make real discussion of subjects such as the pros and cons of contraception possible, are a long way off in most schools, and schools do not even want sole responsibility for sex education. They would be the first to agree that parents have an important, probably the most important, role to play in educating young people for life.

What is not so clear is whether parents actually want that role or are equipped to fill it.

Is parent power the answer?

Judging by our survey, if it were left to parents alone to provide a full and balanced sex education we would have a nation of extremely ill-informed young men. Approaching two-thirds have parents who never discussed the subject with them at all.

Fathers, you might think, are particularly well equipped to explain to young men the physical and emotional changes they can expect during puberty, the likely strengths of their desires, the natural ways of releasing sexual tension, the challenges and responsibilities they will have as they start forming a different kind of relationship with girls. Not a bit of it!

Only one in ten (11 per cent) of the men had fathers who talked to them even 'fairly openly' about sex education. The fathers of a large majority of the rest had never once discussed the subject.

You might think that the supposedly more articulate middle classes would discuss more with their sons, but the subject is usually cloaked in silence whether Dad is a lawyer or a lorry driver.

Richard, 20, a post office worker, said: 'My parents have always covered sex up, never discussed it. I shall tell my children (when I have them). I'd like to have that closeness, to know that they could come to me and talk. Relationships and sex are the roots of many young people's deepest anxieties.

'As a child I had nightmares and worried constantly because I kissed and hugged a girl and thought she would get pregnant. It lasted two years.

'I was the first boy in my year to reach puberty, when I was 12, and I felt such a freak. I shaved my pubic hair and the hairs on my legs for about eight months, so I would look normal in the showers after games, until the others started reaching puberty. All because I didn't know anything about what was happening.'

George, 44, a shop-owner, remembered: 'Even during National Service I didn't really know what some of the other men were talking about. I didn't have any sex education from my parents or from school. All I knew I learnt from a book called *The Red Light* which a friend's more enlightened father had given me to read.'

If Dads can make the effort to talk to their sons, they can obviously identify with some of their worries and can play a valuable role in both educating and reassuring.

Derek, a 19-year-old student: 'I was only 10 or 11 when I started to think about sex. I started to masturbate then and my father found out. He never criticised me in any way or laughed at my questions. I worried that my penis wouldn't get big enough and he gave me a book which explained everything.'

Nick, 28 a product manager: 'My father told me everything he considered relevant in an adult way and answered all my questions. In my later sexual relationships this helped me speak openly and understand what was needed.'

If fathers will talk to their sons, it gives the adolescent not only information but a chance to see an adult male talking calmly and openly about sex, linking it with the often confused and intense feelings that can be aroused; admitting there can be difficulties, but also giving the message, 'It's OK. It's a little weird but it can be wonderful and we all want to do it.'

Men are finding it very hard to change, however. *Just 3 per cent of men in their forties and fifties say that their father discussed sex really openly with them.*

Some are very bitter, like Harry, an office worker aged 56. He complained: 'I grew up in the late forties and I can see now that we were sold a totally false bill of goods by our parents, by other adults and by the then media. Observing the world of the 1980s, I can hardly believe that we were so naive with regard to sex, love and marriage.'

These men are themselves the fathers of those now in their twenties – yet only 6 per cent of those younger men say that their father talked frankly with them. Not very dramatic progress!

Mum's the word!

Very few young people can talk comfortably with either parent about sex or seek reassurance for their anxieties. *Only 16 per cent of mothers have talked even 'fairly openly' to their sons about sex education.*

Douglas, 22, a salesman in an electrical shop: 'My parents told me nothing. I later learned they were under the impression that they should wait until we asked about sex. I have three brothers and two sisters and we were embarrassed to such an extent that we *dare* not talk to Mum about S-E-X.'

David, a 32-year-old office worker, remembered: 'At the age of 12 I asked my mother what masturbation was. She said "You don't need to worry about that yet." We have never discussed sex since.'

However, Mums are making more of an effort than Dads to start talking to their sons.

While more than half (52 per cent) of the 16 to 18 year olds still say their Dad never discusses sex with them, only two out of five (40 per cent) say their Mum **never** *raises the subject.*

Roger, a 27-year-old van driver: 'My Mum told me nearly everything about girls and sex. My father only worried about me bringing VD into the house.'

Even so, only one in ten men in their twenties says that his mother talked really openly with him.

As we have seen, there are many differences in the ways men and women feel about sex. Most mothers of teenage sons will have a fair idea, from their own lives and those of their friends, of the sort of sexual and emotional misunderstandings that can bedevil relationships.

It is mothers who are best placed to talk to sons about the ways female sexuality varies from the male – and from the myths put about in the playground. It is mothers who can emphasise how for most women sex is just part of the whole relationship, and it is going to be no good her lad expecting a wildly happy sex life if he lets his partner feel unhappy in every other aspect of their life together.

It is mothers who can make sure their sons know that their desires will be welcomed and shared by women, as long as they see them as people, not mere objects for relief. It is mothers who can give their sons a chance to experience talking to a women honestly about sex and love, anxieties and misunderstandings.

After all, it is mothers who are most likely to know the frustration of being married to a man who *cannot* talk about them!

If mothers do talk to their youngsters openly, and without condescending or 'preaching', it can give men an enormous boost to their ability to communicate openly and effectively with women.

Simon, 20, a student of photograph: 'My Mum isn't too liberal but she's not protective and doesn't treat me like a kid. She talks to me like an equal, but doesn't let me bring girls home to bed while she's there. I don't think I would anyway, because I respect her privacy.

'I like principles in people. I've always admired people with guts, especially girls in view of sex. I've always believed that the girl has the last say in whether to have sex. If it's no, I respect that. It means she's not prepared to go on the pill, not prepared for physical consummation and respects herself in not having men for the taking.

'There's only been one girl I've truly loved, not just been in love with, and we talked about things like sex and contraception without embarrassment.'

We cannot expect men to be able to talk to their partner comfortably about subjects which are so closely entwined with their deepest emotions and vulnerabilities, unless they have been given a model to follow in how their parents talk to them – and also to one another.

Whether parents make the effort to bring sex and relationships out into the open in discussions with their sons does affect their future happiness.

*Seventy-five per cent of those men who are never happy with their sex life had mothers who **never** spoke to them about sex, and 80 per cent had fathers who never talked about it.*

Jim, 36, a financial adviser, said: 'I had no parental guidance and sex education at my old boys grammar school was nil. Therefore a lot of wrong ideas became implanted in my mind.'

Andrew, 45, a customs officer who is now married for the second time: 'I had to find out the hard way. I never had any instruction or education. I've never been sure my approach to sex is right.'

Mike, a 26-year-old student; 'My parents never talked about it. Occasionally I'd find a booklet on my bed about it but I didn't feel I could discuss it with anyone. I think the last time my parents made love was when I was conceived. Not a very loving family atmosphere. Virtually no sex education at school, either. I felt there was something shameful about sex and even now I have guilt feelings and hang-ups about it all.'

Who's the guilty party?

We don't have to voice disapproval to cause sexual guilt in our children. Just think how disturbing this resounding silence on the subject of sex must be for youngsters. Until they reach puberty parents have been interested and supportive in every area of their life – or at least tried to be, or felt they ought to be! Friends, sports, homework, clothes, cleanliness – no area of their life left unturned.

Then a lad of 10, 11 or 12 starts feeling all these surprising new sensations. What do Mum and Dad say? Nothing. If he tries a tentative query, he gets cut off. Since this increasingly important aspect of his life is not talked about, he may assume there is something involved he should feel ashamed of, keep to himself.

Peter, a 24-year-old computer programmer: 'Sex was very much a taboo subject in my childhood, mainly due to my mother's attitude. Even my father, in other matters progressive, is morally conservative. I felt very guilty about juvenile masturbation and was terrified of being discovered, though I never was.'

One in four men says he used to feel guilty about sex.

A few specifically complained about a Roman Catholic upbringing. Jonathan, 38, a work study officer who is now married for the second time and joined the Methodist Church explained: 'I was brought up a Roman Catholic and made to feel particularly guilty about the normal practice of masturbation which was considered to be a "mortal sin" by the Catholic Church.

'I went to an all-boys school where there was no sex education apart from a blanket condemnation of all normal adolescent sexual urges. I think that the Roman Catholic Church has a great deal to answer for in its attitudes to normal sexual development in boys and girls. In many cases they give children hang-ups which will be with them for the rest of their lives.'

The survey showed that a Roman Catholic upbringing did make a man rather more likely than the average to suffer from guilt about his sexuality. One-third (32 per cent) of those raised as Catholics said they felt guilty – but so did nearly as high a proportion (29 per cent) of those belonging to other Christian denominations.

Distinguished by religion, the men who emerged from the survey as suffering least from sexual guilt were those from Jewish and atheist families. These also had the parents who were most likely to have talked very openly with them.

'Self-abuse' and secrecy

The guilt often at least started with masturbation. It is not only because this is the available sexual activity when you're 12 and more vulnerable to parental disapproval. Not so long ago masturbation had a very bad image, and this still affects us today.

I quote from *Biology of Sex: For Parents and Teachers* by T.W. Galloway, published by D.C. Heath about 1930. There is plenty in this book which is easy to agree with. For example, Mr Galloway points out, 'Sex and all that this implies is a perfectly natural, normal fact of life, with nothing unholy or perverse about it.' However, here is Mr Galloway on 'Special Problems of Adolescent Boys . . .'

'*Problem 1, Masturbation among boys.* How can we bring proper cautions to the boys about masturbation, before they have begun to indulge in it, in such a way as to give them more help than harm? Are we not in danger of introducing them to the act of self-abuse rather than of helping them avoid it?' Mr Galloway suggests the warning should be given 'by the right man and in the right way, to as to provide real and convincing reasons that will fortify most boys against this vice.

'The rooster or cat whose testes have been removed in early life will grow fat and soft instead of strong and vigorous; and will tend to be lazy and cowardly. Much the same thing happens in men . . . It is possible for boys to handle and massage their organs in such a way as to injure their development at a critical period of their life . . . Besides, masturbation tends to make the organs and the nerve centres that control them sensitive and irritable; and in this way the bodily and mental development is liable to become unnatural and morbid.'

(By the way, I cannot find a single mention by Mr Galloway of girls masturbating. They had 'The Problem of Right Mental Attitude'.)

It is easy to laugh at *Biology of Sex* as quaint, but such

22

attitudes haunt the present more than we realise. Neil, 36, an acupuncturist, reflected: 'My mother joked about sex but I think her upbringing had left her tinged with guilt. I can recall her hinting when I was a child that I was tired because I masturbated.'

Many men pointed out, like Paul, 27, a computer programmer: 'I used to feel guilty about masturbation but I've never felt guilty about intercourse.'

Discomfort about masturbation is triggered in adolescence but often persists into adulthood. A chap is more likely to tell you whether and how often he makes love with his wife than whether and how often he masturbates.

The difference may be that if you acknowledge that you masturbate – and this applies to men and women – then you are saying 'I have sexual needs which I enjoy satisfying.' You have to take full responsibility for your own sexuality. However, as soon as you talk about a sexual relationship with another person, then all sorts of other emotions and motives cloud the issue: love, power, social success, potency, parenthood. The sexual need can easily get lost in amongst that lot – and often does in relationships. In other words, guilt about masturbation often reflects a more general guilt about the individual's sexuality – not just about that particular activity – and a discomfort over admitting needs, perhaps seeing this as weakness. This will affect relationships.

A dramatic contrast in the figures highlighted this.

Nearly three-quarters (72 per cent) of those unhappy with their current relationships say they suffered from sexual guilt – three times the average.

It is particularly interesting because we are looking here at the whole relationship, not just its sexual aspect. Why should sexual guilt seem so forcibly to block a man's hope of happiness?

Sexual guilt usually results from a young man failing to find the information and encouragement he needs to understand that his sexuality is a natural part of himself and take responsibility for it. We all carry our parents in our heads, monitoring our behaviour. If our parents have not given us 'permission' to be sexual, then our natural desires and urges will trigger guilt.

If a man feels guilty about his sexual urges then he is going to be defensive about asking a partner to help him gratify these needs. Defensiveness often comes across as our seeming angry and unreasonable.

If the man is married he may partly have projected his 'Mother' image on to his wife. He expects her to be 'good' and 'respectable' like Mother, a 'nice woman'; but he also wants her to share this behaviour of which Mother would not have approved. The more he loves the woman, the more torn and guilty he is likely to feel. His partner may also be torn between her own desires, her wish to please her partner, and the 'Mother' who is saying to her: 'Nice girls don't!'

This conflict in feelings inevitably leaks out to poison far more of their relationship than just the obviously sexual side.

Sexual guilt can make it hard for a young man even to attempt to talk to a girl. Because he feels guilty about his sexual desires, and his sexual desires are not only focused on girls but bound up with anxieties and questions to which no one has offered to help find an answer, even saying hello can feel too threatening.

Keith, 27, an electrical contractor, explained: 'When I was younger I had an inferiority complex. I'd always shy away from girls. I think my real anxiety was because my education on the subject was so negligible. It is only since I've married that I've lost most of my anxieties through my wife. I've realised that women are not just "sex objects".'

Parents' silence over sex forces a youngster to treat this aspect of himself as a shameful secret. It is not acknowledged by his parents, so he is less likely to play according to their rules. They effectively shut the whole subject of sexuality and relationships with women out of the value system which they are otherwise trying to instil. They may encourage him to be honest and hard working, but what help do they offer so he can develop positive values in sex and relationships?

Probably more important than any formal sex education in school, or even anything parents may say to their children, is the example they set. Here's a young man who is very likely to go on to form happy emotional and sexual relationships – and also to have a partner who feels the warmth of his affection.

Gavin, is a student aged 18; 'I have always considered sex to be a natural act and nothing to be ashamed of, despite guarded warnings from older generations in my family. Luckily my parents were very open about it.

'However, my girlfriend's parents are very "Victorian" in their attitudes. My girlfriend was never told the facts of life at school or at home. She was never even told about periods by her mother. When I met her she was very confused about the subject

24

and extremely naive. I find her parents' attitude unbelievable but accept that it is too late for them to change and *their* parents led them to be like that.

'My girlfriend's parents never show emotion towards each other. They seem obsessive about holidays abroad, material possessions, the value of their house etc. On her last visit to my parents my girlfriend was perplexed to see my Mum (49) and Dad (64) holding hands and larking about on the sofa just for a laugh. She later cried, saying that in her whole life she had never seen her parents hold hands, kiss or show any fondness for each other.'

You can't stem the tide

Parents talk to boys about sex even less than they talk to girls. They don't have to worry that a son may get pregnant and they may feel subconsciously that 'what they don't know can't hurt them', that if their sons don't know too much about sex, they cannot get up to much, either.

However, puberty is a natural development which cannot be stopped, though as we have seen ignorance can make it unnecessarily frightening.

Tony, 20, serving in the army: 'I don't think either my parents or school provided enough sexual education. I had to rely on schoolground chatter. I had my first sexual experience while at school, rolling around naked with a girlfriend.'

Barry, 38, a clerical worker: 'The old adage of picking up tips as you go along certainly covers my sex education. I can recall a couple of occasions where huddles of third-formers wore out Page 120 of *Lady Chatterley's Lover*, adding a certain amount of fuel to the flame of my juvenile sexuality.'

Not talking about sex does not stop experimentation. It just makes sex a no-go area between parents and sons and means they lose any opportunity to guide, reassure, or even help sort out physical problems.

Edward, 44, a civil servant: 'I was unable to have sex properly until I was 24 due to my need for circumcision.' He must have worried unnecessarily for years.

Philip, 42 and in the Forces, remembered: 'I had no warnings about sex or incest from my very inhibited parents. At about 12 or 13 I began to try out my feelings about sex on my sister, who was 18 months younger, and even attempted intercourse with her.

'I also joined in some mutual masturbation with the older boys in the scout troop and a few somewhat dubious – I now realise – helpers. That was my only homosexual experience.'

John certainly did not learn about sex in the context of caring relationships. He is 25 and works as a butcher. 'My parents never talked about sex. I learned from a girl I knew when I was 15. She used to "Lie down" almost anywhere for me. I hated her.'

Playgrounds and pornography

A young man is going to get information and form attitudes somehow or other. The curiosity about sex and the urge to try is not going to wither away just because it is not nurtured by information and discussion at home or in the classroom.

How is he supposed to know that the news and values of the playground braggart and the porn magazines all around are not necessarily those most likely to bring him happiness, and that the 'facts' passed on this way are often plain wrong?

Sam, 21, a student: 'I've spoken to a lot of male friends and we all agree that we found out almost all the facts of life from school friends, comparing "theories" in the playground or wherever.

'My best friend told me about something called "venerable disease" and that, if I ever caught it, I must tell my parents I got it from a toilet seat. For ages I lived in fear of sitting down on strange toilet seats.'

Those under 30 were the more likely to have read pornographic or semi-pornographic magazines. Lee, 20, a student: 'I learned the more explicit details of sexual intercourse through a combination of pornography (my elder brothers' soft-porn magazines) and talking with my best friend.' (We look in more detail at men's experience of pornography in Chapter Seven.)

Angus, 28, a builder: 'I don't remember being told the facts of life by my parents. The subject was taboo. I did have some friends, four or five years older, who passed on information and introduced me to soft porn.'

Robert, 21, a student: 'At school so much rubbish is talked among the lads concerning sex. Most of them had no experience and didn't know what they were talking about. Normally it related to how many times in a night a person could manage it, that a large penis was better than a smaller one when it came to sex and few seemed to know what a clitoris was or its function.'

A lot of adolescent attention focuses on the penis. After all, it is very obviously there, it is supposed to change during puberty and plays an increasingly active role in this developing area of a young man's life. It is the standard-bearer of the new man.

Yet porn magazines and the playground are not exactly the best places to pick up a realistic idea of the range in appearance and size that is normal for the penis, nor do they make sure the message gets across that penis size is comparatively irrelevant to giving and receiving sexual pleasure.

'I used to worry that my penis was too small but only because of rubbish I read in certain magazines when I was an adolescent,' said Patrick, 36, a writer.

Ian, 19 a student: 'I was worried that my penis was too small. It's a subject of quite a lot of concern to young boys, about 13 or 14, worried about their "status" at school. Now I've been told that it's not the size that matters but what one does with it.'

One third of men (34 per cent) have worried that their penis was too small. Though only 3 per cent had known a woman complain, 10 per cent are still worried.

Gordon, 52, a long-time married chemical engineer, said: 'I learnt all the facts of life in the school playground and regard "teaching" as counter-productive nonsense.' However, in reply to the question asking whether men had ever worried whether their penis was not large enough he replied: 'I do wonder if this could lie behind our problems.' His playground seminars fell rather short of Masters and Johnson!

Some men lose relationships before they have sorted out truth from myth. Gary, 23, a clerk has already been divorced. 'It's only with my current partner I've realised that the extent of penetration is far less important than stimulation of the clitoris – at least that appears to be the case.' (Yes, but please read on, Gary).

Terry, 35, had uncomfortable memories of the sort of trap that can lie in wait for the lad who swallows the playground line of boasting. Like many young men beginning sexual relationships, Terry suffered from premature ejaculation – but playgrounds and porn magazines do not explain much about this should-be minor problem, or how to cope with it. (See Chapter Thirteen).

He pointed out, 'Between boys it is quite a thing to boast about if you have lost your virginity, and therefore it is a great temptation to lose it at the first opportunity.

'If you and a girl are just using one another for sexual relief

27

and you ejaculate prematurely or, horror of horrors, cannot get it up, the girl's reaction may vary from anger to laughter, and it is difficult to say which is more damaging. It can sour a man, not only in his sexual relations, but in any relationship with women.

'If the boy and the girl are in love, then they will both be more tolerant and caring towards one another. A problem such as premature ejaculation is not then as traumatic as it might have been, because the girl will be supportive and forgiving.

'I feel there should be more emphasis on how special sex is and how it should be saved for a special partner with whom it is truly "making love".'

Which is the sort of point parents – many of whom will have had personal experience of such problems – could put across very successfully.

Our survey shows that honest talk about sex and relationship between parents and sons and a wide-ranging sex education in school does help towards happier and more stable adult relationships. Sex education is not a force working against the values of the family, but very much towards strengthening and enriching family life.

However, no matter how hard we try, we cannot stop our teenagers going wrong or too far, feeling hurt as well as happy. Teenagers are learning to be adults – a new generation different from us – who have to make their own mistakes in order to discover how to do it their way.

3 Fumbling in the dark

The search for experience

Most teenage boys know the basics of human reproduction and perhaps contraception from sex education in school. They have picked up some fact and probably quite a lot of fiction in the playground. However, almost none have had the chance to talk about feelings and relationships with responsible adults, or about what really makes for lastingly pleasurable sexual experience for men and for women. Here they are on the threshold of their adult lives, often literally fumbling in the dark.

At this stage sexual exploration often runs ahead of developing deeper relationships. 'It's strange that sex can be a very lonely experience,' said William, 22, a student teacher. 'My first sexual experience, of masturbation, oral sex and intercourse, at a rock festival, left me highly unfulfilled.' It must have been very worrying for a young man to have sex and not enjoy it. Without someone to explain just how completely feelings can affect our sexual response, he must have thought there was something deeply amiss.

Duncan, 23, a computer programmer: 'Our kissing sessions were quite passionate but talk about sexual inexperience . . . She climaxed while I was touching her breasts. She went rigid, shook violently, then went rigid again. I thought I'd killed her.'

Howard, 27, a builder, remembered: 'The first time I fell in love was sexually traumatic. I was 16 and she was 15. We were both experiencing strong sexual desires but we were well aware she was under age. We were afraid to make love and in the end I felt very inexperienced and a failure.

'We were both sexually inhibited for some time after and I believe a better sex education earlier, and a more understanding adult society, could have saved a lot of pain.'

The subject is usually driven underground at home, even if parents know or suspect their son is having a sexual relationship.

29

Shane, 20, a computer programmer: 'I think my parents always knew that we were having sex but talk about sex was always uneasy ground. It made it worse for all concerned when they found out for sure.'

Sex is made to seem a furtive and guilty activity, instead of open and joyous. Fraser, 27, a mechanic: 'It's hard for young people, mainly because it is difficult to find privacy, apart from fumbling about in cars.' Chris, 23, a printer: 'The fact that we can't enjoy proper sex and closeness in my parents' house made me sad. I have been going out with my girlfriend for five years and we love each other very much.'

Although parents may set an example that sex is something you don't talk about even with those close to you, they don't stop it happening, of course – in the shadows, in cars and darkened front rooms, outside discos and school dances. And very enjoyable many find it.

Lionel, 43, a technical supervisor, 'There was no sex education except the playground variety, and looking back some knowledge of the technicalities would have been useful. But I enjoyed the fumbling about trying to learn.'

Derek, 34, remembers happily: 'Finding out that they want to get inside your clothes as much as you want to theirs.'

William reckoned, 'Most men's sexual relationships during adolescence form a pattern, from a hand inside a bra . . .' However, they vary far more widely than is realised in how soon they have intercourse, not necessarily even seeing it as the culmination. Matthew, 24, a draughtsman: 'I was very happy not to go all the way, but to feel the girl's body and then have the girl masturbate me. Many girls seem to think this is frustrating but it's not at all to me.'

Others hold back from intercourse because they don't feel they are in the right relationship. Gregory, 21, an office worker: 'You don't just have sex, you make love. Although I have been close on a few occasions I have stopped because I didn't feel as though I loved her enough.'

The 'first time'

Most young men are keen for 'experience'. If no one gives you the information you need to be a sexually competent adult then you have to get out to find it by practical experiment – trial and error.

Figure 1

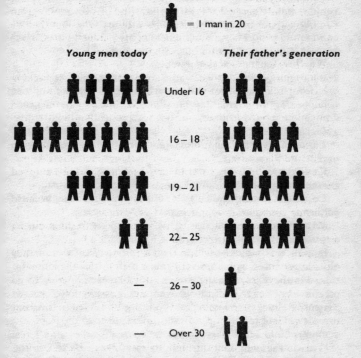

How old were you the first time you had intercourse?

= 1 man in 20

Young men today | **Their father's generation**

Under 16

16 – 18

19 – 21

22 – 25

26 – 30

Over 30

(The younger men on whom I based this illustration were aged 22 – 30 years at the time of the survey but figures will not prove very different for today's teenagers. The 'fathers' were aged 41 – 50 years).

As many as one in four (24 per cent) of adolescent boys has intercourse for the first time under the age of 16.

From an older viewpoint it may seem that an awfully large number of boys is having sex very young. The rate is higher than among older generations, but under-age sex is not something that has been invented in the last decade.

One in eight (12 per cent) of men now in their forties also had intercourse while under 16. (See Figure 1 page 31).

Though some wait until their twenties or later, by the age of 18 nowadays nearly two out of three young men has had intercourse. Yet there has not so much been a wide sexual revolution as a steady shift of a few per cent towards having intercourse at a younger age. Puberty now arrives earlier. Twenty years ago a schoolboy of thirteen might have made it into long flannels, but he was not fashion-conscious like today's lad, who is using gel on his hair and has to have the right socks for the school disco.

Whether the new sexual scares such as AIDS will start a gradual shift back again remains to be seen, but our sexual behaviour is a very deep-seated part of human nature and not going to change overnight, no matter what the newspaper headlines and latest government policy on sex education might be.

Ironically, in view of all the pressure to gain experience, three out of ten (31 per cent) of young men do not enjoy the first time they have intercourse.

Reality may be miles from the myth. Anxiety and ignorance are the main problems: 'Initial sexual experiences were usually of frustration and confusion'; 'We found it very difficult because neither of us knew what to expect'; 'A disaster'; 'I couldn't climax – it was so embarrassing'; 'I was unable to maintain an erection and did not enjoy it'.

Ian, 18, a computer salesman, was 'initiated' by a beautiful, older experienced woman. Every young man's dream? Not quite: 'She was six years my elder with a body like Miss World. I was petrified but eager to find out what sex was like. We became "friendly" by way of kissing and cuddling which led to involved foreplay . I let her lead me until she pulled me on to the floor and demanded that I make love to her.

'The only thing going through my mind was, "Is she on the pill?" I asked her and she said yes, so we went through a very uneasy 25 minutes of "sex". I enjoyed the foreplay better than the actual act.

'When it came time for my climax my penis went soft and it was a terrible *anti*-climax for me. I just wanted to crawl into a corner and die, but she ignored my feelings of guilt, trying to comfort me. Altogether rather a let down.'

Some, like Graham, 18, who works in a music shop, don't repeat the attempt for quite a while: 'I had sex with my first real girlfriend when I was 13. I know now I was too young and I wish it hadn't happened so soon. After that, I didn't have sex until I was 15 or 16.'

However, whereas we found that girls who had intercourse very young were far less likely to enjoy it than those who waited until they were older, there was no such clear-cut link among the boys.

Raymond, 24, a garage manager, had also only just turned 13 the first time he had intercourse. 'I was actually with my girlfriend's older sister. We ended up in the local graveyard, of all places. We lay down on the ground and started kissing, while letting our hands wander. One thing led to another and soon our clothes were off. It was only at this point that I realised what was going to happen and that we were both far too gone to stop it. We both enjoyed it immensely. I felt magic and it became a regular occurrence.'

In fact, older teenagers have often had longer to build up expectations and anxieties, feel they have more at stake and are more worried about getting it wrong. Girls may worry more whether they are doing the right thing morally and whether it will hurt. Boys may be equally nervous that they won't 'do the right thing' – that they are inexpert, lack technique. Boys feel they carry the responsibility for making sure that sexually it is a success.

Neil, 24, a clerk: 'The first time was rather a shock for me. I wasn't expecting my girlfriend to be on the pill, but she sprang this on me in the middle of a kissing/cuddling session. I was only rather shocked and frightened.

'Suddenly my head was full of worries about "Will I be okay?" and "What about getting it up as and when we finally get to bed?" When we did she was too tense and I was rather relieved. We then proceeded to talk about the worries we both had and it seemed more natural after that.'

Once Neil and his girlfriend could behave towards each other as people who cared for each other, but had naturally rather mixed feelings, rather than as male and female trying to achieve some conveyor-belt norm of sexual behaviour, they relaxed and all was well. Most young men find it a wonderful relief if the girl takes some initiative and responsibility.

Julian, 20, a student: 'I was very paranoid about having sex for the first time – how to do it, worried about penis size, premature ejaculation, partner being unsatisfied. I imagined she would be very unhelpful, had visions of her saying to friends: "On a scale of one to ten, I'd only give him . . ."

'In reality, I liked the girl, wanted to know what sex was like, she was the first person actually to tell me *she* wanted sex with me, and at the time was the only girl with whom I'd have had enough confidence to go through with it. She was not a virgin but quite experienced.'

Did the earth move?

Just one in four (23 per cent) of young men enjoy the first time they have intercourse a great deal, while nearly half (45 per cent) enjoy it reasonably well.

Anything less than ecstasy may cause disappointment: 'I was worried it wasn't earth-shatteringly enjoyable,' said Rod, a 27-year-old computer programmer.

Phil, 19, a student: 'I think so much now is put on sex and it is built up so much in novels and media that, before you actually have it, you expect it to be brilliant straight away. When you do it for the first time, it tends to be an anti-climax. Like most things it gets better with practice.'

Many are conscious that their partner is not having a very good time, and mostly blame themselves – again the men take responsibility for both their sexual pleasure, though their partner is nearly always there willingly – only one young woman in ten (11 per cent) says she was talked into having intercourse the first time.

Denis, 24, a cab driver: 'I was 16. It was good for me but I don't think it was good for my partner. I used to ejaculate prematurely and was not experienced enough to indulge in foreplay, caressing, oral sex and so on.'

One good aspect of feeling that you ought to 'wait' before having sex, is that it encourages a couple to enjoy an extensive period of 'petting' before they have intercourse. This gives them a chance to explore their own and their partner's sexual responses and is particularly important for women since many, if not most, continue to find stimulation other than intercourse most satisfying. Simon, 22, a student teacher: 'We have a very happy sexual relationship though we have not had intercourse. We were both inexperienced and my fiancée's parents were quite old and brought her up to believe she should wait for marriage. However, we learnt together, finding out what made the other happy and shedding our inhibitions with each other gradually. We make love through mutual masturbation and oral sex. In many ways this has been an asset to our love-making and not a hindrance.'

They certainly sound as if they're enjoying their sexual relationship more than Alistair and his girlfriend did, for all they 'made it'.

As Alistair, 24, a chiropodist, pointed out, a young woman may have too high expectations. Though neither she nor the young man have much knowledge of what can help a sexual experience be pleasurable, she may assume it is up to *him* to make the earth move for her. 'When I was 17 I had intercourse with my girlfriend at a party, having consumed a fair amount of alcohol. Although the experience was fine for me, the girl was disappointed it had not amounted to more. I think girls are brought up on the idea that when they lose their virginity to a boy, whether he is experienced or not, the earth shall move, they will have stars in their eyes and their heads will be on Cloud Nine.

'As a result of that disappointment the girl would not have intercourse with me again and we split up shortly afterwards. With a typical fragile male ego, it was a year before I had intercourse again. By then I had read up on the skill of foreplay. The next encounter was a bit better for both sides – though the earth still didn't stand still for the girl.'

While some men may agree with Alistair that women take too romantic a view of sex, exactly the same proportion of men as women save sex for love and/or marriage. *One quarter (24 per cent) say the reason they had intercourse for the first time was that they were with a girl they loved. Three per cent had just got married. A further quarter (25 per cent) were with a girl they liked a lot.*

Gerry, 32, a civil servant: 'We were both in love and saw having sex as a further step in our relationship, which I believe is as it should be. There was no pressure to do it or not, but we were both virgins and not sure what to expect. It wasn't as relaxed as it might have been as we were in a conifer plantation and pine needles don't make the best beds, but we were both glad we had crossed the barriers, so to speak, and neither had any regrets.'

However, some girls should take the stars out of their eyes. Simply wanting to know what 'it' is like motivates around half the young men having intercourse for the first time.

Forty-three per cent of men say that the first time they had intercourse it was out of pure curiosity.

Mike, 19, a pipe-fitter: 'I have only had sex with one girl in the past, and that was because I wanted to know what it was like. I had no feelings towards her.'

Those who start having intercourse when they are under 16 are far *more* likely to be acting out of curiosity on a quest for experience.

Of those men who first had intercourse under 16, only one in twenty (5 per cent) says it was because they loved the girl, two in three (68 per cent) that it was out of curiosity.

Alan, 36, a postman: 'When I was in my teens, sex was something to boast about. If you were a male virgin at 17 you were a poof! So every girlfriend had to be "tried". If you got nowhere after two weeks, you dumped her. Sounds harsh, but I think it's still true today with teenagers.'

Only 5 per cent said that they first had sex either because all their friends had – though peer pressure must increase curiosity – or because they had been drinking.

Colin, 27, who's in the Royal Marines: 'I was blind drunk at a school disco when I had my first attempt. I can't remember a lot about it. The girl put it about the school that she'd been with me. I was supposedly a Jack-the-lad beforehand, which was totally untrue, though I never denied it. That was how I finally did "it" – I was 15.'

'First time' experiences provide a very clear illustration of the differences that really do exist between men and women's reactions to sex and their sexual responses.

In Figures 2a and 2b, pages 37 and 38 we compare the reasons and the rate of enjoyment of men and women who first had intercourse when they were aged between sixteen and eighteen – the most common time.

Men are more likely to enjoy the first time – six out of ten women do not enjoy it compared with only three out of ten men.

Men are twice as likely to have sex just out of curiosity – 47 per cent of men compared with 20 per cent of women.

Women are extremely unlikely to enjoy the first time if they have sex because they are curious, have been talked into it or have been drinking, but have a reasonable chance of enjoying it if they are with a partner they care for and who cares for them.

Being with a partner they are fond of makes men more likely to enjoy the first time, but they have a good chance of still

36

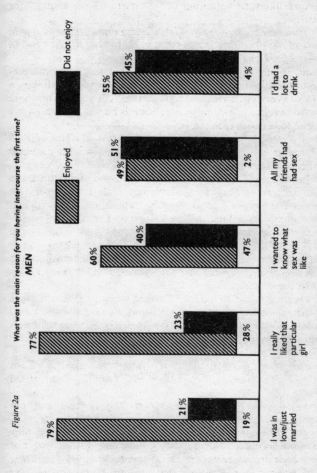

Figure 2a

What was the main reason for you having intercourse the first time?
MEN

Enjoyed | Did not enjoy

| I was in love/just married | I really liked that particular girl | I wanted to know what sex was like | All my friends had had sex | I'd had a lot to drink |

79% / 21% (19%) · 77% / 23% (28%) · 60% / 40% (47%) · 49% / 51% (2%) · 55% / 45% (4%)

Reason: Men who first had intercourse between aged 16 and 18

Figure 2b

What was the main reason for you having intercourse the first time?

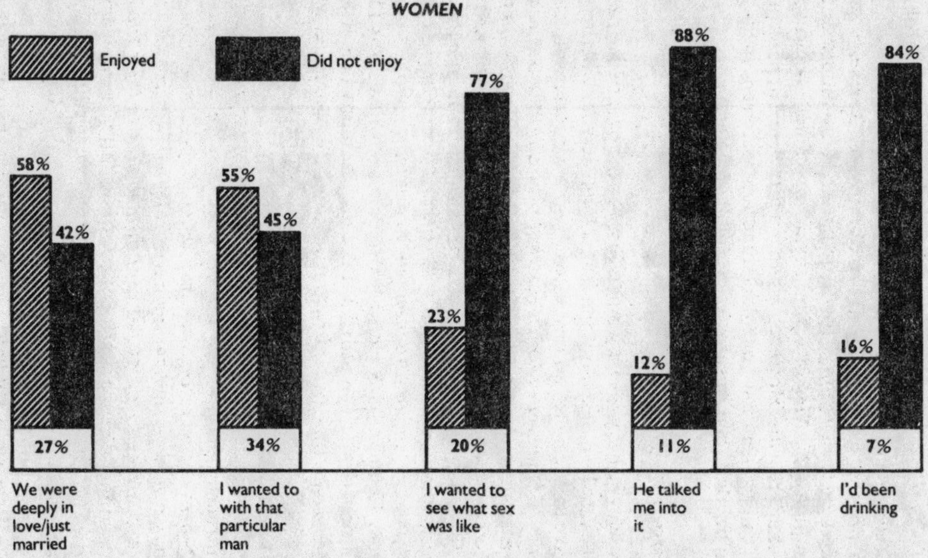

WOMEN

▨ Enjoyed   ■ Did not enjoy

	Enjoyed	Did not enjoy
We were deeply in love/just married	42%	58% (27%)
I wanted to with that particular man	45%	55% (34%)
I wanted to see what sex was like	23%	77% (20%)
He talked me into it	12%	88% (11%)
I'd been drinking	16%	84% (7%)

Reason: Women who first had intercourse between ages 16 and 18 *enjoying it even if they are experimenting just out of curiosity, or because they've been drinking.*

If men don't enjoy the first time they are more likely to put it down to lack of experience, than anything to do with their relationship with the woman concerned – a performance problem rather than one to do with their relationship.

Men are more likely to want and enjoy sex for sex's sake, regardless of their feelings for their parter. This should not be over-emphasised. Men are not sexual machines uncaring of whom they are with. However, there is a difference in perception which causes genuine misunderstandings between men and women in adult relationships, as we shall see later.

Taking a chance?

A man who has sex with a woman just for the experience rather than because he cares about her is less likely to care whether she may have to cope with an unwanted pregnancy as a result.

Overall, 51 per cent of men say that they did take contraceptive precautions the first time they had intercourse – or made sure their partner did. However, among those who first had sex under 16 – the group most likely to be having sex out of curiosity and least equipped to cope with parenthood – only three out of ten (28 per cent) made sure pregnancy could not follow.

Steven, 18 and a bank clerk: 'I first had sex when I was 15. It was with a girl who was only 13. I decided to try my luck when I saw she was getting excited by our petting. I was amazed when she said yes, if I had protection. I didn't, but I talked her into it anyway.'

The cheering news is that today's young men are *more* likely to use contraception than their fathers when they were young.

Sixty per cent of young men now aged 16 to 18 who have had intercourse made sure that they were protected the first time they had sex, compared with 46 per cent of men now in their forties.

More young men are sharing the responsibility for preventing unwanted pregnancies and it shows that such education programmes as the Family Planning Association's Men Too campaign are not falling on stony ground.

Phil, 19-year-old student: 'I was curious what sex was like from a fairly young age (11-12) but was determined that the first time I did it, it was going to be with someone I felt I loved. I'd had chances with a couple of other girlfriends. Although tempted, I felt I didn't love them enough (if at all) to take any responsibility if anything went wrong.

'My girlfriend and I always take precautions but if she did become pregnant I think we are stable enough in ourselves to stay together and bring up a child.'

Wild oats?

While many single young men who took part in our survey had gone through an earlier phase of curiosity and careless experiment, they certainly were not the wildly promiscuous crew feared by those who believe a sexual revolution has wrecked moral standards.

Nearly nine out of ten were in steady relationships, and little more than one in ten of those who currently did not have a special girlfriend did not want one.

Of those with a steady girlfriend, nearly nine out of ten (86 per cent) say they are in love.

We will look at the qualities men believe make for lasting and successful relationships in the next chapter, but the overwhelming majority of young single men seem to believe in sexual fidelity.

Of those who had had intercourse, nearly nine out of ten (87 per cent) only made love with a steady girlfriend. Of the others 6 per cent were not having sex with anyone and only 6 per cent were having casual sexual relationships.

Noel, 27, an assembly-line worker: 'Casual sex is not a patch on making love with a person you are deeply involved with.'

A few spoke cheerfully about many conquests, like Adrian, 19: 'I'm in a band, which helps for pulling women. I just love the challenge of getting a woman to spend the night, usually at my best mate's house, where we'll both take a girl back.'

More viewed one-night stands with mixed feelings. Jerry, 19, a photography student: 'Why I did it I don't really know, except that I had an on-off relationship with my girlfriend. This other girl started chatting me up, we fancied each other and I couldn't resist. The lads' whistling and envying encouragement helped, so I went off with her.

'We had a hell of a night by her fire. She had a blanket down and in the excitement it caught alight. She was a real laugh, a bundle of energy, and I suppose I wanted what she could offer.

Afterwards I didn't feel very proud of her or myself. I suppose I'm a bit old-fashioned, thinking sex is an act of love and endearment.'

Jerry is not old-fashioned but caught, like so many, between wanting to explore the wonderland that sex has been portrayed as being and yearning for one close, loving and faithful relationship. It is a conflict that pursues many men into marriage, as we shall see later.

The younger the man the more likely he is to believe that a sexual double standard still operates.

Four out of five (81 per cent) of 16 to 18 year olds agree that girls who have sex with several boys get a bad reputation. Two in five (41 per cent) believe that boys who have sex with several girls are admired.

Men who have been the faithful type often later regret that they were not *more* promiscuous while they had the opportunity.

Giles, 29, an engineer: 'I often wish I had been less emotional and intense about relationships and been able to experience more casual relationships when I was younger without getting too involved. I wish I could experience purely sexual relationships for physical excitement and variety, but it seems that's not the way I am.'

Naturally the number of previous lovers young men had had was related to age. Today's 22 to 25 year olds are the most 'experienced'.

Just over a quarter (27 per cent) have never had another lover before their current partner. Thirty-four per cent have had up to four other lovers, 20 per cent between five and ten, and 17 per cent more than ten.

Glen, a 25-year-old insurance salesman, explained: 'I have never been in love but I have had 16 sexual partners since I was 16. Three girls have wanted to marry me, but I have declined. My two regular sexual partners are girls I went out with in the past. They insist on visiting me for sex because they say I am good in bed. I am always in search of new sexual partners. I believe sex should be enjoyed and talked about more openly. I tend to get bored with the same sexual partner within three to four months.'

Few men are as systematically casual in their sexual relationships as Glen, who perhaps has a problem with real intimacy. However, at present men certainly don't regret periods of promiscuity the way we found women do. They tend to see them as experience gained – experience which they see as enriching current sexual relationships, and which they feel they need, since the responsibility for making their sex life satisfying and successful is probably seen by both partners as lying with the man.

If men have regrets when they look back, it is usually to bemoan lack of experience rather than worry that they had too much (though AIDS may change this). Peter, 29 and now married, spoke for many: 'If only I knew then what I know now!'

'Getting to know you . . .'

Not only is the man expected to take responsibility for a couple's sex life, he is also generally the one who has to set the wheels in motion to get to know the woman to start with.

Four out of five single men (78 per cent) say that it is men who are still usually expected to make the first move to start a relationship.

What does not help, many complain, is that the women leave them in the dark about how interested they are.

Noel, 20, works in a newsagents: 'Girls don't show if they like you or give any signs. They don't start talking to you. There are lots of things they could do but they don't do anything. It doesn't say much for women's lib.'

The one in five who disagree point out that a woman may not be the one who actually offers the invitation, but she has often paved the way.

Roy, a 22-year-old motor mechanic commented: 'I think it's a myth that men make the first move. Women do it, but subtly.'

'Relationships usually begin in a traditional way, with me asking the girl,' explained Robin, a 24-year-old teacher, 'but I only make the move after some kind of encouragement on her part, be it a wink, smile, a look or sometimes a more sexual come-on.'

Girls may assume that most lads are carefree and confident, and relish the freedom they have to pick and choose, while the girls have to manoeuvre and wait to be asked. They are very wrong.

Only one in five young men is happy to be expected to make the first move – either because he likes feeling he can choose or does not like pushy women. One in ten finds it a real strain and half think it out of date – and a pain!

'Why don't women come straight to the point,' moans Kevin, a 19-year-old shop assistant (with overtones of Professor

Higgins' 'Why can't a woman be more like a man?') 'The other night me and my mate went out to a wine bar,' explains Kevin. 'We saw two women who were smiling at us, so we started talking to them and they asked us to sit down. We talked to them all night, we all went at the same time, and we asked them if they would meet us another night. They just gave us a funny look and walked off.

'Now we did not do anything wrong. We were very nice to them, so why be so ignorant? I would rather they said, "Get lost" to start with. Why don't women say if they like a man, and say if they don't? It would be better than doing things like that.'

Rejection is bad enough, without feeling humiliated because you've indirectly been led to believe that you are liked and welcomed.

It is fear of rejection which makes so many young men wish that they were not expected to be the one who takes the risk all the time. They have discovered no magic confidence pill.

'I can never tell if a girl fancies me,' said Martin, a 21-year-old office worker. 'I always think, "Oh, she wouldn't like me." While I'm trying to decide if she does like me, I miss the boat. They think that, because I'm taking so long to act, I don't like them and they find someone else.

'I suppose I'm frightened of rejection. That's why I like the idea that women should take the initiative. My longest relationship was with a girl who asked me out. I was so flattered.

'I'd been with her every day for four weeks and never realised she liked me. When I caught her looking at me I thought it was because she hated me.'

Byran, 32, an insurance clerk, was only too relieved when he was the one to be picked up. 'I fancied her and was trying to pluck up the courage to go and talk to her, when she came up to me and started talking. Brilliant, I thought. That's one hurdle I don't have to jump over.'

Some men use alcohol to give them courage to bridge the great divide – 'brave beers' one man called them. As Nick, 23 and unemployed, discovered, this can cause more problems than it solves, though it had a happy outcome for him. 'I found it very hard to talk to women because of my shyness. The only way I managed to meet them was in a pub after a few drinks.

'Once I had to go to court for being drunk and disorderly. Working nights then, I got my days mixed up and turned up for court a day late. I went to the pub. When the barmaid heard about me going to court on the wrong day, she curled up with laughter – so we got talking.

'A few days later I went into the pub again. After having a few drinks I asked the barmaid for a Christmas kiss (it was the middle of February). She did, we kept meeting and have been together ever since.'

Other men work out face-saving manoeuvres to try to cut down the risk of outright or public rejection.

Clive, 21, a radiographer: 'Before asking a girl out I always get a spy to find out if she is interested in me. I hate being turned down.'

Howard, 22, a medical salesman, remembers, 'At school I generally got girlfriends by asking a friend to ask them if they would go out with me.'

Trevor, 32, now unemployed, explained, 'I have inevitably made the first move but have always done so in such a way as to be able to "save face" should my advances be rejected.

'For example, on arranging a drink with my "lover-to-be" I told her that I would be in the pub anyway because I had a job to do nearby. In other words, "Don't come for a drink purely on my account." Needless to say, the talk about the job was a fake but, due to my strong sense of pride or whatever, I feel unable to cope with outright female rejection.'

'Pride', like love, can cover a variety of different emotions depending on who is using the word. Fear of rejection so strong that it distorts behaviour and stops a man from being able to say openly to a woman, 'I would like to know you better', certainly does not spring from a feeling of strength and self-esteem. But then how many women would have the confidence to say anything like that to a man?

Women tend to cook up all sorts of reasons why it is out of the question, largely to do with what's accepted behaviour. In fact most men would welcome it, but this is one difficult task in relationship-building that women are usually only too happy to leave to men.

'Like they were Martians or something'

One in three single men says he finds it difficult to meet partners.

Some have particular problems which do not always meet with understanding or lack of prejudice. Robert, 33, a film cameraman, remembers: 'My experience of meeting partners

44

when young was hampered by acute acne, shyness and self-consciousness.'

Ryan, 32, a nurse: 'I love meeting partners at discos but they are too shy to say yes because I'm black.'

Keith, 36, an office accident manager: 'I have a slight disability, a limp, and most girls seem to turn their noses up at this sort of thing.'

Another group of men who have problems in meeting partners are those whose disadvantage lies inside – those who have developed stereotyped images of women, often through lack of friendly contact with girls, and so look on them as almost an alien species.

Geoff, 26, a student remembered: 'I got really hung up when I was in my teens because I was shy and immature, didn't have a girlfriend and everyone else did. I very rarely spoke to any girls at all because I just couldn't relate to them – like they were Martians or something.'

Ken, now 42, spoke of his 'feeling of near terror as an adolescent meeting girls'.

Stephen, 27, a research student: 'I have found meeting partners very difficult because I believe it's unlikely I will have anything deeply in common with the girl I'm trying to chat up.'

Max, 43, a HGV driver: 'I was never any good at talking to women, couldn't understand them, didn't speak their language, not on their wavelength. Perhaps it was me being too abrupt, calling a spade a spade.'

Ross, 36, a bank official, said sadly, 'I did not enjoy my teenage years as I was very shy and very naive. I am still waiting for my opportunity to be one of the lads and put it about a bit. Desperation tinges my approaches.'

Single-sex schooling can be a serious drawback when it comes to forming relationships. Alan, 29, a manager with British Telecom, said: 'I went to all-boys school and found it difficult to see women as people. They were "different".'

Mixed schooling is an early asset. Alex, 32, a manager, said: 'On leaving school it was difficult to accept that meeting partners was not so easy and the relationships formed were not so intense as they had been.'

*Our survey showed that while 25 per cent of 16 to 18 year olds, who are at school or have only recently left, say that it is **very** easy to meet partners, the percentage drops dramatically among 19 to 21 year olds to just 13 per cent.*

Friends first

Young men may worry that they do not dazzle the disco and have not the muscles for Marbella. Yet when we asked how successful relationships had actually started, we found that having a chance to get to know one another as 'people' – friends, classmates, colleagues, fellow students, or whatever – usually gives a relationship the best chance of success. (See Figure 3, below).

Nearly two-thirds of men say that their most important steady relationships grew out of friendship, shared work or interests.

Figure 3

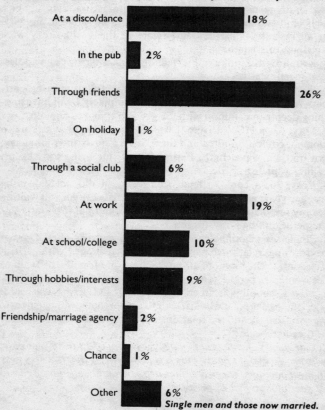

Where did your most important steady relationship start?

At a disco/dance	18%
In the pub	2%
Through friends	26%
On holiday	1%
Through a social club	6%
At work	19%
At school/college	10%
Through hobbies/interests	9%
Friendship/marriage agency	2%
Chance	1%
Other	6%

Single men and those now married.

'We got to know each other first as friends,' said Eddie, 21, a temp worker. 'This was very important since neither of us was putting on a "chatting-up" act. We knew exactly what the other person was like.'

Tim, 25, a production manager: 'I find it easiest to meet partners through shared interests such as badminton club or night school. Then I can find out more about a person before I let her know I like her.

'I have tried approaching girls "cold" at pubs or discos, but a relationship might start which is only brief, because first impressions can be very misleading. I remember one incident especially. I met a girl at a party when I was not wearing my glasses. We arranged a date and went out. It was good fun again – and I had not worn my glases. On the next occasion I wore them. She seemed to go cold towards me and did not turn up for our next date. I now wear contact lenses.'

Meeting through the obvious chatting-up stamping grounds like pubs, discos and the beach, the accent is on appearance rather than personality and the fast talkers rather than the caring listeners. However, these are not the qualities which actually seem to lead to lasting relationships. And that should be a relief!

Not many men have the ease and confidence of 20-year-old Bruce, a squash pro and model: 'I often meet girls in a disco but I like to think I can chat a girl up in any situation. My feeling is that, if you see an attractive girl and you'd like to take her out or sleep with her, then if you don't try to talk to her, you may never know if she would have gone out with you. If she says no, at least you've tried!'

More men feel like Russell, 27, a car salesman: 'I've always found it easier to approach partners through a more relaxed work or social situation where things could develop more easily, than in a market situation – discos, across a crowded bar – or public place, such as on a bus or in a cafe.'

Terry, 23, a milkman, 'I found it quite difficult to meet girls and start talking. I met my partner as a customer's daughter on a milk round. (You know what they say about milkmen, don't you?)'

James, 24, a chemist, pointed out: 'I have always considered myself unattractive to females. I find it impossible to approach women at a disco, but when I have to talk to them at work, I find communication easy.'

47

Figure 4

Which characteristics are important for you to feel attracted towards a possible partner?

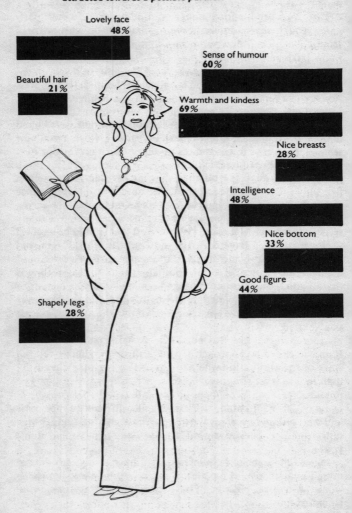

Lovely face
48%

Sense of humour
60%

Beautiful hair
21%

Warmth and kindess
69%

Nice breasts
28%

Intelligence
48%

Nice bottom
33%

Good figure
44%

Shapely legs
28%

Based on the views of single men.

Figures don't count

It is personal qualities rather than physical attributes which most men say are important for them to feel attracted towards a woman. (See Figure 4, page 48).

Seven out of ten men rate warmth and kindness and more than half say a sense of humour is important. Nice breasts and bottom, together with shapely legs, came bottom of the poll with three out of ten men or fewer saying these mattered to them. Intelligence matters to just under half.

It is true that you do not hear many wolf whistles and cat calls of 'Like your sense of humour, darlin'.' But could the emphasis on anatomy in men's *public* appreciation be more closely linked with impressing other men than with what they really feel about women, especially those close to them?

Bruce, the squash pro: 'It is important what my friends think of my girlfriend, as I think it is to a lot of men, and they can influence my opinions.'

There certainly are men who put looks before personality, like Hugh, 44, a business manager: 'I find few women approach my requisites of attractiveness. They may have one or two good points but the drawbacks usually outweigh them.' He sounds as if he is buying office equipment!

Others are so dazzled by appearances they forget there is a real person underneath – flesh, blood and feelings like the rest of us. Sean, 33, a civil servant: 'I always find it difficult or impossible to approach girls that I find most attractive. I usually go for the "easy" girls. My first thoughts on meeting a woman have nearly always been sexual.'

These men, not surprisingly, are less likely to form happy and stable relationships than those who have tumbled to it that women are people above all.

Men who are now in unhappy relationships are more likely to say a good figure and breasts are what count.

While listing priorities can reveal quite a lot about men's attitudes towards women, and even give some indicator of likely future happiness in relationships, in reality there is usually a complex interplay between all these qualities.

Rick, a civil servant, 34: 'When I look at a woman, I suppose I check out the essentials – breasts, bottom, legs, but may have been initially attracted by her hair or any attribute. I then generally look at her face. If it's warm and cheerful, then I would be

49

interested and look again. To me it is the person underneath that is the most important. If she has attractive features then that's a bonus.'

In a sense we are all fumbling in the dark when we try to understand how and why we feel attracted to some people and not others. As well as those qualities men note consciously – if asked – there are others which will have affected them subconsciously – body language, pheromones (body odours triggering sexual excitement), dilation of the pupils indicating sexual attraction – and these affect women, too. This is probably what John, a 19-year-old student, is reacting to: 'You can always tell when there is a chance that a girl likes you by eye contact – it's sort of electric.'

Women are now thought to be attracted more by physical attributes than they admit publicly – or to themselves. Some careful research with a camera revealed that when women claim to have been noticing a man's conversation their eyes have been checking out his crotch.

Yet these days women are also more likely to object to a man showing approval of their body rather than their mind or deeds. Andy, 28, a nurse, thinks men are now forced to deny natural admiration which would only add to the richness of relationships between men and women.

'If women (and I'm sure many do) look at men with an appreciative eye, men feel more proud, pleased. If men do this, a lot of women now feel threatened, harassed, and straight away believe the man is leering at them, undressing them mentally. This is one of the reasons men nowadays feel more uncomfortable with women, especially feminists who deny men the right to look at them and appreciate their feminity and not, as they say, just as sex objects.'

We probably will find a happier balance in time, but those men are unlikely to be made half as uncomfortable by the feminists as women have been made to feel by men who have assumed it their right to pat any female bottom in reach.

There is also an interesting contrast between men's usually easy-going tolerance of what many women feel is harassment by their fellows, and their reaction when the woman involved is their partner – their girlfriend or wife. Steady relationships often bring with them a marked change in men's attitudes and expectations as well as in their assessment of their sex life.

4 'Why spoil a wonderful evening?'

– Sex and steady relationships

F ew men can imagine a good relationship let alone a good marriage without good sex.

Four out of five (81 per cent) say that understanding each other's sexual needs is important in marriage and nearly all (94 per cent) say that a good sex life is important to them.

Perhaps surprisingly, it is not young men eager for experience who lay the most stress on the importance of a good sex life. Older men are more likely to say that it is *very* important to them, and married men more than single.

Douglas, a retired lecturer, is 68 and believes: 'A satisfying sex life is the cement which bonds you together.'

Right in line with all the saloon bar jokes, most men say that they do not get enough.

Three out of five (60 per cent) of men in steady relationships (including marriage) want to make love more often.

This proportion holds remarkably steady across the age groups. The dramatic variation is in what men see as preventing more frequent sex. (See Figure 5, page 53).

While most single men (62 per cent) blame lack of privacy because of parents, the commonest reasons mentioned by married men were that their wife doesn't feel like sex that often (57 per cent) and that she's too tired (55 per cent).

Leonard, 44, a teacher: 'My wife and I courted for five years. We had a very close friendship and loving relationship. As the courtship progressed, our love-making became more physical until we were indulging in very heavy petting, each giving the other manual orgasm. By mutual agreement we never had intercourse before marriage but, during this time, my wife was as interested in sex as I was. We invariably had orgasms when together, as often as six times a week.

'After marriage her whole attitude to love-making changed. She reckoned that as it was no longer a "forbidden fruit" there was no longer any element of excitement. Over the years her interest in love-making, whether sexual or not, has waned. She now only occasionally (about once a month) shows any interest. And only at night. In bed.

'After an enjoyable, romantic evening out, she has often commented when we have returned home and I am showing amorous intentions, "It's been a wonderful evening. Let's not spoil it." '

That's certainly a punch below the belt to a man's *amour propre*, but what happened to turn Leonard's wife from a young woman enjoying sharing orgasms with her fiancé nearly every day to a wife who allows loving contact so reluctantly? *She* has lost so much pleasure and richness, too.

What happens to women's sex drive when they get married? Is the answer simply: marriage?

Leonard's wife told him she had lost interest in sex because it no longer was a forbidden fruit. Knowing that you are breaking the rules and the danger of getting caught can add excitement to sex (see Chapter Eight on affairs), but there were other obvious factors involved which Leonard and his wife seem to have avoided discussing.

It was after marriage that Leonard started having intercourse with his wife, and we don't know what happened to all the heavy petting and manual orgasms. It was after marriage that they started sharing a home and later had children.

It is after marriage that all sorts of attitudes we have absorbed about the 'proper' way for a husband and wife to behave start to emerge. Before they married, Leonard and his wife were both on the same side – young people rebelling against their parents' dicta. Their sex life was an important secret bond.

Once married, Leonard's wife may have picked up all sorts of messages from him – implied rather than spoken – about how he expected a good home to be run (probably rather like his mother's). Immediately she is thrown into confusion – made worse by the fact that she has standards set by her mother in her head. Is she the wild wanton lover or the good housekeeper? Leonard would say he wants her to be one by day and the other by night, but we cannot change character at the flick of a switch.

52

Figure 5

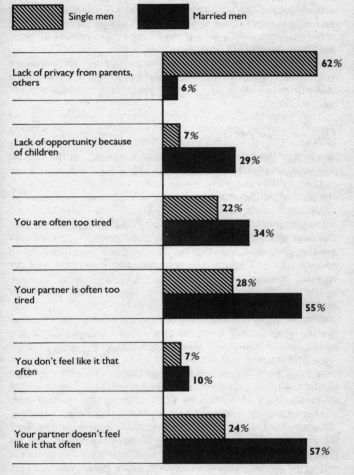

If you wish you made love more often what gets in the way?

Single men	Married men

Lack of privacy from parents, others
Single men: 62%
Married men: 6%

Lack of opportunity because of children
Single men: 7%
Married men: 29%

You are often too tired
Single men: 22%
Married men: 34%

Your partner is often too tired
Single men: 28%
Married men: 55%

You don't feel like it that often
Single men: 7%
Married men: 10%

Your partner doesn't feel like it that often
Single men: 24%
Married men: 57%

Being married is not 'naughty' but 'nice', and 'nice girls don't' – at least not to please themselves.

This is not to say that men do not suffer from the expectations of marriage. Many men lose their sex drive from driving themselves too hard at work to be a good breadwinner, and if they lose their job many lose their ability to make love entirely. But generally marriage suits men rather than women. Married men tend to be healthier than single men, for example, whereas single women tend to be healthier than wives. Perhaps until we throw our ideas of our married roles into the melting pot, there will be many men who agree with Tony.

Married for 12 years, Tony, 36, said: 'I believe most women have much less sex drive than men. They tend to view sex as conferring reward, or as a pleasant game, rather than as a regular, basic need.'

Happy ever after?

Most single young men are pretty enthusiastic about the idea of marriage. 'I want to share all I have with someone else and have children,' said Paul, 27, a surveyor.

Four out of five single under-25s intend to marry sooner or later.

It was only older men who talked of a fear of 'getting caught' and who seemed to think men had to be dragged, kicking and screaming, to the altar. Owen, 38, a postman, remembered, 'I never found it easy to say what I meant to a girl. My teenage years were in the sixties when all you said to a girl was, "Want a dance?" and that was it. She'd be with you for life if you didn't watch it!'

Even if today's young men have relished a period of being 'footloose and fancy free', once they meet the right girl at the right time for them, they seem to embrace the prospect of marriage with enthusiasm.

Neville, 23, a butcher: 'I never believed in love or marriage before I met my partner just under one year ago. I didn't even fancy her the first night. We just ended up together through friends. After three weeks I had told her I loved her, and after three months I had proposed, down on one knee, in the garden, on a Monday afternoon. Now I worship her. We are getting married this year.'

The strength of their feelings can make them suddenly feel very vulnerable and very possessive.

Fraser, 24, a shop worker, explained: 'I used to make it quite clear that I only wanted to get laid and not get involved.

Unforunately nearly all girls fell madly in love with me, which I hated, and I treated them very badly. When I met my wife she was so different from any other woman I've met. When I realised I loved her I was very frightened. Even now that we're married I feel bad. Now it's me that's clinging and doing all the things I despised in the girls who fell in love with me before!'

Most of the men who were in steady relationships (including marriage) said they were generally happy with their partner. Only one in twenty (5 per cent) said he was actually in an unhappy relationship. (There were others who were unhappy because they were in no relationship at all, but we talk more of their problems in Chapter Eight).

However, even men who were generally very happy with their partner said they were unhappy with their sex life.

Frank, 42, who works in local government: 'I have been reasonably happily married to a "text-book perfect" wife. She's good-looking, intelligent, excellent manager of household affairs, good cook and so on. The only thing that mars our otherwise near perfect relationship is her lack of interest in sex, coupled with her inability to understand my perfectly normal needs.'

Ted, 62, and now retired, said, 'It makes me sad that over 35 years of marriage we have never had any communication sexwise. My wife goes "funny" if I even try to talk about it. Sex does not move her. It *never* occurs to her.

'It's such a shame that she has made love (not initiated it) only as a reward for something I have done that pleased her.

'In every other respect she's wonderful. A tireless worker, clean, capable, humourous, kind and always thinking of others and their wants and needs.'

Only one in three (35 per cent) of men feels no need for improvement in his sex life.

Married and older men are rather more likely to be discontented than younger men, though this need not necessarily imply that older men have worse sex lives.

We found that older and married women were less content with the quality of their sex lives, too. It may be that sex which seems exciting and satisfying when you are thrilled to have found one another and any opportunity for sex at all, doesn't seem so perfect ten years later when you have pledged yourself for life. It is during the late twenties and thirties that the rates of sexual satisfaction noticeably begin to drop.

Geoff, 28, a centre lathe turner, is very fed up because his wife will not make love more often. 'Before we married sex was whenever the opportunity arose. Once we were married and beyond the honeymoon stage, we settled down and were making love two or three times a week. Sometimes this was an act of tender love and sometimes it was just for the pleasure of physical sex (on both sides).

'Now we make love perhaps once a month. Usually it is a hurried affair because my wife is getting tired or is worried that our little girl might wake up. Our sex life has suffered.

'However, this does not appear to have bothered my wife, while I still feel like making love two or three times a week. This leads to many rows.

'I agree that my wife should be able to get out sometimes without me, so she goes out for a drink with the girls, often until midnight or later. Yet if I want to make love after 9 p.m. she's too tired. I say that, if she can make the effort to go out, she should make the effort to show some affection to me.'

How often?

How often a man makes love is often thought to be the most important indicator of whether he has a good sex life or not. Generally the man who has intercourse every day is assumed to be enjoying a far better sex life and expected to be more content than the man who makes love once a week or once a month. If boys covertly compare penis size to be sure they are at least average, men like to be sure that they are having sex at least as frequently as the average for their age.

Overall, the average British couple make love once or twice a week.

The figures we obtained in this survey of 5,000 men tally remarkably with those we obtained from our surveys of women and we believe them to be very reliable. (See Figure 6, page 57).

While younger men do tend to make love more often, the contrast is not as dramatic as it is supposed. *While three out of ten men in their early twenties are making love only once a week or less, three out of ten in their fifties are making love two, three or more times a week.*

Ernest was born in 1899: 'My wife and I both enjoy sex though we are both over 80 years old. We sleep in the nude in a double bed. Recently I asked my doctor if this sex did me any harm. He

56

Figure 6

How often do you and your partner make love?

Frequency	All Men	Single Men	Married Men	Men according to age groups						
				16-18	19-21	22-25	26-30	31-40	41-50	51-60
Less than once a month	8%	4%	10%	6%	5%	3%	4%	6%	10%	16%
Less than once a week	14%	11%	16%	11%	10%	12%	15%	14%	12%	1%
About once a week	25%	19%	28%	17%	13%	17%	21%	26%	28%	31%
Two to three times a week	33%	35%	32%	39%	33%	38%	36%	38%	33%	21%
Four to five times a week	13%	19%	9%	15%	23%	22%	16%	11%	12%	5%
Every day	5%	11%	3%	11%	15%	7%	6%	4%	2%	1%
We don't make love now	2%	1%	2%	1%	1%	1%	2%	1%	3%	4%

Men with current sexual relationships

consulted a heart specialist who said it relaxed me and did no damage. Now if we feel like a good cuddle, we just do it with no holds barred.

'We live near a golf course and play a lot of golf and a lot of bridge. And we make lots of love!'

The dramatic contrasts cross all the age and class barriers. Among men of any age and any background there will be those who are making love every day and those making love less than once a month or not at all. Moreover, the frequency with which they make love will not *necessarily* reflect how happy they are with their sex life.

It is true that three-quarters (74 per cent) of those who make love every day say they are very happy with their sex life, but half of those who make love once a week or less say they are very happy or happy most of the time.

Other factors can be far more important than frequency in influencing how happy a man is with his sex life. We will look at the part played by the ways in which couples actually make love in the next chapter, but problems which are orginally nothing to do with sex can also show up in bed.

Martin, 29, and now unemployed: 'My job involved me being abroad a lot. When I was at home I was always expecting the telephone to call me away. I gave it up as we wished to start a family and my wife was beginning to put pressure on our marriage.

'Our sex life was good, though not regular, before. It improved shortly after my resignation but has declined ever since. I am still unemployed, my wife dislikes working, she is expecting and, even though I am well qualified, things currently look bleak. Sex is supposed to bring people together when life is very difficult. In fact it has had the opposite effect. My hope for the future will be a lot brighter when I have a secure job, when we know whether or not we shall have to move and when my wife can give up her job.'

Terry, 27, a musician and driving instructor: 'Our marriage has come under great pressure over the last two years and has brought sexual incompatibility to the surface. Sex is now a major problem rather than a consolation.'

A couple's sexual relationship can be all the more likely to break down because so many women feel they cannot make love unless they and their husband are feeling loving towards one another. They have been raised with the idea that sex is only justified by love. Many men, on the other hand, see sex as a way to bring a caring couple closer. They see it as a way of reaffirming an important bond as well as sharing one of the few pleasures that may be available in bad times.

It can lead to a miserable impasse, but it helps if men remember the importance of lots of hugs – stay in touch even if you are having problems – and if women at least consent to try, even if they add the proviso: 'I may say stop if it doesn't feel right.' Once they have got going, it usually does feel more than all right and can bring much needed warmth back between a couple.

Some men clearly are seriously deprived of physical love but some seem to have a chronic 'I'm not getting enough' belief programmed into them. No matter how often they are making love, they will always feel they should be at it more often.

Half (52 per cent) of those men who make love two or three times a week and three out of ten (31 per cent) of those who already make love four or five times a week want to make love more often.

It could be this doesn't so much reflect physical need for some as conforming to the image that a 'real man' can never get enough.

Women want more, too

There are not quite so many women who want to make love more often, but it is still a substantial proportion. Feeling you are not getting enough is certainly not an all-male prerogative.

The figures that follow are men's assessments of their partner's desires but where they overlap with questions we asked in our women's survey, they show that men have a very accurate grasp of their partner's feelings.

Two out of five (38 per cent) of women in steady relationships (including marriage) would like to make love more often.

It's not only young women with parents limiting their opportunities who want more sex either.

The partners of three out of ten (29 per cent) of men in their fifties would like to make love more often.

However, while virtually no young men in their teens have partners who admit to wanting to make love *less* often, the partners of two out of ten (19 per cent) of men in their fifties do. Older couples are, it seems, more likely to suffer from a troublesome disparity in their sex drive.

Donald, a farm manager in his fifties: 'The first 20 years were very good indeed. Then at about 40 my wife's libido became less and I started to be refused sex.

'My wife blamed her lack of interest on the menopause, although this was still ten years away. She later blamed my preoccupation with my job as a farm manager.

'A medical check has revealed my wife has a serious blood-pressure problem and I feel this may have had some effect on her libido. I don't press her and our life together – sex apart – is good, but there is still a problem with the tension lack of sex causes me.'

We will look at specific problems which can affect sex drive, particularly in middle age, in Chapter Thirteen. The sort of pattern Donald describes here of a general falling off of sex, with each partner having a different view of the causes, seems common enough.

There was a noticeable lack of men willing to talk in more detail about situations where they were the one who said no while their partner wanted more sex. However, we put the question 'If you wish you made love more often, what gets in the way?' to wives, in our survey on them, just as we did to husbands in this survey. Here you can compare the reasons they give. (See Figure 7, page 61).

More than half (52 per cent) of wives who want a more active sex life complain of tired husbands, nearly as high as the percentage (55 per cent) of frustrated husbands who complain of tired wives. In both cases there's usually more involved than unavoidable physical exhaustion.

Tom, a 29-year-old engineer, says forcibly: 'I think that the excuse "I'm too tired" for making love is 90 per cent bull. In my profession I have a very tiring job but I recognise the need that, when I come home, I should not have the problems of the day weighing me down. I need to "save" some of myself for my wife and home, because I regard it as being important.

'This isn't to say I am lax on responsibility or shirk tasks. I think it's more a state of mind and a recognition of one's marital responsibility can go a very long way in overcoming tiredness.'

It's true that men and women can make time and energy for sex, as they can for other areas of their lives, if they make it their priority. They might have to be prepared to insist on leaving the office by six, or even to move into a less pressured but less well paid job. They might have to give up a demanding sport. They

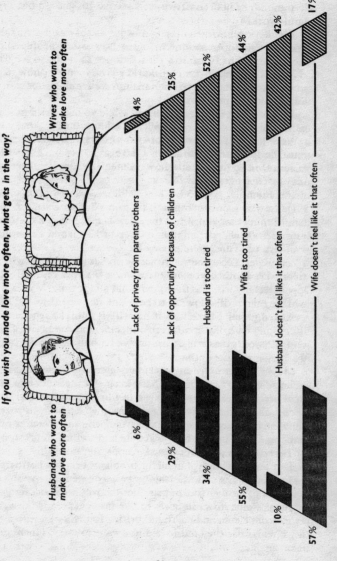

Figure 7

If you wish you made love more often, what gets in the way?

Husbands who want to make love more often

Wives who want to make love more often

	Husbands	Wives
Lack of privacy from parents/others	6%	4%
Lack of opportunity because of children	29%	25%
Husband is too tired	34%	52%
Wife is too tired	55%	44%
Husband doesn't feel like it that often	10%	42%
Wife doesn't feel like it that often	57%	17%

61

might have to live in a grubbier, less tidy house – particularly if they have children. They might have to share more of the housework.

Reordering priorities like this is not as easy as it first seems. We are usually quite quick to see how other people should reorder theirs to fit in with ours, but not so quick to see where change is possible in our own world view. No matter how fair we may try to be, in personal relationships we are all on our own side and cannot be unbiased.

We have all been 'programmed' while young. Perhaps it is to believe that it is our responsibility to achieve at work, that it is up to us to give our children priority over ourselves, that our home must be spick and span. As we have seen, few men have been encouraged to understand how women's feelings and sexuality may differ from their own.

For example, Alec, 39, states baldly, 'After 18 years of marriage, sex is much more important to me but much less so to my wife. I think many men feel the same as me. I have a reasonable job, £13,000 plus per annum, a three-bed semi and a reasonable standard of living, hobbies etc.

'However, I feel I have to tolerate my sex life with my wife. If I went with another woman and divorce was the result, I would lose. I feel my wife has the upper hand all the time. My sex life is what my wife will allow me to have and not what I would like.'

Alec does tend to talk as if his wife is another acquisition in life, along with the comfortable income and semi. Her fault is that she won't perform at the press of a button like the car and washing machine. Perhaps she feels she *is* the washing machine!

Maybe sex is more important to him now than to his wife because the *sort* of sex they have been sharing suits him better than her. Maybe she does enjoy a feeling of power in witholding sex because it is the only thing she has in which he is prepared to show any interest. Does he expect to spend his evenings on his hobbies and then find her tucked up and waiting in bed for him on his return, like an hyper-active hot water bottle?

This is not to imply that all the problems between partners can be blamed on the man. Certainly the way we educate young men has a lot to answer for, but so does the way we bring up young women. Remember the girls in the last chapter, who walked away from Kevin and his friend 'with a funny look', rather than say openly that they did or did not want to talk to them or see them again.

Rather than talk openly about what they want, in daily life let alone sexually, women too often are defensive, indirect or manipulative. Unable to ask or discuss, they silently resist – often hurting themselves and their own happiness in the process as well.

Tom, the 29-year-old engineer, talked of the problem of 'my sex drive which far and away outstrips my wife's'. Like many men he seems to see sex drive as an unalterable characteristic like the colour of your hair – and which, like hair, could gradually but inexorably fade away. Separately, however, he talked of the saddest times in his marriage being 'when I unknowing hurt my wife. She then, being the hurt party, deliberately sets out to hurt me, being unreasonable to the point of childish, withdrawing sex, putting on a spirit of "I don't need you".'

Francis, 36, who has once been divorced, explained how it upset him 'not knowing what my partner is feeling at any given time. She doesn't always freely explain how she's feeling or why she may be depressed. There's a lack of communication which can cause friction if left to "boil over" too long.'

Women's anxieties about voicing needs or criticisms often lead to them adding to tensions rather than clearing them. Rowan, 45 and married for the second time, pointed out, 'Women often assume that one is angry at being laughed at, when what makes one angry is the woman's habit of using laughter as a cover for shying away from situations in which she feels insecure.'

Whenever the differences or difficulties which need airing for a relationship to progress involve sex, then this already anxious scenario is further complicated by ladlings of sexual guilt, usually on both sides.

If we do not raise young people to consider their sexuality comfortably in the context of the rest of their lives, but force them to develop this side of their nature and relationships in secrecy, in the dark, it is going to take more than simply saying 'I do' to break down the barriers.

'Silence is a killer of relationships'

It is an accepted truth of this era of counselling and 'talking-it-through' that men find it hard to talk about their feelings. Many do, but many men also complain that *women* find it hard to talk about their feelings, at least with their partner, and many men believe it to be important. It is not a female preserve.

Francis continued, 'I've recently tried to be more considerate. What makes me happy is knowing my partner is happy and she's got no worries. It's not possible to be content yourself if your partner is not content also. But if for some reason you're not aware of any discontent in your relationship, you can't act to put it right. My advice to any woman (or man) is TALK to your partner. Silence is a killer of relationships!'

We asked men what qualities they considered most important for a relationship to last successfully, and which they considered least important. (See Figure 8, page 65).

Since they could pick several qualities, it shows how level-headed they try to be that only two out of three (64 per cent) mentioned love.

Men were noticeably less romantic as they grew older. While 72 per cent of 16 to 18 year olds picked love, just 58 per cent of men in their forties thought it essential. Probably Ian, 38, and married with children, reflected a common view. 'The most important ingredient for a successful relationship is without a doubt love. By this I don't mean the romantic "moon in June" feelings but a strong sense of emotional attachment to one's partner, coupled with understanding insights into their character. In my view this is the fundamental requirement for a stable relationship of worthwhile intensity.

'That is my ideal at least. In practice, of course, it's a little more complicated.'

After love, 'talking openly about feelings' was the next most commonly named ingredient essential for a successful and lasting relationship, mentioned by 52 per cent of men.

Colin, 27, a sign-maker: 'I have come through many upheavals and learnt a great deal through it all. Love is probably the central point to my marriage but without understanding and harmony, talking openly, pain and confusion easily occur.'

Mark, 20, a student: 'We are totally honest. Sharing ideas, thoughts and feelings is probably more important than sharing a bed.'

The importance of talking about feelings is appreciated more by men under 25, and some older men have only recently come round to this point of view, but it is clearly gaining ground. It was one of the subjects on which most men wanted to expand.

Nigel, 39, a chartered accountant, said too modestly: 'My wife should take most of the credit for our pretty near perfect

Figure 8

Which qualities do you think most and least important for a relationship to last successfully?

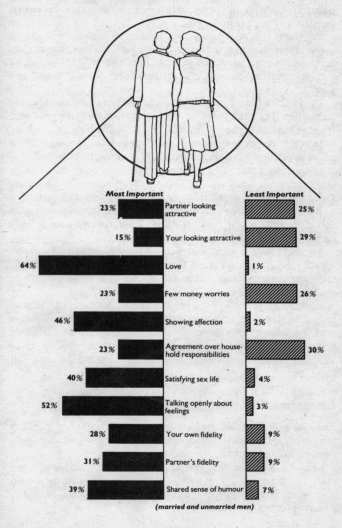

Most Important   *Least Important*

Most Important	Quality	Least Important
23%	Partner looking attractive	25%
15%	Your looking attractive	29%
64%	Love	1%
23%	Few money worries	26%
46%	Showing affection	2%
23%	Agreement over household responsibilities	30%
40%	Satisfying sex life	4%
52%	Talking openly about feelings	3%
28%	Your own fidelity	9%
31%	Partner's fidelity	9%
39%	Shared sense of humour	7%

(married and unmarried men)

relationship. She makes sure I don't become too chauvinist – very easy in my profession. She insists we talk out problems which otherwise I would have bottled up. We really enjoy each other's company and want to try to share everything like a true partnership. We make joint decisions now, although she has let me steam-roller her in the past.'

Of course it is not enough that women encourage men to talk about their feelings more. Women have to ask *themselves* honestly whether they are prepared to give up the feeling of security that reliance on a traditionally 'strong man' can give.

David, 25, a bank steward: 'I have found not all girls like guys to be so open. My basic views on women are that they like guys with feelings but not to show their softness and sensitivity.'

In other words, some women in effect give the message 'Show me your feelings but only the ones I can cope with easily!'

It is not just a myth that talking truly openly about your feelings is good for relationships. Men who did not believe in discussing feelings were far more likely to be in unhappy relationships.

While 54 per cent of those in very happy relationships believe in talking openly about feelings only 30 per cent of men in very unhappy relationships give it any priority.

There is a similar trend that men who are enjoying a very happy sexual relationship are more likely to believe in discussing their feelings than those who are invariably unhappy with their current sex life.

Andy, a 25-year-old brewery labourer: 'We can both sit and talk to each other openly about any problems. We have an active sex life and both enjoy this very much. We have no inhibitions here and can talk about sex easily. What makes the relationship so happy is that we know each other so well, both physically and verbally.'

Caring and sharing

Showing affection was the next most popular choice of qualities important for a relationship to last successfully, mentioned by 46 per cent of men overall.

Kenneth, a retired clergyman suggested, 'A recipe for a happy marriage: Four good hugs a day. This I saw in the *Church Times* some years ago and have ever since passed the advice on to couples when preparing them for marriage.'

A satisfying sex life, so important to so many men, neverthe-less is fourth down the list of priorities, named by 40 per cent.

Jonathan, 24, a student teacher: 'An excellent sex life is not enough to keep a couple together. Interdependence, trust and support in a warm and secure relationship are required.'

Sharing a sense of humour, picked by 39 per cent of men (ahead even of fidelity) seemed to reflect a desire to be good friends as well as lovers, rather than wanting to share a bed with a stream of wise-cracks.

Lloyd, 20, a student: 'My girlfriend is my best friend as well as being my lover. We are always totally open with each other about problems and our feelings. We don't get bored with each other's company and have a good laugh together.

'We can act the fool, be childish or whatever without feeling embarrassment. If something genuinely embarrassing does happen to one of us, we can laugh it off rather than making a fuss.

'We are always totally honest and do not put on a show to try and impress. We tend not to argue but to "agree to disagree". If we have an argument, we always make up, with either one of us apologising, and are not pig-headed.'

Peter, 28, said, 'The greatest pleasure in our relationship is a shared sense of humour and the close support that two people, more friends than just lovers, can lend to each other.'

Close sharing with independence was volunteered by many men, particularly young ones, as the ideal balance for a success-ful relationship.

Greg, 19, an office worker: 'She's very intelligent and inter-esting, has independence and insists on going dutch everywhere we go. She doesn't cling and gives me freedom.'

They like women who roll up their sleeves rather than embroider a fine seam. Joe, 23, a tyre depot manager: 'She helps me with anything. Recently she helped me rebuild my car. She doesn't mind getting dirty because she loves me and I love her very much.'

Of course there are those who still see their girlfriends almost solely as support, as carers – a replacement Mum with sex thrown in for good measure.

Oliver, 24, a disc jockey: 'She is very proficient in bed, makes an excellent meal and really looks after me.'

Malcom, 23, a research student: 'She takes a keen interest in my work and will listen attentively for long periods to my ideas.' Yet Malcom was made uneasy by his girlfriend seeming to regard him as a 'passport to wealth' and the frequent references to girl-friends being appreciated for paying their way showed how uneasy many men are now at being regarded as a meal ticket.

Lack of money worries vies with the attractiveness of both partners for being the qualities regarded as among the least important for a relationship to last successfully.

Not surprisingly, the unemployed and those in low paid occupations were much more likely to see finance as affecting happiness.

Gordon, 33, an insurance clerk pointed out: 'For me money worries are now least important on the list, but it hasn't always been the case. I suppose now that I earn a reasonable salary it assumes less significance.'

Topping the list of men's least important considerations is agreement over household responsibilities.

From our surveys of women it is clear that those seething over what they see as an unfair division of chores do not make responsive partners. It could be said that they should make a better stab at negotiating fairer shares, but this survey also reinforces the impression that men generally underestimate how important such practical – yet tiring and time-consuming – considerations are.

Men who are not at all happy in their current relationship are even less likely than the average to have given any priority to family finances and sharing the chores.

It looks as though they are paying the penalty for not understanding how their partners feel.

Do you understand your wife?

'My wife doesn't understand me' is supposed to be the classic plea of the erring husband, but in fact British husbands seem to feel a pretty well understood bunch.

Three out of ten (27 per cent) of husbands say their wife understands them completely, six out of ten (60 per cent) reasonably well. Little more than one in ten (13 per cent) feel misunderstood or aren't sure.

'My wife tells me she understands me completely. I don't agree!' protested Paul, 34. 'Trouble is, she is usually right in these matters.'

There is a slight lessening of confidence over how well they are in tune with their wife, but most men rate their skills in understanding equal to their partner's.

Just two out of ten (18 per cent) of husbands say they understand their wife completely but, again, only around one in ten (12 per cent) says he doesn't understand her well or not at all.

We received a number of notes slipped in with questionnaires, such as this one from the wife of an electrical engineer in his late twenties: 'My husband has answered all these questions honestly and to the best of his ability. The only thing is, where you've asked for the partner's viewpoint, in many instances he's wrong!'

Overall, however, through cross-checking with our survey on women, we found that men did understand their wives and partners well. For example, they showed a good grasp of the fact that kissing and cuddling, showing affection generally and not just as a prelude to sex, may be of more significance to women than sexual intercourse itself – even if the men themselves are rather less likely to feel this is true for them.

We asked men in steady relationships whether they thought kissing and cuddling was more or less (or equally) important than intercourse to their partners.

Twenty-seven per cent of husbands judged that kissing and cuddling was more important to their wife than intercourse, 61 per cent said it was equally important and just 8 per cent said it was less important to her.

These figures are remarkably close to what we were told by wives about their own feelings. Then 25 per cent said kissing and cuddling was more important than intercourse, 67 per cent that it was equally important and just 8 per cent that it was less important.

Husbands know that for their wives intercourse is far from the be-all and end-all of sex, and there are many husbands who agree that kissing and cuddling are equal in importance to intercourse. David, 28, an engineer, said, 'The most important feature of our relationship for me is the tenderness we show to each other. Although I do want sex more often at times, as long as we talk, show affection and cuddle, it's all right.'

However, husbands are three times as likely as wives to believe that intercourse is more important than kissing and cuddling.

We asked men how often they kiss and cuddle with their partner apart from as a prelude to sex. The contrast in replies between husbands and single men with a regular girlfriend at least in part answers the question we ran up against early in this chapter: of what happens to women's sex drive when they get married.

69

Seven out of ten (69 per cent) of single men, kiss and cuddle with their partner very often, compared with less than four out of ten (37 per cent) of husbands. Fewer than one in ten (7 per cent) of single men rarely kiss and cuddle or don't at all, compared with three out of ten (29 per cent) of husbands.

Kissing and cuddling apart from as a prelude to sex is important to women, whose sexual responses and ability to feel desire reflect more closely than many men's appear to the emotional currents in the relationship generally, and the feelings aroused by day-to-day life together.

Men who kiss and cuddle their partner often and not only as a prelude to sex, make love more often and they are happier with their sex life than those who do not.

Seven out of ten (69 per cent) of the men who are very happy with their sex life, kiss and cuddle their partners very often. Half (50 per cent) of those who are not at all happy with their sex life are those who rarely kiss and cuddle.

It is not just that the men who kiss and cuddle their partner love them more and so might be expected to enjoy a better love life.

Overall, roughly one-third of men tell their partner, 'I love you' every day and a further third frequently.

A few men may cynically agree with Barry, 36, a security officer: 'The word "love" is a pain, I just use it as a tool to get the ladies on the hots, chiefly my wife. I've no idea what love is.' For most, however, being willing and able to say 'I love you' to a regular partner is at least a sign of caring. Husbands say 'I love you' to wives with nearly the same frequency that single men tell girlfriends they are in love with them. It is the kissing and cuddling that seems to go out of the window after marriage and with it much of wives' interest in making love.

5 Ecstasy and the Big Bang

The pleasures and problems of intercourse

S ex is regarded as so important that to admit you have a poor sex life feels like admitting you are a wash-out. Few of us like to think that we and our sexual partners are even average lovers, though of course most of us by definition are just that – average.

We may admit to this difficulty or that unfulfilled desire but, though few of us would lay claim to be Superstud or Superlay, their myth overshadows us all. It makes it that bit harder to sort out any snags without anxiety and fears of failure. Who would admit they need to improve their skills in bed as easily as they might agree they are less than expert cooks?

Nearly four out of five (77 per cent) of men rate their partner as a good or excellent lover. Very few say she is downright poor.

The men were more modest when asked to rate themselves, but not too modest. *More than three out of five (63 per cent) believe that their partner considers them above average and only one in ten (11 per cent) merely passable or poor.*

However, there is a telling shift of opinion between single men and married.

How do you rate your partner as a lover?		How do you think your partner rates you?	
Single Men	Married Men	Rating	Single Men	Married Men
46%	34%	Excellent	33%	18%
40%	38%	Good	45%	38%
10%	16%	Average	16%	25%
1%	7%	Passable	3%	10%
—	4%	Poor	1%	3%

For most men the central sexual experience of their lives will be with their wife. This is what everything else has been leading up to. They are no longer novices fumbling in the dark but have a full-time sexual partner with no overt parental prohibitions hanging over them. They have gained experience, yet what do their memories or expectations lead them to believe? That they are poorer lovers.

When a young couple are going out together sex usually has a clear and important place on their agenda, whether or not they are actually having intercourse. They go out together – to a pub, to disco, to see friends – then they park the car or go to one of their homes and kiss and cuddle and perhaps more. They may spend a whole evening listening to music and thrilling to each other. If they are not enjoying that part of their relationship together, they are unlikely to carry on going out together long.

Once married, sex has to find its place in a life together which includes going out to work, household chores, caring for children, responsibilities – stress. Instead of going out and relaxing together, especially setting the scene for romance, sex is expected to be a naturally occurring part of day-to-day married routine.

In itself this change presents few problems to men. *More than three out of five (62 per cent) of husbands say they* **never** *have any difficulty becoming sexually aroused.*

A lot of men would agree with Peter, 35, a work study officer: 'This sounds arrogant but I don't need a lot of encouragement to feel in the mood for sex. I feel in the mood for sex most of the time.'

This is not to say that men run like Gold Seal batteries. A third do admit that occasionally they can be slow to rouse, and this percentage rises to around 50 per cent among men in their fifties. However, only tiny numbers of men in any age group often find it difficult to feel sexually aroused.

The picture is very different among women. Only one in five wives **never** *has any difficulty becoming sexually aroused, compared with three out of five husbands. Only a tiny 2 per cent of husbands* **often** *have difficulty becoming sexually aroused, while 19 per cent of wives find this a regular problem.*

Obviously stress can and does affect men's libido, but it seems to take a far more devastating toll on women.

Ewan, 27, a production manager: 'Our relationship generally fluctuates from good and innovative to poor and mundane. This

72

is dependent on external factors such as her work, family problems, holidays and so on.'

Eric, 42, a lorry driver: 'We have a diabetic son and a hyperactive daughter. I do understand the stress my wife is going through but a little love my way would help me to help her.'

Too often there seems to be a breakdown in communication between couples. The husband feels like making love while the wife feels rushed off her feet. He tries to show her affection which she shrugs off because it's practical help she wants, not what she may register as a prelude to sex – the last thing she's in the mood for at that moment.

Barry, 33, a civil servant: 'I've always rated a good sex life as being important. We frequently tell each other "I love you" and always mean it. We used to kiss and cuddle often until we started a family, but this has virtually stopped now. Perhaps I do try at inappropriate times, but she rarely reciprocates. As with her refusals to make love, it makes me feel rejected, and reluctant to try again. I wish my wife would be more responsive.'

And it is still usual that the man proposes and the woman responds – or not.

Nearly three out of five (56 per cent) of married men say they always or usually make the first move. Among only a minute 4 per cent of couples does the wife usually make the first move sexually, and among the rest husbands reckon it is about 50:50.

There may have been discussions about whether the sexually liberated women now supposedly stalking the land are putting too much pressure on men with their sexual demands, but they are a rare phenomenon. Only 4 per cent of men believe that women these days are too demanding sexually. In fact, most want them to be a whole lot more demanding.

Tom, 36, a teacher: 'I find it very annoying how women seem to be conditioned to being passive generally. It seems to be tied in with the old double standard of sexual mores that boys should gain as much sexual experience as they can, but good girls don't.

'No matter how much my wife and I talk about this, she still finds it extremely difficult to make the first move and initiate love-making.'

Seven out of ten (68 per cent) of married men wish their partner made the first move more often.

Marriage may have made it officially OK for a woman to be sexual, but the parental prohibitions are still there in her head. It takes more than a ring to turn a 'nice girl', the 'sort that men marry', into a sexually bold adult. 'Mother' is still in there, making her tense when her husband approaches her sexually, blocking her from making a pass when she feels sexy.

It is not only inhibition that gets in the way of women being the ones to suggest sex. Men and women seem to respond to differing sexual triggers. Men are far more likely to feel aroused by a visual trigger – a picture of an attractive woman, the curve of their wife's breast under her dress. Women generally respond more to touch and feeling. There is a question mark over this differentiation. It could be that women are aroused by visual triggers in the same way as men but don't admit it to themselves (see Chapter Seven on pornography), but in effect the result is the same.

A woman with, say, the housework and dinner on her mind is fairly unlikely to drop everything at the sight of her husband in his underpants. If he walks into the bathroom and finds her bending over cleaning the bath, with her bottom in the air, however, he may well feel roused and make a pass.

If he does, how likely is he to have picked the right moment?

Just one in five (20 per cent) of wives **never** *turns her husband down. Three out of five do occasionally and the other one in five refuses often or always.*

Few men now seem to believe that they should never be refused and will try to accept refusals with good grace as long as they are not too frequent.

Gary, 21: 'Refusals to make love are usually due to outside matters causing worry, and tension. Otherwise, if I'm turned on she will not refuse but is more than willing to have sex.'

Bernard, 71: 'My wife used to make an effort to give me satisfaction manually, insisting I didn't touch her. She made excuses for 25 years. Now she says sex is obscene "at our age" and won't make any form of contact – saying it would only lead to sex. I am totally frustrated and unhappy.'

Men say no, too

While Bernard is over 70, the peak period in life for men being refused is not in later years as we might expect. The late twenties and thirties are the years during which women are most likely to refuse to make love most often, and these are also the years during which *men* are most likely to refuse to make love if their partner has made the first move.

More than half (56 per cent) of married men of all ages say they never refuse their partner's suggestion to make love and only 1 per cent refuse often.

Ken, 36, a lorry driver: 'We touch each other a lot, and kiss, hold hands in front of everyone, get into passionate clinches in front of the children. We really love each other. I usually make this first move but if something has reversed the situation, I have never refused her ever.'

Obviously the late twenties and thirties coincide with family demands being commonly at their greatest. Gregory, 34, a freelance biologist: 'There have been periods of our relationship when we made love every day at least several times a week but circumstances at present do not allow (i.e. twin babies). When we find more time, in future years, I imagine the frequency will rise again.'

However, these years are also a peak time for couples who are living together rather than married (and who are less likely to have children) to refuse one another. Generally the years from 26 to 40 seem the most stressful for couples' sex lives. As we have seen, it is from the late twenties that men are less likely to rate themselves and their partner as generally good lovers.

The honeymoon (literally or not) period is over. The thrill of simply finding a partner and having a regular sex life passes and both men and women become more quality conscious. It is not enough just to have sex, it has to be good sex.

There may also be considerable stress in adjusting to living with one another, and these years can be very tiring ones for anyone trying to build a career or business.

Robert, 30, a manager with British Telecom: 'Sometimes my wife complains because I fall asleep while making love, though if she really wants an orgasm she wakes me up or masturbates.'

It's among this age group that we find most men saying that what gets in the way of their making love more often is that they themselves are too tired.

Two out of five (38 per cent) of men aged 26 to 40 say they would like to make love more often if only they were not so tired as well as three out of five (58 per cent) who say their partner's tiredness is a problem.

Neville, 36, a retailer, describes the mix of pressures that can threaten even the most flourishing sex lives: 'When we first met we screwed very often and I was actually worried my lady's sexual desires would be too much to cope with (what irony)! She almost always reached orgasm by just intercourse. Indeed she only wished to climax with me inside her.

'We made the extremely difficult transition from her working full-time/me out of work, to me working full-time/her at home. I started my own business and I had to work very hard. At this time we made love two or three times a week.

'Eventually she became pregnant and our son was born a year ago. Sex was great during pregnancy but since the birth my wife's libido is quite low, possibly due to breast-feeding or a demanding baby who sleeps badly, or just feeling very tired, or a combination!

'For myself, I am very overworked and I have actually decided to sell off part of my business. This will enable me to see my family more and, I sincerely hope, to make love with my wife a lot more (the book-keeping is also playing a heavy role in my wife's life).'

Neville has been able to see a way to reduce the stress in his sex life. Not everyone is willing to make such changes, even if they are able, but the rate of refusals and levels of dissatisfaction do level off after 40. Some men, and women, do stay bitter and unhappy but some obviously come to terms with differing sex drive and attitudes. Tom, the teacher: 'I used to try to pressure my wife into being the one to take the initiative, but now I accept her difficulties and we play down the problem. I can accept her for what she is, not what I would like her to be.'

Setting the scene for sex

If major changes are impossible or unnecessary, it might help to encourage a change of mood from the domestic or work day-to-day to set the scene for sex.

Yet what many men said they prize above all is for sex to happen spontaneously. Andrew, 38, a civil servant: 'I enjoy making love in bed but would like it in other places – outside, in other parts of the house, in the back of the car. Most of all I would like to be able to take advantage of making love spontaneously, whether sun bathing on a secluded beach or at the kitchen sink.'

Stuart, 44, a teacher, certainly had very happy memories of secluded beaches: 'We spent odd days on a beach in Sweden and my wife sunbathes topless. We swam nude in a river there, too.

During a week in Wales my wife sunbathed topless among the dunes and we swam nude in the sea. My wife really enjoys the sun on her naked body and I really enjoy the sight of a completely naked woman. All this leads to sexual arousal in due course. During last summer we made love naked in the sun on the river bank in Sweden, in a forest clearing in England and among the sand dunes in Wales.'

Spontaneity is wonderful when it is possible. After a day lazing in the sun many women could manage to feel spontaneously sexy. The trouble is that if asked to be 'spontaneous' as Andrew hoped, while standing at the kitchen sink up to their elbows in washing or dishes, the feelings first to surface may well be more tired or snappy than sexy.

Relaxation – quite literally letting tense muscles relax and the body calm down – is a physical necessity before many people can respond to sexual stimuli. If they are feeling too dull, then they may need brightening up. Either way many women, who are slower to arouse sexually than men, need a switch in mood if they are to feel responsive.

We asked men 'what do you usually do to help you or your partner feel in the mood for sex?'

Nearly two in five (38 per cent) of husbands could think of nothing they do to help them or their partner feel ready to make love.

As John, 21, pointed out: 'The pace of modern life is so detrimental to creating that relaxed climate in which lovemaking flourishes. If men were more affectionate and less obsessed by the physical act, they might meet with more response. Relaxation coupled with mutual understanding can resolve problems.'

Men who don't take the trouble are less likely to enjoy a happy relationship with their partner.

More than half (53 per cent) of those who are currently very unhappy make no effort to encourage a loving mood before suggesting sex – though some may have lost hope, of course.

Most men do realise it's worth making an effort to warm the atmosphere – as well as pleasurable – and most of these start with kissing and cuddling.

What do you usually do to help you or your partner feel in the mood for sex?

	Husbands
Kissing and cuddling	31%
Foreplay, massage	12%
Drinking/wining and dining/special outing	9%
Sexy talk	6%
Dressing/undressing in special way	5%
Looking at erotic books, magazines or video	5%
Taking a bath or shower together	5%
Dim lights, music	2%
Other	2%

The happiest relationships were those in which sexplay could arise naturally out of affectionate kissing and cuddling. It was much more common for those who were not very happy with their relationship to be making special efforts like wining and dining or trying to loosen inhibitions with alcohol.

However, quite a few couples think variety is the spice of a good sex life and some mentioned more than one option on this list.

Patrick, 52, a teacher: 'Variety is the key – quietly cuddling and then touching each other up, looking at an erotic picture, making a grab at each other.'

Alan, 24, a research officer: 'We don't make a special arrangement every time but often a relaxing evening listening to music, or sharing a bottle of wine, or watching TV leads to our making love. Sharing a shower seems also to excite us both and invariably we make love afterwards – or during.'

Dressing the part?

Many couples also believe that variety is the key to dressing – or undressing – for sex.

Harry, 28, a store owner: 'Variety is the spice of sex. (I've heard that somewhere before!) While making love naked is best (I feel closer, more "with" my wife), to see her dressed erotically is a great turn on.'

Men often have strong preferences over what they like their partner to be wearing – or not wearing – when they make love.

Approaching half (46 per cent) of men prefer their partner to be naked to make love and three out of four of their partners agree. (See Figure 9, page 80).

There was remarkably little difference in tastes between men of all ages, married and unmarried, so the figures we quote here are for all men. If you believed stockings and suspenders are only really popular with men old enough to have been courting in the days before tights, think again. If anything they are most popular with men in their twenties, whose *mothers* must have taken to tights before they were even born.

'We have a varied sex life,' explained Simon, 25, an investment consultant. 'We sleep naked but I prefer her dressed up in some flimsy thing when we make love. Suspenders are best.'

Some partners are less eager than others, however. David, 23, a policeman: 'I would like my wife to wear stockings instead of tights all the time. I find the greatest visual turn on of all to be the sight of the bare flesh just above the top of the stockings, especially when a woman has just crossed her legs. Unfortunately she will only wear stockings about once every couple of months, although she looks absolutely stunning in them.'

One in five (19 per cent) of men like their partner in a sexy nightie – which half of them wear – and just 7 per cent prefer some sort of special outfit, which seven out of ten of their partners do wear.

Terry, 24, a student teacher: 'We make use of lingerie, vibrators, magazines. All of these add some variety and spice to our sexual relationship but we are not dependent on any of them. Lingerie, in particular, offers my lover a chance to display her exhibitionist streak. We have bought a number of items from such shops as Anne Summers and also my fiancée makes her own items from scarves, net curtaining and so on. All of these succeed in arousing me no end.'

Just one in ten (11 per cent) of men gave no special preference, and there's no doubt that some women feel very uncomfortable if their partner has got very strong ideas about just how he wants them to appear by the bedside. They can feel as though they are being pressured to fit in with some fantasy rather than being desired for themselves, or worry that it's the lingerie which is the turn-on rather than their partner's love for them. (See Chapter Seven).

Gordon, 46, a chartered engineer, explains: 'I have an occasional desire for my wife to wear clothes which are sexually

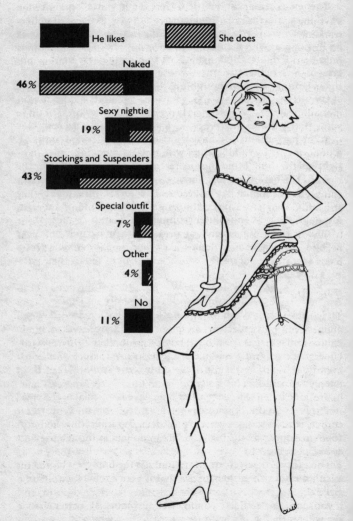

Figure 9

Do you like your partner to dress/undress in a special way for sex?

■ He likes   ▨ She does

Naked
46%

Sexy nightie
19%

Stockings and Suspenders
43%

Special outfit
7%

Other
4%

No
11%

stimulating. It's more exciting if she uses these clothes coyly, without being brashly sexual, for example, if I catch a glimpse of suspender when sitting normally at home.

'My wife's view is that I am perverted and she will not give me anything as I "would only want more". There is a lack of understanding by woman that physical aspects and stimulating clothes do not detract from a loving relationship. With such "goings on" the relationship is enhanced. Without them the relationship is very poor.'

Setting the boundaries, finding the limits which are comfortable for both partners can often be difficult. A woman who does not mind wearing suspenders might baulk at Frank's preferences. 'I am very turned on by a girl who seems to hurt herself to be attractive, for example, very tight belts with anything or nothing, knickers pulled high into the crutch and very tight corsets.'

Whatever the preference, it's more likely that a partner will comply if she is first asked how she feels about it and whether she would find it exciting to dress up – or down. Many a woman is going to feel pressured by the man whose Christmas present to her is a full set of erotic underwear, and as grateful as if he had given her *his* favourite record – which in a way he has.

The Big Bang theory of sex

Those of us old enough to remember, have been reading articles about female orgasm for decades. Male experience of intercourse and climax is presumed to be far more straight-forward. Unless a man has a 'Problem', he is supposed to operate according to the Big Bang theory of sex. It is what every boy learns in the playground and he may run across little to contradict it later in life.

The theory goes that there is foreplay, followed by intercourse, followed by a period of frenzied thrusting activity, followed by the Big Bang – climax and ejaculation. Cause and ecstatic effect.

The extra bits of information that will probably get bolted on to this theory at a later date are that if you know how to find a girl's clitoris, there is a better chance of her reaching orgasm, and if you learn how to delay your own climax there is a better chance she will reach hers during intercourse.

How closely does men's central sexual experience follow the Big Bang theory?

In fact, only one in three (34 per cent) of men never has difficulty with either reaching a climax or controlling its timing. (See Figure 10, below).

To start with, men far from inevitably reach climax *every* time they make love, though they do with more regularity than women.

Fewer than three out of four (72 per cent) of men always reach climax when they make love. One in four says he usually does, and it is only a tiny 2 per cent who say they climax during love-making only occasionally. While there is some variation according to age, since just 60 per cent of men over 50 say they always reach climax, it is not dramatic. Even among 22 to 25 year old men, the age group who climax during love-making with the greatest regularity, one in five (20 per cent) say climax is not inevitable for them.

Figure 10

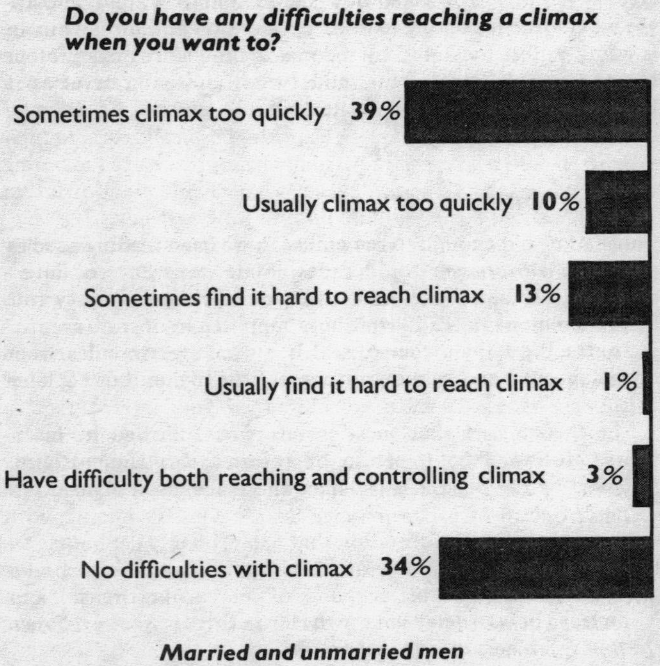

Do you have any difficulties reaching a climax when you want to?

Sometimes climax too quickly   **39%**

Usually climax too quickly   **10%**

Sometimes find it hard to reach climax   **13%**

Usually find it hard to reach climax   **1%**

Have difficulty both reaching and controlling climax   **3%**

No difficulties with climax   **34%**

Married and unmarried men

Overall, one in six (17 per cent) of men say they sometimes have difficulty reaching a climax.

Especially the first time this happens, it could be pretty reassuring for a man to know how common an experience this is.

Two out of five men have difficulty keeping an erection at least occasionally.

There is a similar trend that this is more of a problem for older men – fewer than half (45 per cent) of men over 50 never have this trouble – but it happens to at least 30 per cent of men in all age groups.

GPs and problem-page editors are always being asked for help by worried men whose erection has let them down at the wrong moment for the first time, and who react as if their arm had dropped off. They believe something is irreparably wrong and will never be the same again.

Even more worrying – since those men can be reassured – are those who are so frightened and ashamed that they dare not ask anyone for advice. Having difficulty keeping an erection occasionally, or for a short spell of stress, is so common as to be normal. It is important for men to know that, since anxiety alone can block the sexual responses and turn what should have been a small difficulty into a major problem.

Men who want to be good lovers, bringing satisfaction to their partner as well as themselves, usually want to control the timing of their climax. The standard piece of bolt-on information is that a 'real man' can delay his climax for as long as it takes.

Sean, 33, a nurse: 'I feel very sorry for women who are used by men to satisfy their lust without attaining satisfaction. I have a rule that I never climax before my woman reaches her orgasm. It's difficult but it can be done.

'After kissing and cuddling for at least 10 minutes, then fondling and licking her breasts for at least 15 minutes, I lick her vagina for at least 10 minutes and we then begin intercourse.

'I begin slowly and increase speed. If I feel inclined to ejaculate I slow down and then speed up again to her demands, only ejaculating when her moans tell me she has reached orgasm.'

Far from all men can manage Sean's control, nor would it always be desirable.

It's not that all the less controlled men are careless or uncaring lovers.

Half (52 per cent) of men say that they have difficulty delaying a climax as long as they want to.

One in ten (10 per cent) say that they usually climax too quickly and the rest that this is sometimes a problem.

As we shall see, Superstud control is far from necessary for a mutually satisfying sexual relationship, yet, if a man regularly reaches his climax before his partner, it does seem to cause problems in some relationships.

Overall, one in eight (13 per cent) of men say that they always climax before their partner, but among those who are very unhappy with their sexual relationship, one in three (32 per cent) men always climax before their partner can reach orgasm. (See Chapter Thirteen for help for such problems).

Did you come, darling?

For a man to climax before his partner has reached orgasm need only be a problem if one or both of them wants her to reach orgasm during intercourse. However, only half of the women who reach orgasm usually do so during intercourse – and that's if you accept what men believe. If you go by what women themselves say, the real figure is even lower.

When we asked men what usually causes a climax for them and their partner, just 49 per cent said that their partner usually reaches orgasm during intercourse. (See Figure 11, page 85).

Nearly one in three said she usually reaches orgasm through manual stimulation, one in ten through oral sex and nearly as many that it varies.

Chris, 29, an engineer: 'My girlfriend usually climaxes through oral or manual stimulation or a combination of the two. Quite often she climaxes through simultaneous intercourse and manual stimulation which we both enjoy because we usually climax together. Sometimes I find it difficult to hold back in this situation, as her increasing excitement further excites me to climax. On a few occasions she has been able to climax through intercourse alone after a period of manual or oral stimulation, and she would like to be able to do this more often.'

Far from all women seem to see this as a goal, however. Bruce, 20-year-old squash pro: 'I think foreplay is as important as intercourse and in my experience girls seem to enjoy clitoral stimulation more than vaginal penetration.'

Julian, 25, a computer programmer: 'I can often easily make my wife climax by oral sex before we have intercourse. I think she enjoys oral sex more than the act of intercourse itself.'

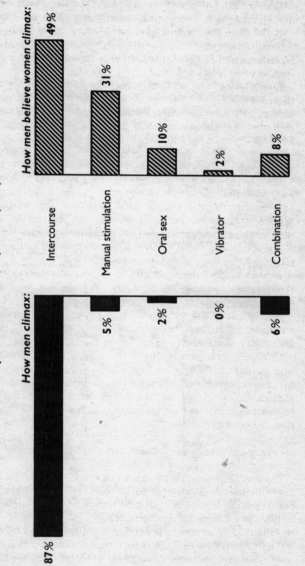

Figure 11

What usually causes a climax for you and your partner?

How men climax:

Intercourse 87%
Manual stimulation 5%
Oral sex 2%
Vibrator 0%
Combination 6%

How men believe women climax:

Intercourse 49%
Manual stimulation 31%
Oral sex 10%
Vibrator 2%
Combination 8%

In fact, when we asked women how they usually reach orgasm, even fewer said it was through intercourse. The gap between what the men believe and what the women say is particularly wide among the unmarried, where the pressure to conform to the Big Bang theory, and for a girl to fulfil her boyfriend's expectations, are particularly strong.

While half (51 per cent) of single men believe that their girlfriend usually reaches orgasm through intercourse, only half as many (24 per cent) of unmarried women say that this is true. (See Figure 12, below).

We know from our surveys on women that two out of five, married and unmarried alike, fake orgasm, but not many men rumble them. Just 7 per cent know that their partner sometimes or usually fakes. Ten per cent say that they suspect she does and 17 per cent admit they don't know.

Figure 12

Faking? How single men believe their partners climax – and how they say they do themselves.

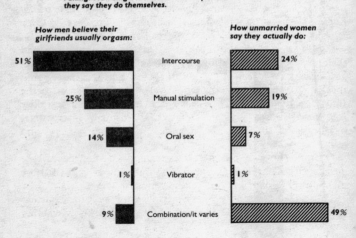

How men believe their girlfriends usually orgasm: / How unmarried women say they actually do:

	How men believe	How unmarried women
Intercourse	51%	24%
Manual stimulation	25%	19%
Oral sex	14%	7%
Vibrator	1%	1%
Combination/it varies	9%	49%

As Alex, 21, a health authority administrative assistant points out: 'How do you know if someone is faking an orgasm?' Though he feels bound to add: 'My fiancée never does. From her point of view, what's the point of it. You only fool yourself.'

Which is quite true, of course, and faking prevents a couple discovering mutually satisfying ways of making love which don't involve one of them implying that there is something wrong with her sexuality, so wrong that it has to be concealed.

However, the pressure on women is understandable.

One in four (26 per cent) men is not happy with the frequency of his partner's orgasms.

Anthony, 38, an accountant: 'I'm happily married in all respects but one. I find my wife's apparent failure ever to have experienced orgasm deeply distressing. Perhaps I regard it as a criticism of me by her.'

If men and women could accept that we are all responsible for our own sexual fulfilment, then men would not need to take this as a criticism of themselves but simply join with their partner in finding what would bring her greater satisfaction, if indeed it is orgasms she is after.

From our surveys on women we know that they believe it is twice as important to their menfolk than it is to themselves that they should reach orgasm, and it certainly is a key factor for men who consider their sexual relationships to be very unhappy.

Of the men who are thoroughly dissatisfied with their sexual relationship, half (50 per cent) are not happy with the frequency with which their partner reaches orgasm.

Slightly more believe that their partner is unhappy, too, and their answers to the questions we asked about masturbation suggest that the problem for many of these couples is indeed that they are trying to find happiness through fitting in with the Big Bang theory. This involves the man taking responsibility for bringing the woman satisfaction through intercourse, handicapped by generous helpings of sexual anxiety and guilt.

Overall, 71 per cent of men with partners say they masturbate at least occasionally, compared with only 46 per cent of those men in very unhappy sexual relationships.

Thirty-four per cent of men generally know that their partner masturbates, and nearly as many say they don't know whether she does or not.

Many talked happily about shared masturbatory experiences and even those who were not sure whether their partner masturbates added comments like Graham, 35, a clerk: 'I would quite like my wife to masturbate. I think it would help her understand her body more and I would only be upset if she preferred it to making love to me.'

Yet only 14 per cent of the men in sexually unhappy relationships

87

know that their partner masturbates, while the majority state firmly that she definitely does not.

Masturbation is such an effective way for anyone to explore their sexual responses that it is usually one of the first 'homeworks' suggested by sex therapists when consulted for such problems as lack of orgasm. It would so help those couples troubled by the woman's inability to reach orgasm if the man could release himself from feeling a failure – and his partner from pressure to be orgasmic unless she wants to. If she does, then she must first learn that it is the literal truth that the answer lies in her own hands, if only in order that she can guide his later.

6 Call this making love?

The changes men know they want

Three out of four married men want to improve the quality of their sex life and most see themselves as being blocked in this desire by their wives.

A general air of disappointment, of trampled dreams, hangs over what the men say about the quality of their sexual relationship, even when they regard their relationship in general as a happy one. They complain of hurried sex, given little priority in their relationship, far removed from their fantasies.

Men may underestimate how important other aspects of their life together are to their wife. For example, that she will not feel loved and loving if she also feels overworked and taken for granted in the home. However, many women underestimate – or choose to ignore – that for many men sex is not just one element in their relationship. It is the literal embodiment of their love. Mike's wife implied, 'I love you, I just don't like sex' (see page 6), but few men feel loved at all unless they are welcomed physically and joyfully.

Arthur, 52, a chemical engineer: 'Making love does not, at least for me, consist of the absolute minimum of foreplay required to produce lubrication and erection with a totally pre-dictable result. In that sense I wonder if my wife and I have ever truly "made love" as I like to think of the term.

'If I could make a change it would be to change me so that I could accept my wife's lack of warmth or, preferably, improve my performance (in all senses) so that we could introduce into our lives the warmth I so sadly miss. It might help if we could discuss our intimate problems (not just sexual). I think I might be able to do so. I know she can't.'

Improved performance, Sir?

We asked men what changes they would like to make in their own and their partner's love-making. Here we are concentrating on married men's responses because it is within marriage (or marriages) and the pressures of day-to-day life together and family responsibilities that most men can expect to have their main lasting sexual relationships.

Only one in four (26 per cent) of men was completely happy with the way he made love and saw no need for change.

Roger, 28, an assembly-line worker: 'I believe 70 per cent of a lasting relationship is based on a good sex life. When we make love we take care to make sure both get as much pleasure as possible, in other words plenty of foreplay. Timing is a thing we seem to have when reaching orgasm, which makes us happy in our sex lives. When I do something which I know will make her happy, this in turn makes me happy. We are sexually suited.'

What men see as their most common fault is lack of skill. *Among the majority of men who want to make changes in the way they make love, two out of five (40 per cent) say they want to be more skilful.* (See Figure 13, page 91).

'I would like to be more skilful in my love-making but I don't know how to go about it,' said Rod, 21, unemployed.

They are particularly likely to worry about their skill if their partner does not reach orgasm or does not climax during intercourse – though of course only a minority of women do reach orgasm through intercourse.

Chas, 39, a labourer: 'The saddest part of our relationship is my inability to satisfy my wife. To be able to do that would have put "icing on the cake".'

Arthur earlier talked of 'improving my performance so that we could introduce into our lives the warmth I so sadly miss'.

Of course, any such coolness may have absolutely nothing to do with the way they make love at all. A woman may be unresponsive and unorgasmic because of her upbringing, her health, conflicts in the relationship as a whole, or for a whole host of reasons, as we have seen.

However, men place great emphasis on being good sexual performers, knowing techniques and putting them smoothly into practice. They take responsibility for having the sexual expertise to please both partners, for being more skilful came next to

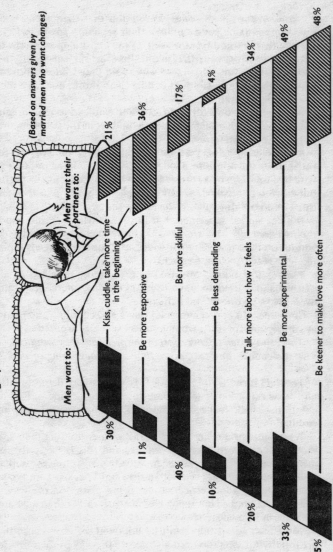

What are the changes you would like to make in the way you and your partner make love?

(Based on answers given by married men who want changes)

Men want their partners to:

Men want to:		
Kiss, cuddle, take more time in the beginning	30%	21%
Be more responsive	11%	36%
Be more skilful	40%	17%
Be less demanding	10%	4%
Talk more about how it feels	20%	34%
Be more experimental	33%	49%
Be keener to make love more often	25%	48%

bottom of the list of changes they would like their *wives* to make in *their* love-making.

Women, too, have some expectation that their men should possess the magic key to unlock their sexuality for them. That their partner should be more skilful was third highest on the list of changes wives said they would like in our survey of their feelings. However, what most wives said they wanted above all was for the man to kiss and cuddle them more, and take more time in the beginning.

All this stress on skill and technique can lead to men missing the point as to what their partners would see as the problem, even in purely physical terms.

Women can find very deliberate technique chilling in its effect rather than the opposite. Don, 38, a writer, pointed out that his wife had told him of a former lover who was 'technically perfect but far too controlled. Oddly enough, her sister said the same thing of an off-duty gigolo she met in the Seychelles!'

It's not sexual supermen, but husbands who kiss and cuddle their wives a lot, who are six times more likely to be rated excellent lovers than poor by their wives, and the wives are also more likely to reach orgasm frequently.

Elaine, 22, told us, 'We used to spend more time kissing and petting and I used to have orgasms during intercourse fairly often. Now he doesn't take the time.'

Some men do appreciate that kissing and cuddling and petting are important for most women to feel sexually aroused.

Three out of ten (30 per cent) of the men said they would like to kiss and cuddle, and take more time at the beginning of making love.

Tom, a journalist of 52, said, 'My wife is very demonstrative and is working hard, with some success, to get me out of my emotional shell, to become more affectionate with kisses and cuddles.'

What stops the other men? Many women told us their men thought it 'soft' to kiss and cuddle, and this is likely to be a problem so long as lads are encouraged when young to think of kissing and cuddling, even within the family, as sissy, and to see petting during adolescence as just being a step on the way of reaching the goal of intercourse with a girl, rather than as shared pleasure in its own right.

Some men admit they can't be bothered, often because they are too tired. Being too tired also gets in the way of their making their second most popular change – to be more experimental, to get their lovelife out of a rut.

One in three (33 per cent) of husbands who would like to change the way he makes love wants to be more experimental.

Mark, 24, a taxi driver: 'I'm selfish in bed. I'd like lovemaking to last longer and to be more varied but I work 11-hour shifts, six days a week, so I'm always very tired. She always makes the suggestions when it comes to experiment.'

Most men, however, are more willing to experiment than women.

Only 3 per cent of men ever refuse their partner's request to try a new position or technique.

Eddie, 35, unemployed, said, 'Most men like myself would agree to almost any suggestion a woman may make, if only because it's nice to feel a woman has sexual preferences of her own she wants to share.'

The requests most commonly refused by those few men are for vaginal intercourse approaching from the rear, and for oral sex.

Ten times that many men (38 per cent) said their partner refuses their requests to try something different.

In nearly half these cases their request is for oral sex and, in considerably smaller numbers, for intercourse approaching from the rear and anal sex (which is technically illegal in this country between heterosexual couples).

Many men do not feel able even to make their longed-for request, some because they are so sure it would be refused, others because they are too inhibited to do so, though whether by their partner's or their own feelings they are not always sure.

Max, 35, a medical scientist: 'I never make requests my wife refuses, but that is because I never make any requests at all. I would like to request certain things, but cannot bring myself to do so. In particular I would like her to kiss my body and to use her fingers to stroke my genitals.'

Quite a number of men mentioned that their partner refused to touch their penis.

Stephen, 27, a catering manager: 'I think my wife feels that sex is dirty, or parts of it are. We must have been married at least three years before my wife would touch my penis. Even now I have to take her hand and put it on my penis.

'My wife doesn't seem to mind if I use oral sex on her but she will not respond on myself. I have suggested bathing together or massage, but she does not think it's "nice". She will not make

93

love with the light on and, when she dresses or undresses, it's very carefully, ensuring I don't see her naked.'

Women cannot help being raised with inhibitions, but they can help allowing them to spoil their adult relationships. Feeling guilty about sex seems to work in two ways, not only preventing response but also making the women behave harshly and uncaringly in other areas of their lives. If women want men to understand their needs more, then they must be prepared at least to try and shake off 'Mother', remind themselves they are big girls now and have a partner who is longing to share sensual pleasure.

Convention v. experiment

The most popular change desired by husbands is that their wife should be more open to variety in technique and position.

Half (49 per cent) of the husbands wanting change wish their wife would be more experimental sexually.

Denis, 43, a shop owner: 'Making love is the one personal and private part of a couple's relationship which is totally theirs. It isn't shared with children, family or friends. Therefore, it should be fun, interesting, exciting, and the one thing they can do together in whatever way they like, where and when they like, within reason.

'I would like to be more experimental and make sex more exciting, but my wife is very conventional and only wants to make love in bed, at night, with the lights out. Only occasionally during our married life has she shown any interest in doing something different. This will last for two or three weeks, then we're back to square one.

'If I try to talk about it I'm told I'm being critical, and how would I like it if I was criticised. Yet I only want to make our love-life better. However, I've virtually given up trying.'

Craig, 34, an insurance clerk had made many suggestions but been rebuffed at every turn. 'My wife is very conventional when it comes to sex. These days she will not let me give her oral sex (although she used to) and she has never given oral sex to me. She tried to once but said she didn't like the taste of it. I have offered to put some sort of different flavour on my penis but she still won't try. I've given up trying to persuade her now.

'I have bought her sexy underwear and offered to buy some for me, but she is not interested. She will not wear suspender belt and stockings for sex as she thinks it is kinky.

'I bought a book about women and sex but she won't even read it. That probably sounds as if I put too much pressure on her and she resents it. I merely mentioned that I had the book and would she like to read it. She said she was not interested.

'As you can imagine there is not much excitement in our sex lives. Frankly I am bored by our "always the same" sex but, for the sake of a reasonably settled and otherwise happy home and relationship, I don't complain too much now.'

Craig has given up complaining but such differing attitudes towards sex can put a great strain on a marriage. Mike, the teacher, whom I quoted earlier, ended saying, 'What bothers me increasingly is that if an opportunity for a sexual relationship outside our marriage presented itself, I could find it impossible to reject.'

The post-1960s idea that everyone should have a high sex drive and an intense and experimental sex life is now recognised as a myth, causing as many problems and pressures as the old attitude that sexual desire was something no decent person admitted to or talked about. If one of a couple wants to make love rarely, quickly and quietly and the other with lengthy variety, there is no *objective* reason why it should be the one to whom sex seems less important who is assumed to have the problem and need help.

If the couple do not manage to work towards a compromise which both can tolerate, it is true that the person who feels sexually frustrated may damage or end the relationship by having sex with someone else (see Chapter Eight). On the other hand, a person who finds intense sex a strain may well find a reason to end the relationship, too.

What makes these common cases of couples with apparently differing sex drives so problematic is that it is often confusing to determine just how much of a genuine difference in desire for sexual satisfaction exists and how much one (or both) is inhibited by sexual guilt laid down during childhood.

Colin, 61: 'She endures sex because she loves me and wants to give me pleasure, not for the pleasure it can give her. I try my hardest and did give her an orgasm through oral sex, but she thought it was perverted. She cannot break away from her mother's teaching that all men are animals with only one aim. I wonder if there are any completely uninhibited women who actually enjoy sex, or are they only characters in books written by men?'

'I wish my partner didn't feel guilty about sex,' said Dominic, 24, unemployed. 'According to her quite a few women feel this way. She doesn't like me fucking her from behind because she says it makes her feel used and it's too animal-like. That is what I enjoy about it. I think it's important to be able to feel uninhibited with your partner, even if it sometimes seems as if you're using them.'

Increasing the force of the way sexual guilt works against willingness to experiment is the pressure laid on young women to take the responsibility for 'drawing the line'. It is the young man's 'task' to pressure a girl to go further and further until she goes 'all the way'. It is her duty to set the pace. Yield too slowly and she will be seen as 'frigid'. Yield too quickly and she will be seen as 'cheap'.

It is not necessarily that easy for a woman to know, even in a settled relationship, just how she and her partner are going to feel after the next barrier in experiment has been breached, especially since many men will keep pressing for more and more to be tried. By most people's standards, Brendan's fiancée has already shared in a great deal of experiment. It's not enough, says Brendan, 25, who's training to be a doctor. 'My fiancée is too conservative in her love-making while I am not averse to experimentation.

'Bondage, role playing, kinky clothes and group sex or making love in company do not appeal to her. She will not try physically demanding positions and still baulks at aids such as duo balls and love eggs.

'She does like making love in public risky places. She took some time to accept vibrators but now she loves them. I derive much pleasure from increasing her enjoyment with such aids. We also use love beans, inserted anally, and a vibrating dildo (somewhat more impressively proportioned than myself).' One man's wildest dream is another's conservative restriction!

Elliot, 31, a garage foreman, 'On the sexual level I like to think of the women who appeal to me as in some way like goddesses to be worshipped, rather than seduced. I have a possibly exaggerated respect for women.

'My fantasies tend to be about my partner being in some way dominant, making me show my unworthiness of her by physical worship, particularly the kissing and licking of her feet. I am something of a foot fetishist. More recently my wife has gone some way towards satisfying one of my wishes by caressing my erection with the sole of her foot!'

Mel, 38, a salesman, said: 'I have great difficulty in explaining my feelings. My wife is a great lady and I am very proud of her. However, at times I like her to act like a prostitute with me, and I do have an urge for her to make love with another man.'

It may help women feel more comfortable with experiment if instead of being put to them as a demand, they are *asked* if it is something *they* would like to try or might find pleasurable.

Nick, 32, a project manager, explained: 'My experience is limited, but the women I have known have usually required prompting to admit they would like/enjoy something other than the missionary position – oral stimulation, mutual masturbation. However, once prompted, they have been happy to state their likes and dislikes.'

This apparently obvious answer does not work for couples who find it enormously difficult to talk about sex at all frankly, or where the woman cannot admit to sexual needs and satisfactions.

Wake up, Sleeping Beauty

Nearly half the majority of husbands who want change would like their wife to be keener to make love more often.

We have discussed some factors which can be involved in many women's apparent reluctance to have sex as often as their men would like. One change which seems to follow marriage is that men do less kissing and cuddling, take less trouble to make their partner feel appreciated and aroused. However, men's next most commonly desired change in their partner is also very relevant.

One in three (36 per cent) of husbands would like his wife to be more responsive when making love.

Noel, 21, a student: 'She is very understanding and, due to her responsiveness to sex, has made me feel totally secure and confident about having sex with her, which consequently leads to very enjoyable love-making.'

Some men feel rather hard done by, in that while they are trying their hardest to make sure that their partner has an enjoyable time sexually, she can't be bothered to respond in kind.

Owen, 43, a librarian: 'I am lucky in that my wife enjoys love-making and climaxes every time we make love (unless she is a very good faker.) The only trouble is this perhaps makes her a touch complacent, as she doesn't take as much care (I think) to make sure that I, too, get maximum pleasure, particularly in foreplay.'

Ian, 46, complained: 'I feel I am pleasing her for hours longer than she tries to please me. My wife likes me stimulating her clitoris with my mouth – I could do it to her all day – but when I ask her to get in the 69 position, so I can get some stimulation, too – she often refuses.'

Other men are not bothered by lack of reciprocal stimulation so much as by a lack of response to their loving, which means they actually are not sure whether they are giving pleasure or not.

Wesley, 32, a bank clerk: 'I would like my wife to be much keener on sex than she is now. Her lack of interest bothers us both but we are trying to adjust to it.

'I would like to try anything in bed but have to persuade her a little at a time. This has to be a slow process as nothing destroys an intimate atmosphere quicker than realising she is "closing her eyes and thinking of England." She must enjoy it as well.'

Many husbands would like to improve the quality of their wife's sex life and, if she could be sure of having a good time, it might indeed encourage her to want to make love more often. The trouble is that while many women seem quick to make clear any technique or touch they do *not* enjoy or feel comfortable with, they are often slow to respond equally to what they do enjoy or would like to try.

Many women find it hard to 'own' their own sexual desires and pleasures. Secret, silent guilty sex while a teenager can lead on to secret, silent guilty sex even after marriage.

Ralph, 27, a dairy worker: 'My wife never wants to make love while we are on holiday because she is terrified the people next door will hear. In fact, we didn't even make love on our honeymoon for the same reason.'

It is a powerful prohibition and deep shame which makes a woman prefer to refuse sex with her new husband rather than let anyone hear her participate in making love.

Other women cannot bear their partner to see them making love. Russell, 52: 'Making love always has to be in the dark. I would much like to see her body intertwined with mine in as many varied positions as possible, to have "fun" in the bedroom, not merely to have sex as quickly as possible. My wife is a wonderful mother to our children but could do better as a wife.'

How does it feel?

Even if a man is not literally making love in the dark, he may be in the dark as to what his partner really enjoys or would like unless she tells him. It is unfair to expect a man automatically to be skilful and knowledgeable when we would also be outraged at the suggestion that all women are sexual clones, that if you have had one you have had them all.

One in three (34 per cent) husbands wishes his wife would talk more about how it feels while making love.

Andy, 24 and in the army: 'I love to hear her telling me what it feels like when we make love. I wish she would keep telling me all through having sex whether it's nice or could be better.'

Blake, 43, HGV driver: 'I have no problem communicating my thoughts and wishes, but I find it difficult to get information from my wife, even after 14 years together. I am a normal, lusty male but my wife doesn't seem to take the strength of my feelings seriously. She doesn't respond and I become very frustrated that she won't talk more, meet me halfway in sharing our likes and dislikes. Most of the time I know that if I don't take the initiative, in love-making or anything, then absolutely nothing will happen. If women want to be treated well, then they should be prepared to treat men with consideration.'

Even when a man is unselfishly trying to give his partner sexual pleasure, some can seem too guilt-ridden to respond in any way freely or openly.

Cliff, a computer analyst: 'After four years of marriage, I read in a sex manual that oral sex might give my wife pleasure. When I tried it she got angry, told me that I could "get my sex somewhere else" and sulked for many months. It was for her benefit, not mine.'

If couples can talk more openly together about how sex and different ways of making love feel, it can turn sex into the shared communication of physical love and pleasure, rather than the route march of a blindfolded man with an out-of-date map.

Gavin, 28: 'I was disappointed with oral sex but since filling in your questionnaire I've talked to my wife. She said my clumsiness made it uncomfortable for her and now I can try to be more gentle.'

How often is it not prejudice which puts women off a new technique, but the need for some simple adjustment which they are too inhibited to spell out?

Only two out of five (41 per cent) of men say that they and their partner talk completely openly about sex and their sexual feelings.

While most of the others claimed to talk fairly openly, as long as there are any constraints, it is always the most difficult and embarrassing points that do not get discussed.

It can be hard to make the effort. Leslie, 39, a civil servant: 'We don't have any difficulty talking about sex and our bodies but this tends to be clinical. When it comes to our sexual feelings it is awkward, I probably broach the subject more than my wife, but I find it very difficult. I can't find ways that don't seem critical – even if they are – and I don't want to hurt her feelings.

'I find it hard to choose the right time. It's no good just after making love saying, "Well, that wasn't much good", even if you're feeling it, and it's hardly the time over the cornflakes in the morning.'

Yet talking completely openly does make a dramatic difference to a couple's chances of sexual compatibility.

Thirty per cent of the men who are very discontented with their sex life *never* talk at all about sex or their sexual feelings with their partner, while this is true of only 2 per cent of those who are very satisfied.

Jimmy, 21, who works in finance, said: 'We are very open in our sexual discussions. There's nothing we *wouldn't* discuss. We have a lot of laughs and jokes, so there's never any tension and it does help remove inhibitions.'

Of course it is difficult for those who have been brought up to feel guilty and reserved about their sexual feelings to start talking about them openly, even with their partner. We should remind ourselves that none of us can dictate what another person's sexual experience should be like. All any of us can do is feel how it is for us and ask how it is for others.

Throw any ideas of norms and ideals out of the window, don't launch into techniques from a sex manual without warning. Start with a kiss and a fingertip stroked down the face. Ask, 'Does that feel good?' and go on from there. The only person who can guide you through your partner's body map of pleasure is your partner. It is not number of techniques and changes of position that matter, but the intensity of feeling discovered and shared by both.

7 Dream lovers
Fantasies, pornography and prostitution

T he one place in a man's known world where woman never sets foot is inside his head. There no mother can disapprove of his dirty thoughts. There no girlfriend stops a wandering hand short of its goal, no wife refuses any type of sex as often and long as he wants it. There is no job, no bills, no children, no family responsibilities, no restriction on infidelity. Sexual license is his.

So what do you think he gets up to in there – rape, pillage and orgies? A few do, but not many. He may dream of young girls and virgins, of making love to two women at once, or covet his neighbour's wife in a way that leaves him safe from the divorce court and maintenance payments, but he is more likely to fantasise being dominated than dominating.

Most men fantasise while they masturbate and one in three (37 per cent) fantasise while they make love.

The table shows their most common favourite fantasies.

Making love with a different partner: Young girl or virgin (9 per cent), past lover, member of family, friend or neighbour, stranger seen in the street   18%

Making love in different surroundings: beaches, forests, mirrored rooms   13%

Watching/being watched: wife with another partner or in threesome (9 per cent) making love to wife, lesbians together, taking part in a blue movie   15%

Special clothes: partner wearing stockings and suspenders, high-heels, leather, rubber, uniforms   11%

Making love to two women (or more)   9%

Being dominated by partner or older woman, bondage   7%

Masochism: being smacked, degraded, raped by
woman/women   5%

Famous women: making love with actress, sports-
woman, TV personalities   5%

Oral sex: receiving and giving   5%

Being dominant: sultan with hand-maiden(s), master
with schoolgirl, etc.   3%

Rape, submissive females   2%

Dressing up in women's clothes   2%

Making love with men   2%

Wife being responsive   1%

Anal sex   1%

Extra-large penis, several penises   1%

At first glance a rather disparate bunch of subjects for fantasy,
but looked at more closely, coherent, deeper themes emerge.

Sleeping Beauty awakes

The fantasies of making love to a young girl or another woman
do not usually reflect any real urge for the man to seduce virgins,
or have an affair with his sister-in-law. In fact, some men
pointed out that if there is any real chance of their making
love with the other woman they then avoid her in their fantasy
life. She starts becoming a real person to them sexually, rather
than a fantasy image whom they can direct as they wish in their
dreams.

The key characteristic of these 'other women' is that they are
sexually eager and responsive, sometimes even in spite of themselves. The man, in his fantasy, is sexually irresistible.

Youth is supposed to equal slimness and beauty. Try telling
that to a teenager worried about puppy fat and acne – but of
course the young girls in men's fantasies are slender and firm-
bodied! However, it is not their physical appeal that seems to
make them such a powerful image. A young girl is sexually a clean
slate. In the dream at least, she does not know what she wants
until the man shows her, and then she responds with abandon.
She is Sleeping Beauty who awakens to her prince's touch and

she cannot resist his magic. He is the man of experience who shows his partner pleasures she never knew existed.

Michael, 24, a computer programmer: 'I take an imaginary girl of about 15 with a firm body who feels randy but thinks she does not want sex. I rub my penis on her crutch until she really enjoys it when I start to enter her.' Like many of the men, Michael is quick to add, 'Though I have no inhibitions about fantasies, I've never wanted to do this in real life, due to the possible mental effect on the girl.'

For married men the fantasy of a young girl may be a way of winding the clock back to his single days, before his sex life got entangled with his and his wife's expectations of their roles as husband and wife, mother and father. Harvey, 46, an explosives engineer: 'I fantasise I am with a previous lover of 25 years ago who was my first uninhibited sexual partner. We were both single then.' John, 61: 'I always imagine my wife as she was when we were first together.'

A young girl is more likely to allow an older man natural dominance, to fall in with his suggestions and then enjoy it – because of course we are all wonderful lovers in our dreams. Paul, 53, a chiropodist: 'My fantasies are mainly of a young, slim girl who would let me make love to her in a secret way. Nothing dirty but abandoned!'

If older men may fantasise premarried days to avoid the restrictions on unbridled sensuality imposed by their mother/ wife figure, younger men may fantasise about the type of girl of whom Mother would not approve, but whom he suspects might be more responsive and relaxed sexually than the girls she accepts.

Robin, 20, in financial services: 'I often fantasise about a young girl in my office. She's about 17 and is very petite but pretty also. She's rather a yobbish and pathetic person with a common accent, but there's something inexplicable about her that makes me attracted in a purely sexual way. She's the last person in the world I'd want to go out with, but I do occasionally fantasise about sex with her on top (my favourite position).'

The more mature 'other women' in the fantasies are usually in humdrum settings but ready for sex at the drop of a washing-up bowl, with the first electric touch of the lover's hand. They are never too tired, too busy or have the children's dinner to put on.

Trevor, 38, an insurance clerk: 'My favourite fantasy is making love to a friend's wife. I know she is more adventurous than

103

my wife because of what my friend has told me. I imagine calling on her when her husband is out. She goes into the kitchen to finish the washing-up or whatever. I approach her from behind and put my arms around her. My hands move up to her boobs (which are not particularly big, incidentally).

'She responds by letting her head fall back on my shoulder and putting her hand behind her back and rubbing my erect penis. She turns round and we kiss passionately. We start to undress each other. As I remove her G-string I pull her vagina towards my face and kiss it. I lick all round her vaginal area. We then both fall on to the floor and get into the 69 position where we arouse each other to a state where intercourse does not last very long.'

Wayne, 28, a bus driver, often fantasises about making love with his next-door neighbour. 'She's in her mid-thirties, with four young children and she's very attractive. I go home, it's quite late and nobody's home, so I go to her house. She comes to the door wearing a see-through nightie with very sexy underwear and invites me in. She offers me a drink and then comes and sits next to me. Pretty soon we are kissing and I'm fondling her breasts. She's stroking my groin and then I perform oral sex on her and she on me. We go upstairs and make love in lots of positions.'

Such fantasies sound very much like what men want to be sharing with their wives in real life. Wayne might not be quite so keen on his own wife answering the door in a see-through nightie, but that is the overall message.

Some men specifically draw the comparison: 'I fantasise someone who is a more active and willing partner than my wife.' 'I suppose if my wife were more sexually active I would not need the services of another woman in my fantasies.' Others fantasise about their wife, but not responding as she does in real life. Lee, 23, a shopworker: 'My fantasies are always of my wife. I would love to really turn her on. I'm sure she's never had an orgasm. It would make me very happy to do this for her.'

Older women feature in such fantasies because they are assumed to 'know what they like'. Andy, 37, who works on a production line: 'I fantasise about making love to an older, uninhibited woman. A kind, considerate, warm woman who appreciates a man, especially in bed. A woman who loves sex, who enjoys the sex act without feeling dirty or guilty. A woman with experience of satisfying a man – usually a widow. It is important she is not a prostitute or a tart. This would make me feel cheap. She will do anything in bed to please me, not because she feels she has to but because she wants to.'

The fantasies about particular sexual techniques such as oral and anal sex also focus on women who are willing and permissive partners. Morgan, 23, a technical sales representative: 'I often fantasise about making love, including oral sex, with different women I meet in my job, whom I'm too scared to tell how I really feel. I am married. I like to think of them giving me fellatio and wanting me to make love in any position I care to imagine.'

Philip, 43, an accountant, says gloomily: 'I fantasise oral sex. My wife enjoys having it done but not doing it.' He might be disappointed if she did. Stewart, 27, a historian points out: 'I find the fantasy of anal intercourse more exciting than the reality.'

Cutting the apron strings

The very turn-on of such a fantasy may not be the physical sensation of the act, but the thought of it as something beyond the pale of the nice behaviour of which 'Mother' would have approved (which may be just what is holding his wife back from participating in reality, of course).

Remember we are not necessarily talking about what a man's own mother really felt, but the attitudes he assumed 'respectable' women held because the whole subject was screened off by silence. If as a boy he gets the feeling that his very sexuality is threatened by this suffocating 'niceness' then anger and force are more likely to play a part in his fantasies. He needs them to fight off the tight controls which he subconsciously feels are being placed on his manhood. In these fantasies the women have no choice but to enjoy his rampant sexuality. He may be raping them (men's fantasies of rape are just as different as women's from the reality) or find himself in a position of power over them.

Men fantasise about being a schoolmaster with a schoolgirl, a plantation owner with a slave, a sultan, a pharoah. Vivian, 37, a teacher: 'I am surrounded by sexily dressed attractive women, who are trained to give and receive my pleasure whatever they may be. Two will dance provocatively with each other or with well built men, while several more will bathe me, dry, oil, massage, kiss, lick and suck me. We drink and eat exotic fruits, wine.

105

We use ropes to bind one another and restrain and increase the pleasure. We may whip or beat one of the girls tied to a post or wall. I may have two girls make love to each other, sexual and manual activity.

'The tempo increases and I find myself fucking or being fucked by one of the girls, who is using one hand to pleasure herself, while the other girls are masturbating themselves on my hands, feet or mouth, or making love to each other. All around me are the sounds of people abandoned to their sexual pleasure, noisily sweating and gasping, we climax together, and slowly recover in a warm, satisfied glow, released and satisfied.'

Once Vivian has used the force of his position of power to throw off the constraints of normal behaviour, to shut 'Mother' out of the party, everyone has a good time. The anger in a fantasy like those of Adam, 33, a solicitor, feels far more menacing to most women. 'My fantasies are of being naked with a Page Three girl in a shower, pissing on her arse and then ramming my two-foot long penis inside her, pinning her against the wall.' Even the language of such fantasies is violent, abusive.

Adam went on: 'I don't consider that these fantasies affect my marriage. As long as I can masturbate them out in the privacy of the bathroom I am satisfied.' Sexual fantasies, like our sleeping dreams, cannot be judged by normal standards of morality. We cannot usually control what we dream. In fact our dreams and fantasies are often a very healthy sign that we are relieving anger and hurt that we do not want to affect our behaviour towards others, acting out our revenge in our head where it hurts no one except ourselves.

That does not mean we should just ignore the material of our dreams and fantasies. It can often tell us a great deal about ourselves that we are too frightened to look at. If we deal with it in our conscious thinking and real lives, it can release us and those around us from the legacy of old wounds. Perhaps Adam's wife has no inkling of his sexual fantasies but if he has had a great deal of anger about women bottled up inside him since childhood, he may well reveal this in other ways that make them both unhappy. Has he distinguished his wife from his mother?

Women, too, have fantasies which may not tally with how they like to think of themselves. Women fantasise about being raped. Not only do they abhor the reality (which they know is not the same as the deliciously enjoyable rape scenes of their dreams). It is not comfortable for a woman today to have to admit to herself that far from being sexually liberated she uses a mental image of being taken against her will, so that she can say to her 'Mother' image, 'See Mum, I didn't *want* to do it.'

Some couples talk each other through such a shared, 'liberating' fantasy. Charles, 27, a company director: 'I fantasise about raping a woman. I follow her each night for about a week till I know her pattern. It is usually by some bushes, then one night I grab her and push her to the floor. I slowly take off her clothes – her blouse first, then her bra, I suck her tits. While I'm doing this I've got my hand up her skirt feeling her vagina, then I rip off her knickers and undo my trousers, then rape her viciously. I rape her about three times then I go.

'I tell my wife about it and it seems to excite her more. We play it out. Not that she wants to be raped, or I would rape anyone. I have a sister and two daughters and I think what it would do to them and me if they were raped.'

Sometimes the twist in the tale is that it is the man who is the 'slave', who is forced into releasing his lust, but then dominates through the sheer power of his sexuality. Perhaps it is no coincidence that Iain, 38, is a clergyman in daily life. In his fantasies: 'I am in an erotic, Abrabian or Eastern setting. I am a slave and my wife is an empress or queen. I am lined up with a number of other male slaves and she inspects us all – intimately. She chooses me and leads me to her private quarters. Once we are inside the door is locked. She wants to do exciting things to me but, green or not, I can be in control and be masterful, and do what I want to her. I often share this fantasy – or variations of it – with my wife.'

Desert island dreams

One in five men chooses to transport his loving to a more exotic setting or to share it with a more glamorous partner.

Most of the different settings men imagine for making love are romantic and luxurious. Good sex is part of a good holiday and these are holidays men are taking in their minds. The lovers' bodies are caressed by sun and sea, the breezes blow through the wide open spaces, and there is a bottle of champagne at their elbow. Would not most people swap their semi for the Seychelles for a night or two of romance?

'We're making love on a tropical beach with the waves coming in over our naked bodies.' 'We're having sex outside, in the countryside, or in a log cabin high up in the mountains, completely private, with log fires, champagne etc.' 'A forest or a room full of mirrors, or in a very plush and high-class car.' 'A bigger bedroom, luxury bed etc., or maybe somewhere exotic, sunshine, beautiful setting, sea.'

It is a yearning for glamour that most men also seem to express by their fantasies of making love with famous women. They did not give detailed descriptions of scenarios, just names of women they imagined to be sharing their caresses. After all these years, top of the list, including for young men barely out of their teens, came Marilyn Monroe. Next? Well, no one quite liked to say they imagined they were making love to Princess Diana but, 'I imagine my wife looks like Princess Diana and we are very rich.'

Some are greedy: 'I suppose my all-time fantasy is to have Tina Turner on one side and Dolly Parton on the other!' Newsreaders such as Jan Leeming and Carol Barnes, sit-com stars like Gwen Taylor from *Duty Free*, Page Three girls such as Samantha Fox, and female performers like Cyndi Lauper and Toyah Wilcox, all made the ratings. Twenty-two year old Geoff imagines: 'I am with an older experienced woman, like Jane Fonda or Elizabeth Taylor, in a massive great bed.'

The onlooker

For one in six men his favourite fantasy is of watching or being watched: watching his wife make love with another man or as one of a threesome, watching women make love together, being watched while he makes love himself.

Bryan, 35, an air-conditioning salesman: 'My wife was engaged when I met her and, as I suspected, having regular sex. Some years into our marriage I reminded her of the occasion when her ex had met her from work and they'd had sex for "old times' sake". Admittedly this was before we were married.

'My wife was surprised that I should want to know all the details and that I was aroused by her story. I once suggested during love-making that she could handle more than one at the same time – me making love to her while she performed oral sex with another. Although my wife did not agree she did not say no. I kept on with this suggestion at odd times, until one evening we sat down and discussed it in detail.

'I said that I found anything that would excite her or be arousing to her of interest. To watch her with someone or as a threesome would be the ultimate. Again she did not say no.

"Maybe, one day," was the reply! I have not pursued this any further, as I am aware that as a fantasy it's a turn on, but in reality it could be a disaster.'

In such fantasies it seems that the imaginary competition heightens excitement. Another man desiring and arousing your wife makes her more desirable and arousable – though it might be very disruptive in real life. Some men did tell us of their experiences with wife-swapping and threesomes (see Chapter Eight), but most couples find this best left in the realm of fantasy.

It is not only the competitive element which stimulates men having these fantasies. Seeing couples making love in the mind's eye focuses the attention, helps shut out distractions just like a blue movie. Men especially are responsive to visual triggers and the images help send the hormones flooding round the system, to increase desire and sensation. In many of these fantasies the onlooker appears to be sitting happily in front of a mental video, his excitement building.

'I imagine my wife with another woman, any close friend. I come home early, unexpected, and catch them at it. I watch from behind the bedroom door until I can see that they are very carried away and then I join in.' 'I like to imagine that I'm watching my girlfriend and I making love from above or through a window.' 'I often fantasise with my wife of her with another man or without me there. When watching a blue movie on the video it turns us both on very much and we always end up making love soon after watching one, if not before.'

One in ten men's favourite fantasy is making love with two women at once.

These fantasies rarely have any suggestion in them that the man really wants to try this experiment. They focus on sensation, four hands being better than two, etc.

Joel, 33, a telex operator: 'When we go to bed in my fantasy I lie naked between my wife and another woman – for want of a better word, my mistress. They are equally naked. I am usually on my back to start, with my arms around them. They snuggle up and entwine themselves round me, their hot bodies tightly woven about me, their hands wandering over my erect penis. One by one, I kiss and make love to them each in turn. Both eagerly try to outdo the other, but with mutual respect.'

Like the fantasy of being an onlooker, dreaming of making love with two women is a way of heightening sensation, of turning sex into an all-enveloping experience. Mark, 28, fantasises: 'about the idea of having several penises with which I can have intercourse with my partner.'

Dressing the part

One in ten men say their favourite fantasy is of their own partner or another woman dressed in clothes or underwear they find particularly exciting.

As we have seen, one in five women do dress up in stockings and suspenders to make love, but some men prefer the fantasy or have to make do with it. It is a line of sexual day-dreaming that starts with women being dressed in provocatively sexy clothes, clothes that leave no doubt what they want, through fetishism and beyond.

Dudley, 28, in the army: 'I am with some girl I know, whom I slowly undress to reveal stockings, suspenders and high-heeled shoes. I make love to her while she is still wearing them, feeling the silk against my body – er . . . I think I had better calm down.'

Gareth, 36, a financial representative: 'I finally persuaded my wife to wear stockings and suspenders when we make love. Now I always have the same fantasy of my wife (no one else) being clad in a leather (preferably black) or rubber outfit with studded belt and thigh-high boots and holding a whip. I feel I must pluck up the courage to buy such an outfit, but my wife says she will not wear it.'

What is the attraction of leather and rubber, high-heeled shoes, silky fabrics and snapping elastic? To start with we have been conditioned to see them as flagrantly sexy. The underwear seen as signalling 'Come and get me' dates back to the music-hall era, when for a respectable woman to flash an ankle was daring.

In those days if a man got a view of suspenders and stays they were probably on a 'fallen woman'. Even his wife might undress with more modesty, and many a husband went to his grave never having seen his wife naked. Just as a nun's habit is merely the day-to-day clothing of the Middle Ages which has become an accepted uniform, the underwear of the turn of the century, the days of Gay Paree, has become the uniform of a woman who is interested in sex. The partner who dons the stockings and suspenders is showing her man that she is on the side of his sexuality, and willing to rebel against the 'Mother' in herself and as well in him.

For some men, that is as far as it goes, but others progress beyond overtly sexy underwear into rubber, leather, and boots which, even if in fantasy form alone, can be extremely important for them to feel sexual arousal and release.

Psychiatrists do not agree about the exact causes of these sorts of attachments to fetishes, except that the pattern is laid down in early childhood.

Freud saw the overriding factor governing a man's childhood as his rivalry with his father for his mother's love, and the fear that his father would castrate him. According to this theory the fetish symbolises the penis. As long as the fetish is present the man is sexually safe.

A more recent theory, which seems more generally applicable, is that the fetish is not connected with fear of the father, but with anxiety about losing the mother's love. It is this anxiety, laid down when the man was a helpless baby, that can be seen as fuelling so much anger against women, who seem to choose to hold it back, to say, 'No! Don't touch! Don't do that!'

As a baby, the theory goes, the man knows security and sensual pleasure being dried all over after a bath on mother's waterproof apron, the bliss of feeding cuddled close against her silky underwear. Crawling around on the floor he feels a sudden panic. 'Where is Mum?' Then he spots a familiar feminine shoe. Relief – 'There she is!' Yet Mum can also seem strict and stern, witholding the food or cuddle he wants, and saying no to all sorts of lovely experiments day after day.

Refined and embellished over the years, the fetish objects and clothes become necessary to sensual/sexual pleasure, part of his inner programming for arousal, but also associated with a woman who dominates and says no, who has total power over him. Mother did not need boots and a whip to have her way, but as he grows bigger and stronger he may add these to strengthen her image for him.

For some men the fantasy is not that important. Occasionally re-enacting his childhood conflicts in symbolic garb in the private spaces of his mind is enough to deal with them. Kelvin, 23, a salesman: 'I imagine my lover being very dominant, ordering me to do this and that. She wears (in my fantasy) high-heeled thigh-length boots, stockings, a whip (which she does not hurt me with, it just symbolic, my masochism is purely psychological violence!), a black skin-tight basque. I am usually tied up, spread-eagled on the bed.'

Peter, 35, an acupuncturist, is sure he does not want to act out his fantasy: 'Although I would run a mile if I ever found a woman like it, my fantasy is of a well-built lady in very aggressive, kinky gear who wants to beat me. Alternatively I am beaten by a very slight lady in ordinary clothes, but I know she has stockings on because I get a glimpse of the stocking tops as she lifts her arm to strike. I dislike pain, but my fantasy is always of a masochistic nature.'

Roger, 38, a garage manager, would like to act out his fantasies: 'I don't fantasise over other girls, only what I like to have done and do with my wife. Favourite is me being tied on the bed, having my wife smack me a bit and then forcefully have me. After me coming, she would sit on my face and let her/our juices run over my face and mouth. I don't know to what extent I would actually enjoy it, but I want to try.'

Tim's girlfriend willingly co-operates (he is 23, a roofer): 'My fantasy is for my partner to dress up in uniforms, and special outfits. Boots, long gloves, basques, suspenders and fishnet stockings. I can't explain why I like these things, but I just seem to go into top gear when she walks into the room all dolled up for me. I also like to be dominated by her, the naughty boy and teacher act, and getting punished. I'm just a pervert I suppose!'

There is nothing perverted about something two people both enjoy doing together, but fetishism and masochism do cause problems in relationships when the partner – it is usually the woman – gets the feeling that it is not so much her who is turning her partner on, but the special clothes or the 'punishment'. Once she gets the feeling he does not care *who* is wearing the boots or wielding the whip, so long as somebody does, she feels very threatened and usually calls a halt.

Attachment to fetish clothing is an element in transvestism. It is not such a big leap from being excited by the clothes on your partner to being excited by them on yourself. We look in more detail at transvestism in Chapter Twelve but, again, when a partner feels it is the clothes that provide the excitement and not her presence, she often withdraws her co-operation.

Erotica

Blue movies and sex magazines are now a regular part of the majority of men's lives.

Only one in five men (18 per cent) says he never sees erotic literature and films.

However, they are a staple diet for only one in six men. Teenagers of 16 to 18 are less likely to see pornography often, but they are also less likely than the average to see none at all. Steven, 17, a student said: 'My fantasies are usually based around soft porn images, as these magazines were generally available at school off mates.'

It is teachers who are also parents who express the most concern about the effect this material must have on developing adolescent minds. Alec, 42: 'Some of the magazines that my 15-year-old son can get his hands on border on hard porn. It is violence with sexuality that I find most disturbing in books, magazines and the media. I occasionally write about it to the publishers. The most pornographic book I came across concerned death, cars and sex. It was in a college library, part of the county stock, and the librarian did not know it was there. It was withdrawn. I rate it a serious book, but most would not read it like that.'

Gerard, 37, also a teacher: 'I once had a *laissez-faire* attitude to pornography, but now I am strongly against it. While one can argue that it does no harm, I do feel that it can affect attitudes to women in impressionable minds. It certainly degrades men and women into being objects and not human beings, and it appears to feed on itself, demanding ever more sensational material so that we now have the ultimate, the so-called "snuff movies" portraying real murders.

'I know for a fact that young children obtain this material, which concerns me. One of the greatest shocks I had as a youngster was to discover some pornographic photographs which my stepfather owned. At that age I felt it degraded my father and I found the experience hurtful.

'My wife and I went through a stage where we obtained some porno mags and films but, after an initial response of excitement, we began to feel sorry for the people in these materials, that they should degrade themselves as human beings, and they became decidedly unerotic.'

Michael, 36, an accountant, enjoys some soft porn videos with his wife. 'We tend to have a good laugh but feel that stricter laws should be enforced re hard porn videos. We're adult enough to take it lightly, but too many youngsters who are easily influenced have access to these videos. They can't have a normal outlook on life and sexual relationships if they've seen this kind of porn.'

Some magazines and videos 'act out' men's anger against

women, making abuse seem almost acceptable. Even milder material can shape men's ideas of the 'sexy' woman's appearance and trappings – the basque and suspenders – and what the full range of sex play should include. A young man arrives at his first intimate relationship, not just with an urge to explore together what they would both find pleasurable, but a list of techniques that he wants to try because he's seen them in magazines or on film.

Neil, 19, a student: 'I very often buy porno magazines as I am still a virgin and find them useful methods of sexual release. I started by buying the occasional magazine from newsagents. More recently I have ventured into sex shops, but have not always been satisfied by what I have bought, as sometimes it isn't as strong as the ones you get from the newsagent. My favourite ones are those which feature oral sex. I find it fascinating and hope to try it one day on my girlfriend. Buying these magazines becomes rather addictive so I've built up quite a secret collection.'

Perhaps Neil's girlfriend will be as keen as he is to try oral sex but, if it is not something she is ready for yet, she is going to feel under pressure and he is going to feel disappointed in her sexually, since he has built up quite a head of steam through the magazines he has been reading. Without them, perhaps oral sex is something they would have discovered together in their own time, when both were ready to enjoy it.

Gary, 21, an acrylics engineer, saw another drawback. 'Erotic materials may heighten one's sexual activities but may also be detrimental as they can enable a person to feel incompetent after seeing a "perfect" sexual act.' Pornography, even soft pornography, sets standards in physique and performance which are unrealistic and can leave many feeling inadequate unnecessarily.

We asked men to say whether they mostly saw hard or soft pornography though, of course, this has to be a very subjective judgement. Hard porn may just be what *you* find too strong.

One in three men (36 per cent) said that the material they see is hard pornography or a mixture of hard and soft.

Soft porn is accepted as having a useful function by most men, even those who don't use it. 'Before I was involved in a permanent relationship I used girlie magazines as a sole source of sexual pleasure.' 'I only read erotic material when I am away from my girlfriend for a long period.' 'Better than being unfaithful.'

Chris, 27, who is in the Royal Marines: 'I enjoy masturbating while reading girlie mags. If people want it, let them have it. In my line of work, you need it!!'

Giles, 29, a GP, suggested: 'I think pornography is useful in some cases and can relieve tension.' Alistair, 67, and disabled, agrees: 'I get a lot of enjoyment from girlie magazines. They all turn me on so much. That is the only way I can enjoy life any more.'

Matthew, 28, summed up: 'Window shopping is fun for a lot of people but hard pornography for the sake of it or financial gain from others' weaknesses should be controlled more strongly. Moderation is best – in all things.'

While some men spoke up for hard pornography: 'In general hard-core porn should be available to those adults who want it,' nearly all draw a line somewhere. Ross, 27, a ship's engineer: 'The hardest porn that I would entertain would be up to pictures of group sex. The ships that I've been on have probably had the hardest stuff available, including lesbianism, child sex and sadomasochism. I think some of these types are revolting and should be stopped or at least controlled. I think video nasties – of which I've seen one – are over the top, and that with some people they could be dangerous.'

Men raised various objections: 'I'm put off by violent sex. I like a bit of unconventionality but violence is sick.' 'I do not agree with child pornography or bestiality. This type of material should be banned.' 'I object to those which could be classed as medical catalogue: the spread-legged close-ups.' 'Bad pornography represents women as "a hole to be filled".' 'Some of it I find offensive and degrading to women.'

However, very few women seem to put up any strong objection.

Most men say their partner knows that they look at pornographic material at least occasionally and only one in four (25 per cent) says she minds.

Ian, 38, an insurance clerk: 'My wife used to read my magazines but she said she got bored by them and thought they were rather sordid, so she doesn't read them now. I still buy girlie magazines but I keep them out of sight under the bed.'

Women often have very conflicting feelings about the material available, not sure whether they are being aroused or sickened. Colin, 27, in the army: 'My wife is curious about porn, but finds she is in the end so mixed up inside she's turned off by it, and feels it is dangerous.'

Few women seem to object to all erotic material but they are, perhaps not surprisingly, quicker than men to feel that it is degrading. Tony, 21, a student: 'My girlfriend and I enjoy looking at and reading sexual material. It turns us both on and heightens our love-making. However, on one occasion she was sickened and felt cheap when we bought one type of magazine. This seemed more smutty than the others, more close-up genital shots (of women only).'

One in ten men often looks at erotic material with his partner and a further six out of ten occasionally.

William, 25, a joiner: 'I had seen a couple of hard-core pornographic videos and my wife had never seen one. I borrowed a tape and a machine off some mates at work and asked my wife to watch it with an open mind, working on the theory that you don't know until you've tried it. I agreed to turn it off if she found it offensive. The result was that she enjoyed it very much, and we both got incredibly turned on by it. I think the effect stunned us both. I reckon if you view it as a bit of fun and a turn on, then it's great. If you take them seriously, you have a problem.'

Erotic material, like some of the fantasies both men and women have, certainly works in focusing the attention and encouraging sexual responses to come into play. Clinical research has shown that more women respond sexually to erotic material than can consciously admit it, as Ken, 26, an electrician, noticed. 'While watching soft porn videos my wife has said that they don't do anything for her, despite obvious heavy breathing. I wonder if this is a conditioned response.' Perhaps she has good reason.

Cliff, 23, a shop worker told us: 'I find girlie magazines horny but I've just found out that my wife likes most porn and I feel shocked.'

Now more women are able to shut 'Mother' out and openly admit they enjoy and are aroused by sexy images. This does not mean that women want or will allow themselves to be pushed further and further along a limb towards more and more hard-core material. Now that women want to join with their partners more in sharing this stimulus, the demand is growing for a change in the nature of the material available.

Howard, 29, a shop owner: 'The problem with most girlie magazines is that they often portray women as recipients of sex and aggression rather than as participants. The magazines require improvement. It would be nice if someone launched a magazine for men and women to read together.'

Ben, 32, an architect: 'My wife likes watching blue movies and usually finds them stimulating. However, they are mostly aimed at fulfilling men's fantasies rather than women's, which she finds disappointing.'

Paying for the dream

One of a prostitute's most important functions, as men see it, is in fulfilling sexual fantasies.

Three out of ten men (28 per cent) say they believe prostitutes provide particular types of sex men cannot get in their relationship.

'Prostitutes sell sex as a commercial article,' commented Vincent, 36, a dentist, 'and there is a shop for every taste. Wives do not always have such interests. A whore is like Harrods. With money you can get anything.'

Men whose partners will not share in the particular forms of dressing up or treatment they desire, may pay for their pleasure – if they can afford it. Colin, 35, a lorry driver said wistfully: 'I would only visit a prostitute to satisfy rubber-related urges. They cost a lot of money so it's out of the question, but wishful thinking is OK.'

Edmund, 23, had no regrets: 'I went to a prostitute because I wanted sex of a different kind. It was quite expensive but she dressed up in leather for me and I climaxed about three times. I felt very good after and I would have no hesitation in going again.' Francis, 50, a domestic engineer, says: 'Prostitutes provide oral sex which my wife won't either way.'

Bob, 38, self-employed, is very embarrassed by the memory of his visits to a prostitute to act out his fantasies. 'I fell in love and married my wife when I was nineteen. When I was twenty-five or so, I visited a prostitute twice. I've never told anyone this, out of embarrassment. I had developed an interest in the "seamy" side of life – a reaction to married respectability or a self-destructive streak, whichever you choose.

'A contact magazine provided me with an introduction to a lady called Deborah and I duly visited her. She specialised in dealing with masochists or submissives, myself identifying with the latter. In short I paid her to dress me in women's underclothes and humiliate me. She was quite a pretty woman with long dark hair, her age around twenty-eight or so. (Her ad said twenty-one!) She dressed me in suspenders and stockings, some frilly panties and a pinny, make-up and lipstick and then I was given some household chores to do.

'Eventually I was told to take some tea on a tray into a sitting room and serve it to Deborah and her "maid", a blonde women around sixty in a turquoise Crimplene dress; presumably their teabreak! After serving tea and being used as a footstool while they drank it, there came what became my most humiliating experience. Upon Deborah's instructions I took off the pinny and lowered my panties to my ankles and stood there while they made disparaging remarks about my genitals. They criticised the size (five inches when erect – I worried about it at the time) and then I was made to masturbate before them, Deborah abusing me as the older woman looked on.

'A few weeks later, I returned for a similar session. This time I was permitted the privilege of performing oral sex on the older woman (whose name I forget) while being beaten by Deborah.'

Such fantasies can seem rather pathetic to those who do not share them. Some wives would be very upset if asked to act them out, so it could disturb what may otherwise be a very harmonious relationship and family life. Perhaps there is no harm of itself in someone choosing to give men a safe outlet at a reasonable fee to act out such fantasies which involve no risk to the prostitute.

Prostitution may be something that seems to have little bearing on the lives of most women – though this attitude is one some prostitutes and feminists have been fighting and which the advent of AIDS is calling into question. Men have long been more interested – or nervously tempted. Dick, 43, a librarian: 'I remember when I was about 17 walking past the prostitutes around Hyde Park and feeling terrific lust plus cold feet. I opted for an Italian meal instead. Probably two reasons kept me from going with a pro – being careful with money and fear of VD.'

Just over a half of the men (52 per cent) who took part in our survey have at least wondered about going to a prostitute. One in six (15 per cent) has done so.

Men who are alone – the separated, divorced and widowed – are twice as likely to have paid for a prostitute's services, and men who told us of such experiences often had no relationship at the time or were a long way from home.

One in six men said that what prostitutes mainly provide is sex when a man is away from home.

Some men serving in the Forces, particularly overseas, and overseas salesmen may make regular use of them. Chas, 44, a salesman: 'Prostitutes always made me feel welcome. I used them for years in the Far East, mostly Siamese, Chinese, occasionally Eurasian. They are all very good and really knew how to please.'

Anthony, 29, a sub-postmaster: 'When I was in the navy I had a number of prostitutes but usually only one in any given port of call.' Tom, 62, a librarian, remembers: 'When I was in the army in North Africa, I acted as interpreter for the others in an Algerian brothel. I asked some of the girls why they were on the game: "For our dowry." '

Prostitution now often goes under the guise of an escort agency or massage parlour. Denis, 35, an accountant: 'I enjoy an occasional visit to a massage parlour. This does not always include sexual intercourse, since I always enjoy a sauna, and often it only includes hand relief.'

Henry, 55, took a job in the south but his family stayed in the north, as his children's O and A Levels were looming. 'I rang an escort agency and was asked if I wanted theatre or sex. I opted for the latter. I booked the same girl every three or four weeks for five months – a meal and then back to my rented flat. Then I found out that she was only 19, the same age as one of my daughters, and I felt guilty. I found another of about 25, who talked crude at times, which turned me on. That lasted seven months.

'In the end my wife became suspicious as I was spending too much money, and checked up on me. I tried to pass it off that they were just escorts for theatres or restaurants, but she wouldn't believe me. She refused to see me and we were separated for two years. Then I persuaded her to give me another chance. I have regretted the incidents ever since – both being a MCP and going off to a job just to please myself, and also the prostitutes and what it did to my marriage. Although things are improving, my wife does not trust me away from home even for a night when it is for business. She goes with me.'

Some regretted their experiences at the time. Mark, 27, a graphic designer: 'The only sexual experience I had previous to my current girlfriend was when I visited a prostitute four years ago to find out what sex was all about. It was the biggest mistake of my life. I hated it. It put me off sex for many years.'

Dominic, 25, a chemist: 'I visited a prostitute on two occasions and both times were because I was feeling sexually excited after watching a hard-core porn film at a London cinema club. I felt at the time that I needed sexual relief in a way other than by just masturbation. I did not enjoy the sex obtained in this way. It was so impersonal and remote.'

Quite apart from their personal sexual dreams men build up fantasies about prostitution, particularly young men. Brendan, 19: 'The fact that I have never had sex with a prostitute makes it intriguing.' Nigel, 35, a teacher: 'As an adolescent they figured quite considerably in my fantasies – the idea that you could pay a woman for sex. While girls were attainable, women were not.' Young men often believe that prostitutes may be a short cut in their quest for 'experience'. Warren, 31, in general services: 'I've always believed that a *good* prostitute can teach one far more about sexual technique than any book.'

Warren has never actually been to a prostitute. Those who have visited them with this sort of expectation, and to gain experience of sexual relationships, often seem to have been disappointed. Sandy, 22, a DHSS clerical assistant: 'I found going to a prostitute one of the most unpleasant experiences of my life. It left me very cold. I was a virgin until then and wanted to discover the feeling of sexual intercourse. The experience made me feel very guilty and just the thought of it made me cringe with embarrassment for years afterwards. I have told only a very few people about it. I would not recommend it to anyone for first-time intercourse.'

Bradley, 24, a cab driver: 'At fifteen I visited a prostitute because my girlfriend – my first – had never had sex with me. I was curious to find out what it would be like. I did not enjoy it at all, though I was fascinated by just looking at a naked body in front of me for the first time.'

Older men are more likely to be satisfied with the services provided and to have more realistic expectations. They are not looking for a substitute for a fuller relationship but for something in addition to it, either a particular type of sex they do not get at home, as we have already seen, or simply extra sex.

Three out of ten men say that what prostitutes can provide is extra sex without risking a relationship.

Rowan, 32, a waterboard inspector: 'I have been with a prostitute because I am unable to have sex with my wife due to a difficult pregnancy. What a prostitute can offer is quick and easy relief.'

Mel, 30, a research student: 'They give me a quick sexual release without all the complications and anxieties entailed in proper relationships. I think prostitution is a very important outlet for male sexual frustration. As a liberal male (I hope), I can see it as degrading to women, but as a male with a frustrated sexuality I can understand why prostitution exists and is likely to go on existing. There's no doubt, too, that there's an element of power in the prostitute/client relationship for the male which is pleasing. I see lots of sexually attractive women, knowing that I haven't got a chance of "scoring", but with a prostitute I can choose a nice looking woman and know I'll get sex.'

Very few men condemned prostitution outright. Wesley, 46, an artist believes that: 'Prostitution provides grounds for continued guilt about sex and a view of women as property and toys,' but most saw prostitutes as having a valuable role – if not for them. Tim, 20, an office worker: 'Prostitutes are a good thing for lonely people who need sex.'

Vernon, 53, a chemical engineer: 'Prostitutes provide, at a price, physical relief from frustration. I find nothing morally repugnant in a contract freely entered into between a man and a woman, regardless of its nature. It's just not for me. I doubt if even the most expensive ones can provide the essential prerequisites to truly satisfactory sex – love. It has always seemed to me that if frustration reaches such a level as to adversely affect your nature (and it can), it is better to masturbate and thus abuse yourself, than go with an "on-in-out-off" prostitute, thus abusing two bodies.'

Some men pointed out that if there were less hypocrisy about the subject prostitutes, their clients, and the public would be better safeguarded.

Douglas, 36, a labourer: 'Although I've never visited a prostitute, I believe they are providing a necessary service for those who need the kind of relief they are offering. However, making it illegal just serves to put these girls in the hands of pimps and organised crime.'

Nigel, 35, a teacher: 'The thought of sexual intercourse being conducted on par with a business transaction is a most unattractive proposition to me now, but I believe the British attitude to prostitutes is cant. We should operate a system of legalised prostitution as they do in Germany. It negates the necessity for "cruising", which can cause a nuisance to other women, it is safe from a medical point of view and also for the prostitutes themselves, and they can practice their profession without causing a nuisance to residents on their beat.'

What even regular medical checks cannot guard against, and that may make men far more wary of visiting a prostitute, is the spread of AIDS, at least until such time as a cure may be found. At present a medical check is no protection to the prostitute if her next customer has the virus, nor to the client who follows him up the stairs.

Prostitutes could choose to follow the rules for safer sex (see page 219) but how likely is it when they need the money and customers will pay them to take the risk? Cases have been quoted of young girls selling themselves for £10 with a condom and £25 without. That teenagers are willing to risk a death sentence for £25 should make us all question more seriously than ever before what pressures lead women and girls into prostitution and what can be done to prevent it. More men may confront their comfortable fantasies that 'the girls do it because they enjoy it', rather than because they can find no other way to earn a living, in the face of the risk to themselves, their customers and their partners.

8

For ever and ever?

Fidelity and affairs, divorce and loneliness

'Why go out for a hamburger if you've steak at home?' is the standard answer of film stars being asked if they are *really* faithful to their wife. Along with this goes the assumption that, if a man has an affair, it is because the missus – one way or another but probably sexually – is one of life's hamburgers.

Infidelity is not taken as seriously as it used to be and men no longer regard it as an important ingredient for a successful marriage.

Only one in four (27 per cent) of married men puts any emphasis on his own fidelity and, surprisingly, only fractionally more (29 per cent) on his wife staying faithful.

Even those who believe fidelity is crucial do not cite moral grounds. They take a more pragmatic approach. Their objection is not so much that they see having sex outside their marriage as wrong, as fear of the turmoil such a breach of trust may cause and the wedge it can drive between partners.

Bob, 34, in the Forces: 'I sometimes get an urge to go with other women. I really don't know why. I just assume it's the male chauvinism in me. But I do know it would put my marriage in jeopardy so I would not ever try – though I do enjoy fantasising once in a while.'

Francis, 29, a historian: 'Although I do not consider it morally or philosophically wrong to have affairs when married, both my wife and I consider it a breach of trust. This element of trust for us lies at the heart of marriage as an institution, rather than the outward appearance and moral values.'

Colin, 27, a soldier: 'We are totally open with each other and talk about everything together. People change all the time, day to day. Through expressing our feelings we keep each other in touch with our needs and stay close together. We think that if people were able to talk and were willing to expose some of their inner feelings, yet keep it only within their partnership, they would be much happier and not have damaging affairs and flings of revenge, destroying a valuable relationship.'

Men in the Forces who often spend long periods away from home may ponder the importance of fidelity more than most. Affairs can indeed destroy marriages, and perhaps men who think their relationship could cope with the strain might have a shock if faced with the reality. The men who took part in our survey who had been through a divorce certainly gave fidelity greater priority.

Forty-four per cent of divorced men believe that their own fidelity is important for a relationship to last successfully, and nearly half (48 per cent) that their wife's is important.

Many men stressed how much their wife's fidelity mattered to them. Chas, 25, a security guard, almost sounds to have breathed a sigh of relief on his wedding day: 'What made me happiest when I got married was knowing my wife would be faithful until the day she dies.'

Anthony, 34, a teacher: 'I have had one affair since marriage. I allowed myself, against my better judgement, to have a brief affair with an ex-pupil, aged 18. She did all the running and the idea of sex with a young girl appealed to my poor ego. The whole thing was pathetic and I am deeply ashamed about it. I expect my wife to remain faithful and she has the same right.'

Some admit they have a double standard and that what is sauce for the gander certainly is not for the goose!

Al, 28, and in the Royal Marines: 'I'm getting married at the end of July – I'm quite looking forward to it although friends who are say "Don't!!!" I love the girl although I must admit I've been "off the rails" four or five times, mainly while away. I don't think that there's any harm as long as she doesn't find out. It would kill me to find out she'd been doing it, too. Quite the chauvinist???!!'

Past lovers

Some men find it very hard to accept their wife had other lovers even before they met her.

Tom, 24, who is unemployed: 'My wife had one lover before we met. My feelings are *very* strong about this and it is a continual source of extreme anguish and worry. It has caused *immense* trouble.'

Henry, 36, a project manager: 'My wife was a student at the time when promiscuity was equated with maturity. This resulted in her having an extensive love-life prior to our meeting compared with my limited one. I was – and am – jealous of this.'

These days, however, only a minority of husbands and wives are each other's first lover.

Did you and your wife have other lovers before you met?

Husbands	Number of previous lovers	Wives
39%	None	41%
11%	One	13%
8%	Two	6%
6%	Three	4%
5%	Four	3%
14%	Five to ten	5%
4%	Eleven to twenty	1%
3%	More than twenty	1%
6%	Yes, but don't know how many	5%
3%	Don't know	21%

Just two out of five (39 per cent) of husbands and virtually the same proportion of wives (41 per cent) have not had a previous lover.

However, to this fairly sizeable minority, being each other's one and only lover is often very important.

Denis, 55, a scientist: 'We were both virgins when we married, have developed our love-making and experimented together, so it is as good and as exciting as 25 years ago.

'Sex is not an end in itself to us but a wonderful part of marriage. We have not lost out by not having had other partners. It's nice to know that your wife's body has not been "used" by anyone else and I know she feels the same about mine. As well as still feeling sexual excitement, we also feel untroubled by comparisons. Not having had other partners means contentment to be with one, no restless "moving on" feelings. We have a wonderful marriage.'

In fact, whether a couple have had previous lovers or not does not seem closely linked either way with whether they enjoy a happy marriage, or even a happy sex life.

If anything, there was a tendency for those who said they were very unhappily married not to have had previous sexual partners, but this probably reflected the fact that these couples tended to have married too young. Many men laid marital problems at the door of marrying when they were too immature.

Not having had other sexual partners can certainly leave a man wondering. Dominic, 28, an artist: 'I have not had any other lover besides my wife and I am certainly curious about sex with other partners. However, I still don't believe I would risk an affair if the chance arose, because I have too much to lose. My marriage is more important than passing curiosity or lust.'

For some men feeling inexperienced can be an extra pressure to have affairs after marriage – particularly if their wife has had more lovers than they have.

Nigel, 46, an investment manager: 'I had an affair and felt guilty at the time but subsequently felt pride and gratitude – and a boost from having gone some way towards levelling the sexual experiences of my wife and myself.'

It is interesting that one in five husbands (21 per cent) doesn't know whether his wife had any previous lovers or not – perhaps their wives feared just such an effect from their revelations. If all husbands had been able to fill in the figures for their wives, it is likely that the women would prove to have had pretty nearly as many lovers as the men. After all, to have five to ten lovers doesn't make a person wildly promiscuous if they start having intercourse aged 18 and marry at 25. With an average of around one lover a year, each experience could be in the context of a serious relationship.

Sex before marriage

Most couples have had previous lovers before they met their marriage partner and very few wait until they have exchanged their wedding vows before completing their own sexual relationship.

Some who do wait, have religious reasons, like Michael, 26, a groundsman, who is not yet married. 'My girlfriend and I are both practising Christians and we don't believe in sex before marriage. This may seem strange but we find we can cope. Of course, it is difficult at times but we've set ourselves standards or limits, and we are frank and love each other enough to tell each other if things are getting out of hand. I would say something like, "I love you enough to ask you to stop as I'm finding it hard to control myself." I suppose we indulge in very gentle petting and at the moment this helps us both.'

However, some couples simply prefer to wait, like Mark, 28, a scientist: 'Both my wife and I were virgins on our wedding day. We had no problems with sex and the best honeymoon any two people could ever wish to experience. Sex *after* marriage with the woman you love can lead to a strong and lasting marriage. We are not particularly religious, either. Are we just normal?'

Our survey showed no correlation between whether a couple have sex before marriage or not and whether they go on to share a happy sex life once married, but Mark and his wife are unusual.

Overall, more than three-quarters (77 per cent) of married men had sex with their wives before marriage.

Warren, 23, a music teacher: 'I found it necessary to make love with my wife before marriage. Emotionally we found we did not want to wait.'

Younger men are even less likely to have married as virgins. Ninety-two per cent of men in their twenties slept with their wives before marriage, compared with 59 per cent of men in their fifties. However, this still means that, even thirty years ago, only a minority of women were virgin brides.

How common is infidelity?

If it is so rare for couples before their wedding day to believe that sex must be confined to marriage, perhaps it is not surprising that many do not afterwards, either.

Ned, 29, a musician: 'Is marriage worth it? Is the grass greener? How can I play my part in an institution that was never intended to live up to the pressures of living in the 1980s?'

Of course, sex was not strictly confined to marriage in the 1880s, 1680s, or 1280s, except perhaps for those to whom establishing a clear line of inheritance was important. However, today many couples have very high expectations of marriage. They hope for love, companionship, a high level of sexual satisfaction, caring, sympathy, understanding, providing and being provided for in different ways, fun, spontaneity, enjoyment of shared leisure . . .

Perhaps not surprisingly, not all find all these needs met, or at least not all the time. A sizeable percentage, even among our sample of couples who are mostly at least reasonably happily married, have had affairs.

One in four (26 per cent) husbands admitted he has had or is having a sexul relationship outside his marriage. Twelve per cent said their wife has had an affair. A further 17 per cent didn't know one way or the other.

The simple word 'affair' can cover a wide variety of infidelities, situations, emotions and attitudes. Leonard, 39, a manager: 'We've both had affairs but I think these are symptoms of deeper problems.'

Paul, 35, a security officer: 'My wife knows about the ongoing affair because we are in a swapping situation. We're over the problems of guilt now and it's great. It's made us stronger and we talk more frankly about things – though never about the other's performance.'

Vernon, 38, a clerk: 'I have had a few affairs. I believe that no matter how satisfying a relationship is between two people, one or both will at some time look elsewhere (or take an opportunity if offered) for sexual pleasure, if only for a change from the norm.'

One in three of husbands who has ever been unfaithful is having an affair – or affairs – now.

Sandy, 31, in general services: 'I've found that amateur dramatics can lead to an amorous lifestyle – I love it!'

Bradley, 46, a customs officer: 'My wife is a wonderful person, a good housekeeper and so on. What makes me unhappy is her lack of interest in sex, hence my affair which has lasted a number of years. My lover has given me everything in sex my wife couldn't. I would have lived with her, but she found it impossible to face the problems of leaving her husband (whom she does not love) and setting up home with her two children with me.'

How many affairs do men have?

More than one in five (22 per cent) husbands who has had affairs says he has had anywhere from five to more than 20 sexual relationship outside his marriage. (See Figure 14, page 129).

A further one in ten (11 per cent) says he does not know with how many women has been unfaithful. This is unlikely if he has had only a handful of other relationships. Probably one in three straying husbands has five or more liaisons. Wives seem less likely to have so many 'flings' (and this is confirmed by our survey on wives).

Figure 14

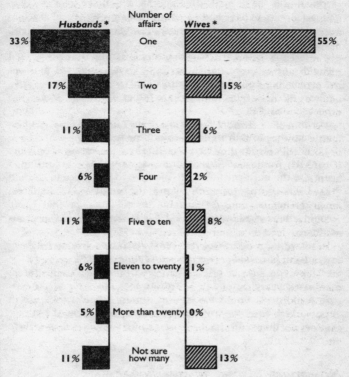

How many affairs?

Husbands *	Number of affairs	Wives *
33%	One	55%
17%	Two	15%
11%	Three	6%
6%	Four	2%
11%	Five to ten	8%
6%	Eleven to twenty	1%
5%	More than twenty	0%
11%	Not sure how many	13%

* Husbands and wives who have had affairs.

The men who have high numbers of affairs often have jobs which give them the opportunity. William, 42, a salesman, 'Since being married I have had 22 separate affairs, 3 of which are still current. I travel a lot and I have never had a row with any of them. They continue until it mutually drifts apart.'

Ralph, 54: 'Being a domestic engineer, I frequently come into contact with bored housewives. Most of my short-term affairs have started that way.'

However, far from all see themselves as worldly philanderers or take their repeated sexual adventures lightly. Len, 43, a

129

newsagent (now): 'Though I quell it, I am preoccupied with sex – I think – which means that my wife, an educated and intelligent woman must be normal. [Len and his wife make love less than once a month.] I have had 13 affairs. This strong sexual urge has destroyed two flourishing careers – both mine. I seem to offend people easily – chatting up *any* attractive woman – so now I believe I am better off working alone as much as possible. I would give an arm and a leg to be psychoanalysed and put straight – but don't know how to start.'

Bob, 42, a lecturer: 'Affairs are rather like drugs to me. The more you have the more you want. But for every drop of happiness one gets a gallon of tears. They simply must end in destruction – usually of one's emotional reserves.

'The pity is that they would be totally unnecessary if only my dear wife would be a little more exciting in our relationship. I suppose the hard truth is that you have to recognise in the end that the most important sex organ is the brain!' As we shall see, men do not have affairs just for sex. It could be that Blake would still be as addicted even if his wife were more adventurous sexually.

Two out of three (67 per cent) husbands who have been unfaithful have had between one and four affairs.

These, too, may be brief. Giles, 37, a financial administrator: 'I had a one night stand in a Mediterranean resort while attending a business conference. It was almost classic caricature in cliché. The boost to my ego was much needed at the time!' However, many affairs last for years, without the marriage breaking up.

What is the longest time an affair has continued?

Husband's affair	Length of time	Wife's affair
21%	Day/night	18%
20%	Few weeks	28%
21%	Up to one year	21%
20%	One to four years	6%
8%	Five to ten years	3%
2%	More than ten years	—%
8%	Not sure	23%

Three out of ten (30 per cent) of men's affairs last from one year to over a decade.

Bruce, 44, a pub landlord: 'I didn't mean to start an affair or be unfaithful to my wife, but for three years I have been having an affair with a very independent lady in her thirties who is single, has never wanted to get married and still doesn't.

'We met on holiday and have met one day a week ever since. She has brought new meaning to my life and we are very good for each other. I still love my wife and wouldn't deliberately hurt her, but I cannot give this lady up. Even if my wife discovered the affair I would still have to find a way to see her.'

James, 46, a company director, has also been having an affair for three years. 'I cannot disregard 22 years of marriage but, if my girlfriend and I had met before, she is the one I would have asked to marry me. We have everything in common.

'We both are married but neither of us wants to cause hurt to our family by going away together. This is not cowardice or deceit or wanting the best of both worlds. It is the right decision for us for the time being. Perhaps one day things will change and we can be together – we'll see.

'We are both professional people with busy, responsible lives, and we have put a lot of thought into our relationships with our children, our respective spouses and the people who surround us socially and professionally. It's not easy to spend your life with the wrong person at home, knowing that the right one is there and feels the same. However, we manage. That's the main thing.'

It probably is best from the children's point of view that James and his mistress stay *in situ* until they are grown up. Whether Jame's wife would agree that their behaviour is lacking in deceit, and prefers to be left in ignorance until he perhaps leaves her aged fifty-plus, is another matter.

Children are often the reason these long-term liaisons do not lead to the divorce court, and not just among 'professional people' like James. Matt, 27, a van driver: 'I started my affair with my next-door neighbour's wife, who one evening "confessed" to me that she fancied me. We kissed and cuddled for a little while but nothing happened.

'Over the next few months I gave her driving lessons (always at night) and we tried to have sex in the back of the car – without success. Then we tried having sex in bed (as I worked shifts this was easy to arrange) but I felt very guilty about it and couldn't get an erection. This lasted for two months, during which time she said she loved me and didn't really need sex to love me. She understood me very well and I fell in love with her. After several attempts I finally had sex with her and it was great. She even enjoys my favourite position.

'This has now gone on for a very long time but because we both have children we are not planning divorce and marriage. (We will only do that if we are "caught".) I love her very much and she loves me the same. I try to be the same when I am with my wife, but it is very stressful.'

Why do men have affairs?

The answer is not as obvious as it seems. To start with, affairs do not necessarily imply an unhappy marriage. *One in five of the very happily married men has had an affair.*

Some of these couples agree to have an 'open marriage' or enjoy swapping. Clive, 52, a ship's captain: 'Other lovers is something my wife and I have agreed to accept, possibly due to the nature of my work. We feel physical sex can be kept apart from love. In our case it has worked very well for over 12 years. This does not mean we go on a binge every time we are apart, but the knowledge that we can indulge at our discretion is very liberating. We have agreed to be frank with each other about our sexual encounters, to stop the gossip-mongers in their tracks, but we also find that recounting these experiences can be very titillating.'

Gary, 34, a salesman: 'Ours is a wife-swap, but not the keys thrown on the table at some party variety. Rather we are two couples who have known each other for years and found that we are attracted to each other. We discussed for many weeks the implications and possible pitfalls until, eventually, we did make love and have continued to do so for three years or so.

'We don't meet every week or even every month, but when we do there's a good chance we will make love to each other's partner. None of us would rather be with the other's partner for good and none of us meets or contacts the other without everyone knowing.'

However, affairs are more commonly secret and, particularly long-term affairs, are more likely if a man's sexual relationship with his wife is not flourishing.

Fewer than two out of five (36 per cent) of men with a very unhappy sexual relationship have not had an affair and roughly as few (38 per cent) of their wives have stayed faithful.

Whether both partners have affairs because the sexual relationship is unhappy or whether the affair undermines it – or at least distracts the partner concerned from making any effort to improve it – must sometimes be questionable.

Douglas, 28, a clerk, 'What makes me happy about my present set-up is that I am now enjoying a fulfilling sexual relationship such as I have never known with my wife, but I am still able to live with my children, whom I love dearly. My girlfriend, being unmarried, is prepared to wait for a while, at least until the children are a bit older and better able to cope with their parents separating.

'My wife's steady decline into obesity began very soon after marriage. I interpreted this, and her lack of interest in sex, as an indication that she was content to have "caught a man". She claims that this was her understandable reaction to the excessive hours I worked and my resultant failure to spend much time with her. Chicken and egg!!!??? We don't make love at all now.'

Nonetheless, a poor married sexual relationship is blamed by only a minority of men who have affairs.

One in four (24 per cent) of men having affairs give a poor sexual relationship with their wife as a reason. Sixty-four per cent say simply that the opportunity presented itself.

What led to your having an affair?

Poor sexual relationship with wife	24%
Poor emotional relationship with wife	17%
Boredom	11%
Being away from home	11%
Her having an affair	2%
Opportunity presented itself	64%

Sometimes it does seem more or less simply a matter of chance. Mel, 37, a policeman: 'I have had two one-night stands outside my marriage. They were both opportunities which presented themselves. I did not go looking for them and I would not.' In other cases, however, the 'opportunity' is combined with other circumstances, often a difficult patch in an otherwise stable marriage, which make the man extra liable to give in to temptation.

Fred, 29, a builder: 'My wife was pregnant and had been ill

(mostly bedridden) for six months. The last month of the pregnancy was spent in hospital, where she had a Caesarian. While she was in hospital I was working 20 miles away, but came home every night in order to visit my wife. I had to organise babysitters.

'One night one of them stayed over and I made up a bed for her in the spare room. The next night she stayed again, but this time asked to share my bed. I had not had sex for over six months and I was extremely frustrated. So we made love all night and had a frantic, exhausting, passionate affair for about two weeks until the baby was born.

'This affair was very exciting and sexually satisfying, but when I saw my son I was in a state of complete turmoil. When my wife came out of hospital I could not bring my lover back to the house and we only met twice after that. She asked me to go to live with her in Greece. I was tempted but I realised I could not go and finished the affair.'

Andy, 24, a production manager: 'Our marriage was not so good at the time. I had not got a promotion and my wife was upset. I went out in Blackpool with friends and we got involved with some holidaymakers. We went to a party and then back to their hotel, where I had sex with one of them.'

For one in six, affairs are a relief from an emotionally unhappy marriage.

Charles, a salesman: 'I feel let down most of the time these days. I am 43 years old, weigh 11 stone, don't smoke, have been drinking three times in the last year, a total of 10 pints – my wife told me that, because she counts. I'm reasonably attractive, have a keen sense of humour and I hope I can last another 10 years because then I'm off. I would not go before and ditch my children because I feel I'm the stable one of the family.

'I love my children. They are always on my lap, I play football with them, swim with them, play hide and seek with them. My wife never joins in. She is very strong-willed and dominant, shouts a lot at me, the kids, her mother. She goes as black as thunder. All of my £10,000 a year goes on essentials. She gives me, *yes gives me*, £10 a month because she thinks I am able to make a bit on expenses.

'My visits to my out-to-town customers are my safety valve. I have some very nice sexual and non-sexual relationships in far flung towns, and more that I am working on.'

What's good – and bad – about an affair?

Affairs are assumed to be all about getting more and better sex, yet only two out of five (38 per cent) men who have had affairs say that they were more satisfying sexually than their marital relationship. (See Figure 15, page 136.)

Of course, in an affair, the very context of the relationship is a throwback to the boyfriend/girlfriend scenario in which sex does not have to compete for time and energy with so many other demands. As Nicholas, 56, a company director pointed out: 'In extra-marital sex your partner sets out to please you in the short time you are together, while a wife frequently adopts an attitude of "There's always tomorrow." '

Many men talked as if they felt 'unmanned' by their wives and their lack of interest in them sexually. For them finding other lovers is the obvious answer. Dave, 42, a salesman: 'I love to feel wanted, I love to be pampered once in a while. I do not get this from my wife, but I do from the other women I make love with.

'My wife has become less and less interested in sex and usually indicates oral satisfaction is what she's after, not intercourse. After this I have to "dive in" and satisfy myself while she lies there quite motionless. My favourite lover is quite different. It is reassuring to me, to my pride, to my ego, to feel a woman beneath me who actually enjoys feeling my penis where it is intended to go.'

Why has Dave's wife become less and less interested in sex? Has he ever asked her rather than just complained about it as if it were her fault? How often does an affair take the place of talking about what is really going wrong between a couple? If what a husband really wants is to sort out his problems with his wife, then he may realise that the affair is really just an irrelevance.

One in five men (18 per cent) having affairs finds them **less** *satisfying sexually than their marriage. Only one in five finds them more rewarding emotionally.*

Jeff, 47, a lecturer: 'I began the affair after being totally rejected by my wife for over three years. The affair started after a quarrel (one of many) with my wife. While I was away I had a few drinks and got friendly with another member of the course. We saw each other for about a year. The affair provided a form of escapism, but the physical side never fulfilled the expectations raised by the excitement I obtained through my wife.'

It is not love or even greater sexual fulfilment that most men

135

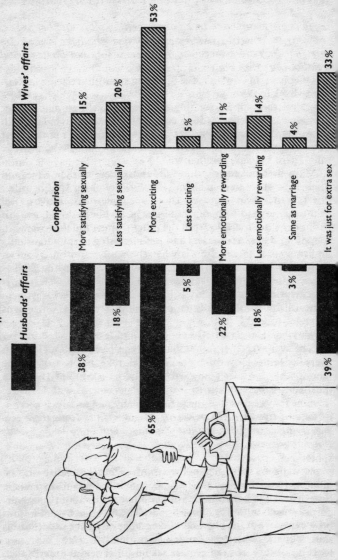

Figure 15

How affairs compare with marriage

Husbands' affairs ▮   Wives' affairs ▨

Comparison

	Husbands' affairs	Wives' affairs
More satisfying sexually	38%	15%
Less satisfying sexually	18%	20%
More exciting	65%	53%
Less exciting	5%	5%
More emotionally rewarding	22%	11%
Less emotionally rewarding	18%	14%
Same as marriage	3%	4%
It was just for extra sex	39%	33%

find through affairs. The top two attractions are that affairs are more exciting than marriage and simply provide extra (not necessarily better) sex.

Phil, 43, a centre lathe turner: 'The best affair lasted 18 months. She liked to meet after my evening job. We would go for a drink and then back to her flat, or we would make love in my camper. My wife would never do this – she would tell me to wait until we got home.

'This affair was so exciting because I knew that she always wanted me. She used to wear stockings and suspenders and lovely bras, or often she would go braless and leave two or three buttons undone to excite me. We never needed much. The affair only ended because, as luck would or would not have it, both couples moved out of the district. Perhaps this was a good thing, because we were getting very involved emotionally as well.'

The respectability of marriage has a lot to answer for! Did Phil's lover take so much trouble to excite her husband, or is it that affairs themselves rev up the pulse rate? If her husband had found out about her affair, he would almost certainly have dismissed it as far less thrilling than Phil rated it.

According to husbands, wives are more likely to find their affairs less *satisfying sexually and* less *rewarding emotionally than their marriage.*

They do concede their wives may find their affairs more exciting, but even then they will not allow them the same degree of certainty as themselves (See Figure 15 page 136).

Greg, 48, a HGV driver: 'She came back to me afterwards and told me that I am a better lover in every way. I want to believe her but I need constant reassurance from her to help me feel better – more secure and to regain my self-confidence.

'I wonder if my wife realises how much of an impact it had on me when I heard that the other man had been bragging that my wife had praised his penis and told him it was bigger than mine. I don't think women take men's feelings seriously enough sometimes.'

It sounds as though Greg's wife does indeed realise and is doing her best to minimise the damage. An obvious difference between the affairs of their own the men told us about and their partners' affairs, is that their wives' affairs have by definition been discovered and evaluated in the light of what the wife then says. If a wife wants her marriage to outlast her affair, she is not likely to say her lover surpassed her husband in every way.

In fact, we know from our survey of wives, women are about as likely as men to rate their affair as more satisfying sexually, and a lot more likely to find it more rewarding emotionally than marriage – 34 per cent do in reality, compared with the 11 per cent whose husbands believe they did. They do agree, though, that it is excitement which is the most widespread benefit – six out of ten wives having affairs say themselves that they are more exciting than marriage.

How tempted are the faithful?

It is enough to make those who have always remained faithful wonder just how much they are missing out.

Two out of five (37 per cent) of those husbands who have never had an affair either wish they had or feel tempted.

Often it is simply lack of opportunity which holds them back.

Clifford, 36, a design engineer: 'I have not had an affair. This is not because I am a devoted and faithful husband (though I feel I am) or from conscience. It's from the lack of opportunity of a "no-risk" relationship. I am very happily married and have no desire to upset it, but I feel I would enjoy other short-term relationships.'

Three out of ten said they would like an affair 'just for a change'. However, as many said they wanted to find a more satisfying sexual relationship. More than two out of ten said they wanted to see if they were good in bed with someone else.

Leslie, 35, an internal auditor: 'My desire for good sex with another girl is purely caused by dissatisfaction with my wife. I love her dearly but also need sex. Regrettably, I may one day seek this elsewhere if my wife's worries about her parents' disapproval of our marriage continue to affect us in the way they do now.'

Mac, 28, in the army, has found another husband in the same boat – as we've noted, fidelity is a very live issue to men in the Forces. 'I've never had actual intercourse with another girl, but it's an AA situation – Adulterers Anonymous, we call it. We often confide in one another, share our experiences, work out the causes and attempt to overcome the guilt. This has not solved the problems, but we get a sort of strength from each other's situation.'

How affairs affect marriage

What makes men hesitate, though sorely tempted, is not knowing how an affair will turn out. Few are so unhappily married that they would seek divorce at the first opportunity, especially if they have children. Most embark on an affair hoping for secrecy and a sexual relationship as well as marriage, not instead of it.

One in four (25 per cent) of the men who have had affairs admit that it worsened the emotional relationship between them and their wives (See Figure 16, page 140).

Obviously the wife learning of the affair can have a far-reaching effect. Steve, 36, unemployed: 'I told my wife about my two one-night stands and they hurt her very much. As a result I feel very guilty and ashamed. Time did heal her wounds, but her trust in me has been affected. My fling can only be blamed on my intake of alcohol, which resulted in common sense going out the door.'

Chris, 40, a manager: 'I told my wife early on about my relationship with my mistress. This had a devastating effect on our marriage. My wife no longer trusts me – and she is quite right not to. I think my honesty was the biggest mistake of my life.'

As well as being discovered there is another way in which an affair can undermine the marriage – by emphasising what's lacking in it.

Rick, 28, a film technician: 'A number of affairs during my marriage did not improve my relationship with my wife. In fact, they pointed up her inadequacies and my desires. Being married at an early age, I had not matured sufficiently for what wedlock demands, and I found I needed outside or other stimulus to make up for what lacked in our marriage, sexually and emotionally. We are now divorced.'

Partners' affairs are more likely to be seen as damaging, of course.

Three out of ten (30 per cent) of the husbands who knew their wife had had an affair believed it had worsened their emotional relationship.

Sebastian, 28, an architect: 'When I met my wife it was magical, extravagant, joyous. Love seems too small a word for what we had. Various problems made life with me difficult. Another man pursued her for over a year and eventually they had a long and unhappy secret love affair. He moved on once I found out, and now we keep going as best we can. The heart of our

139

Figure 16

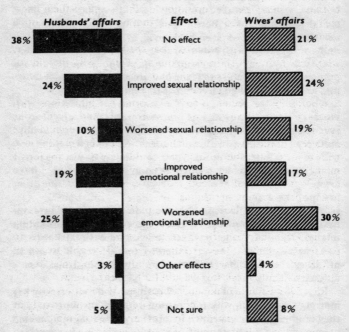

How affairs affect marriage

Husbands' affairs	Effect	Wives' affairs
38%	No effect	21%
24%	Improved sexual relationship	24%
10%	Worsened sexual relationship	19%
19%	Improved emotional relationship	17%
25%	Worsened emotional relationship	30%
3%	Other effects	4%
5%	Not sure	8%

marriage, our love, is dead. There is no magic. My only "extravagance" is of silent hatred for the interloper who has taken the joy of my lovely wife. I would kill him with relish.'

In some cases, the – albeit unacknowledged – competition makes all concerned pull their sexual socks up. Ralph, 54: 'My main affair was with an ex-girlfriend. Her marriage was stale, mine was so-so. We had an affair for eight to nine months when we tried everything – oral, anal. It was glorious. We were very much in love but did not want to break up either marriage. My own marriage benefited. I think my wife knew but she never said anything.'

In other cases it is as though casting themselves in the part of mistress or lover releases inhibitions. This new, more relaxed attitude benefits their married sex life, too.

Greg, 48, the HGV driver: 'One result of my wife's affair, surprisingly, is that we now have a more adventurous and satisfying sex life. I suppose that the circumstances helped. Her lover boasted to many people, not knowing that some of them knew me personally. I heard many details that normally would not be mentioned.

'Eventually my wife admitted that she had done these things with him, although she was unable to explain why she did so, particularly those things that she had always refused me. I imagine she then felt obliged to do the same things with me.

'Gradually she seems to have overcome her inhibitions with me and admits she now enjoys our more varied and adventurous love-making. However, sometimes I wonder how she could have made love to him, and within an hour or so be in bed making love with me. Perhaps she thought she could allay any suspicions I might have had that way. Unfortunately for both of us, I have always enjoyed oral sex and I discovered traces of the other man's sperm around her vagina.

'As the months have passed, the pain and sense of betrayal have receded until we now have an even stronger and more caring relationship. It's not perfect, but at least we both try harder to please one another. I never thought I would be able to accept infidelity, but I realise how much I love her and need her – although I could *never* forgive her if it happened again.'

Ray, 33, a bank official, had recently learned that his wife has a woman lover. 'For whatever reason it has vastly improved our sex life (which was very much in a rut, my wife told me) and my perception and understanding of my wife and women in general. It has helped me to improve my technique and performance (which I reckon was pretty dismal in the past) and has enabled my wife to admit she loves cunnilingus.'

However, while two out of five (38 per cent) of the men who had had an affair believe that it had no effect sexually or emotionally on their marriage, little more than half as many would say the same of their partner's infidelity.

Of course, the wives' affairs had all been discovered and that is the risk that all those who have affairs run. It is hard even for those directly involved to predict how they will react to an affair. For the sake of the excitement and what may be just short-term gains, an affair may cost the marriage and perhaps home and children. 'I was married for ten years,' explained Ken, 48, a driving instructor. 'For most of that time I screwed around as I pleased. Eventually she got fed up with it and divorced me, following the discovery that one of my longer affairs had produced twins.'

Trevor, 40, a British Telecom engineer: 'I was married for 16 years but my wife started having an affair with another man. We're starting divorce proceedings. It's cracked me up. I've lost weight and my hair. I've ended up going on Valium tablets.'

Rick, 28: 'I left my wife because I had found a lady I admire, trust and feel at ease with and above all love, and she feels the same about me. However, the separation and subsequent divorce lasted about two and a half years and were very distressing for me, my wife, my daughter, and my new partner. The effects will stay with me for a very long time.'

Alone again

While the ending of a painful marriage can be a relief, many men spoke ruefully of divorce and the aftermath.

Morgan, 32, a civil servant: 'Although relieved at finally finishing the 10-year ordeal my marriage was, I admit to feeling terribly insecure since and a sense of loss for the waste of a third of my life.'

Three out of ten (29 per cent) of the divorced men said they have seriously regretted parting from their wife at least sometimes. For one in five these regrets are lasting.

Hugh, 56, a journalist: 'Her last words to me were, "I cannot try any more." For me they remain the saddest words I ever heard.'

Alan, 44, self-employed: 'My marriage ended in divorce after only six years. It was by mutual consent but I was devastated by it. I felt as if I had failed in the most important part of my life.'

Ian, 35, unemployed: 'My wife divorced me seven years ago when I was 25. We had three children. I loved my wife and I adored my kids. For the first years away from my wife and kids the pain was just too much. I turned to drink. I drank anywhere, any time, just to forget. I lost five stone in the first six months. I was really ill.

'Every time I thought of the kids or of her, I would cry uncontrollably, almost into a fit of some sort. That lasted a year and a half. I was convinced I would die of a broken heart. I used to dream in my drunken stupor that we were all together and that what I had been going through was the dream. Then I would wake up and find myself in the bedsit. I'd go crazy, grab another bottle and start everything again.'

Many men, at least in retrospect, blame a divorce on marrying too young. Mitch, a dairyman: 'I lived with a girl for three years. We had a baby and because of family pressures (my family are Roman Catholic) we decided to get married. It lasted for exactly nine months. In that time we were never really happy. We were at our happiest before we got married.

'My divorce should be through soon. As my friend said, "Mitch, you've married, had a child and been divorced, and you're still only 23!" '

Some couples who realise they are now incompatible manage to split up without bitterness. Brian, 35, a fireman, 'My first wife and I separated and divorced quite amicably. We are now better friends than when we were married.'

Even then, however, there can be regrets and difficulties in starting life again as a single man. Keith, 33, a dentist: 'I do not regret getting divorced in the sense of losing my partner but deeply regret losing my wife, the mother of my children, my children themselves – in other words, the family unit. Nobody made any effort of conciliation and no efforts were made to persuade us to attend marriage guidance, which I feel should be specified before anybody can apply for a divorce.

'Though I consider myself fairly outward going, I have never been able to make or start relationships outside work or direct social contact.'

Ian, who was so distraught after his divorce, added: 'It took me seven years to find someone I can love and care for.'

We heard many complaints from divorced husbands about the hardship of having to support their first family when they create a second, but most divorced men want another long-term relationship and probably to remarry.

Only 11 per cent of divorced husbands do not want to remarry and 9 per cent are not bothered about either living with someone or getting married again.

In fact, they are a lot less disillusioned about marriage than divorced wives. Half of the divorced wives who took part in our earlier survey did not want to marry again. They had had enough.

Women who are alone again find it very hard to meet men they would want as life partners. Four out of five said it was hard to meet the right kind of man. It is easier for men, but far from plain-sailing for all.

William, 38, a journalist, explained: 'Over two years after my wife's death from cancer I feel a great sense of desolation. People say that up to three years is needed to adjust sensibly. I doubt that one ever really gets over it. The loss of love, companionship and the waste of a vital life seems total. One works for substitutes but they are not the answer. Self-pity is no answer. One just hopes that luck will bring someone else along.'

Vincent, 61, a civil servant: 'After my wife left, many people sought to introduce me to, in their opinion, eligible women. Most fell flat, but often the result was to start off a romance between that lady and someone else. It was rather like the shunting engine that brings the train into the station for another engine to take out.

'Strangely, my present wife and I both decided to look on our own through an agency and then discovered we did know people in common who had never thought of introducing us.'

Many men in their forties and fifties mentioned using introduction agencies and personal advertisements but few were as systematic as George, 53, a farmer. 'The most effective way in my experience of meeting partners, and the only one that I've used in the past 25 years, is to insert an advertisement for a housekeeper in the classified ads of a certain century-old publication. The only disaster was my ex-wife.

'Applicants for the post of farm housekeeper fall roughly into three categories:

1 – those who want no sexual involvement and make it plain at the interview,

2 – those who desire a sexual relationship and make it plain at the interview, in two cases requesting a trial run,

3 – those who are not against a sexual relationship on principle, but need time to decide whether this is a situation that would be acceptable to them.

'It is easy to sort out the likely candidates at the interview. Under no circumstances would I force myself on an uninterested partner. In a successful relationship, both partners must be not only willing but equals. My present partner is the fourth since my ex-wife left. This is because the previous three and I were not entirely compatible and they decided to move on. These partings were harmonious and all three have corresponded since leaving. Although I would have liked to have found a suitable partner at once, I enjoyed the variety found in the others from a near nymphomaniac to a willing partner afflicted with vaginismus at the critical moment.

'I remained faithful to my ex-wife as long as we were living together, but as far as I was concerned, divorce occurred on the day she walked out. Legally speaking, it was six and a half years before the divorce was finalised.

'As a result of my experience in obtaining a divorce I will never again marry in a legal sense. I consider myself married in common law to my present partner, and have been and intend to remain faithful to her. I would be willing to have a family if she wanted one, but never again will I allow church or state to poke their noses into my private life.'

Other men think that divorce has a good effect on relationships and marriage the second time around. Robin, 52, a bus driver: 'One failed marriage for both of us ensures that we work really hard and honestly at our marriage.'

Lawrence, 33, a postman: 'I used to think that marriage was something you had to stick with. Now I realise how easy it is to get a divorce and therefore that marriage is a partnership which has to be worked at constantly. Divorce never used to scare me because I never thought I'd go through it. Now that I have, I would never want to again. This is a good thing because it makes me realise that my wife is not a piece of furniture or an extension of me. She is another human being who needs to be loved for all that she is – good and bad.'

What does still trouble men years after the break-up of a marriage is the loss of their family life with their children. Donald, 56, a clerk, said: 'Fifteen years after the break up of my first marriage I often regret that parting. I have always felt sad that our daughter was taken from me.'

Sometimes the wife makes access difficult and sometimes a second partner resents the child from the first marriage. Rick, the film technician: 'I love my daughter and adore being with her. Unfortunately my partner sees her as part of my marriage and therefore will have little to do with her. This saddens me very much, but so as not to cause any undue strain I see my daughter alone.'

The question of how often divorced men see their children obviously causes a lot of discomfort to men who have remarried.

Of the men with children from their first marriage *who had remarried*, more than half did not answer the question. Presumably, it was just too uncomfortable to think about. One in four either lived with their children or saw them regularly, and one in ten saw them sometimes.

As we shall see in the next chapter, the bonds between fathers and their children are very strong. What pain such severing must cause them all.

9 *Family men*
Fertility and fatherhood

A child is both the fulfilment of a man's sex life and its frustration. Graham, 20, a bricklayer: 'The arrival of our first child was the most marvellous experience of my life.'

'As a father of three children, I feel very proud,' said Richard, 52, a chiropodist. 'My children are the natural product of my wife's and my love for each other. My seed was ejaculated at a moment of great mutual love.'

However, David, 38, a teacher found there are snags: 'Our children are a tangible expression of our love for one another. We thoroughly enjoy being a family, although a sex life isn't very easy when you have to make love with one foot on the door!'

Edward, 35, a civil servant, has run into serious difficulties. 'We had a reasonable active sex life before we had our daughter. In the two and a half years following the birth we had made love about half a dozen times.'

Living with children of any age makes a man less likely to be really satisfied with his sex life.

Forty per cent of men who have no children or whose children have left home say that they are very happy with their sex life. Just 29 per cent of fathers with children in the house are happy with theirs.

A planned baby can start affecting a man's sex life even before it is conceived. Some men find their wives are keener to make love more often. Neil, 42, a teacher: 'Though my wife does not believe in sex solely as a means of procreation, in the religious way, she is happiest when we are trying for a child. Unfortunately, in a way, we are lucky enough to be fertile, so we don't have to try hard for very long.'

Nick, 32, a civil servant, found quantity can seem to impair quality: 'We had a particularly active sex life when we were trying for a baby. We went from an average of about twice a week to five to six times per week. This we found very tiring and it even became somewhat mechanical.'

Feeling pressured to make love in order to produce a child,

146

rather than because his wife desires him, is often the beginning of a tension that runs throughout the years the children are at home – between fierce love and pride in his offspring, but resentment at the amount of his partner's time and attention they take from him.

If conception is delayed, then sex can become fraught with anxiety and the man feel a failure as a lover. Perhaps especially after a few years in which a couple's main aim has been to make sure the woman does not become pregnant, it can come as quite a shock to discover that starting a family does not automatically follow stopping contraception.

Sam, 43, self-employed, remembers: 'The saddest period in our marriage was the year we spent trying for our first son. My wife was so depressed that I almost felt threatened by her moods and despair.'

Peter, 33, a civil servant: 'I had never really thought about children. I would have been quite happy as we were but my wife really wanted them. We started trying about three years after we got married. I was quite pleased when she got pregnant but after three months she miscarried. She was really upset. A year or so later she got pregnant again. It wasn't a very good time for our sex life, as our doctor advised her to abstain for the first three months not to risk another miscarriage. It was all worth it because we had a beautiful daughter nine months later.'

Fertility problems can lead to a couple breaking up altogether. Barry, 35, unemployed: 'My wife and I divorced by mutual agreement. The love had all gone, so we thought it only sensible to part while we were still young enough to start a new life. We'd been married 11 years and had no children – it turned out I'm sterile.'

Some men find their partners are as keen or keener to make love during pregnancy but some women lose all interest in sex, which can put a great strain on their relationship. The men can feel they have been used to start a family but are now being cast aside, their task completed.

Fraser, 27, an oil worker: 'My girlfriend and I had a terrific sex life up to the last two months. Now it is almost non-existent. She is pregnant and not in the mood. I am, and I feel men should not be forgotten during pregnancy. I understand the changes in a woman and I understand the lack of interest, but I feel a compromise should be reached. It seems to cause a lot of trouble with male frustration.

'I may sound selfish but I know a lot of men who are having affairs because of this. To be making love nightly for a long period and then stop dead does not make for a happy man, as he has not had any hormone changes. So much attention is paid to changes in the woman but what about us? To help keep relationships together, women need to understand the needs, the basic instinct in men to have sexual relief.

'One of the main problems with women and relationships outside pregnancy and during pregnancy seems to be that if they are not in the mood for sex then it's lights out and go to sleep. Well, I find that selfish and uncaring. They don't have to have intercourse, but to do nothing is insensitive and unloving and so stupid. More often than not the male partner will then go elsewhere, not because he wants to but because he feels a need to.'

Quite a few men did tell us of affairs during their wife's pregnancy or even while she was in hospital having the baby. Anthony, 34, a teacher: 'My one affair happened during the later months of my wife's second pregnancy. I still feel very guilty about betraying my wife's love and trust.' Especially in cases where the – often uncharacteristic – affair happens while the wife is in hospital giving or having just given birth, it seems it is not so much sexual frustration acting as the spur but a 'last fling' before responsibilities finally close in.

The birth of the baby, especially a first baby, inevitably ushers in a change of lifestyle – and usually a change in the pattern of the couple's sex life – but can also cause specific and sometimes serious problems.

Among men who currently have a problem in their sex life, more than two out of five (42 per cent) with children under five say it is connected with pregnancy and/or childbirth.

Robert, 42, a civil servant: 'At the moment we're having particular problems as, after the difficult birth of our second son four months ago, she has gone off sex. This also happened for a few months after the birth of our first child. I don't want to play at being an amateur psychiatrist but I think that she works it out that sex = pregnancy = pain = work and tiredness. I have complete sympathy with this viewpoint. If I had the baby, I would avoid sex. My impression is that a woman going off sex after a baby is common. I try to be caring and sympathetic but I sometimes think that she "ought to" and guilt puts her under more pressure. I find it all very difficult. It's a good job that I love her.'

It is very common for a new mother to lose interest in sex for a while after childbirth. Painful complications apart, birth is itself a tremendously fulfilling experience, and Nature has programmed her body and feelings to concentrate on bonding with the new baby she's just had, not getting back with her mate to create another.

It's a time for a couple to take it as easily as they can, and snatch as much relaxation as a new baby allows. If this stressful time is combined with other pressures, then it can take a long while for a couple to feel really close again – if they ever manage to. Once a couple have allowed their sex life to die down to being very infrequent, our hormones work in such a way that one or both can find it hard to build up desire again.

Edward, 35, and his wife have lost almost all the physical contact and comfort from their marriage. 'My wife had a forceps delivery which, of course, required an episiotomy. This may not have been too bad in itself but she was stitched up very badly and was in considerable pain for several weeks. We were both very tired, too, from looking after the baby, who was quite demanding.

'We tried to make love, as suggested, before the post-natal visit to the hospital six weeks after the birth, but it was impossible – too painful. The discomfort carried on for many months. We mentioned it to the doctor who examined her, but he said it would heal up given time. Although he has been a good doctor to us, he seemed to be embarrassed talking about sex so we didn't pursue it with him.

'At this time we were also carrying out extensive work on our house, so we were both continuously tired and had very little relaxation time together. Although sex is important to me I also need to be touched and cuddled at other times. This stopped almost entirely as a result of the baby, particularly when she slept less during the day. She sleeps in our bed, all attempts to wean her into her own having failed so far, and she rarely goes to sleep at night until we go to bed. We've made love only about six times in the two and a half years since she was born.

'My wife gets no time to herself except for a couple of hours in the afternoon when our daughter has a nap. It's hardly surprising that, having escaped from her for a short while, my wife doesn't devote her attention to me. I understand the problem and do what I can, but it doesn't make it any easier. On occasions I have been resentful and withdrawn.'

Having a new baby in the house **is** *very tiring. Among those*

149

men who would like to make love more often, nearly seven out of ten (65 per cent) of those who have children under five say the problem is that their partner is too tired. The men themselves are likely to be more tired even than men twice their age.

However, although virtually all couples agree that babies bring changes, they seem to bring serious problems mainly when there were already stresses in the relationship. Many other couples manage to work around them. Patrick, 29, a British Telecom manager: 'My wife was finally given a Caesarian after one of the most awful nights I have ever lived through. This obviously affected our sex life. She was very worried about making love after the birth but we had been given advice about this at the National Childbirth Trust classes we attended just before the baby was born – something along the lines of a candle-lit dinner, a bottle of wine and KY Jelly.

'Our sex life is still not so good because we both get so tired. Hopefully things will get better when the baby is a bit older.'

Howard, 34, a lorry driver: 'Obviously having children does affect your sex life but as long as you are prepared for it – the tiredness and irregular hours your children bring – there is a way around it. In our case we find that both children are asleep between 11 a.m. and 1 p.m. When I'm home at weekends my wife and I spend this time together. More often than not it leads to love-making, irrespective of where we are – the bedroom, kitchen or living room.'

It is perhaps only as the children begin to grown up that many couples realise that teenagers are more of a bar to a spontaneous sex life than the tiredness associated with a young family. The trouble with teenagers – and sons and daughters in their twenties who have not yet left home – is that they don't go to bed before you do.

Even the teachers' strike had unintended complications – Terry, 36, a radio and TV repair engineer: 'The main reason our sex life has decreased of late is that our eldest son is now almost 16. He stays up much later, so we get to bed later and are usually tired, as we work long hours. For a while we went to bed at lunch time and that was great – though we found one hour a bit rushed. But even that had to stop with the teachers' strike and our children coming home for lunch.'

Teenagers often think that sex is their preserve and trigger off sexual guilt in their parents. Simon, 53, in management: 'When the children were young our sex life was affected by their coming into our bedroom at night. Now they are older, it's their disapproving looks and remarks, and the difficulty we have in being alone.'

The parents who are sexually confident know that realising that their parents make love has a good rather than harmful effect on young people, helping them understand sex's role in a strong, loving relationship. They firmly set limits protecting their married sex life. Ian, 40, a sub-postmaster: 'We have always been open about sex. They know and always have known that my wife and I have regular sex. A closed bedroom door means just that.'

Ronald, 53, a bus driver: 'Our children have never affected our sex life as we are a very open family – for example, my wife and I have no qualms about nudity or bathing together. We do keep actual intercourse to ourselves but otherwise our affections are quite open.'

Family planning

Even loving fathers feel that enough is enough. Glenn, 28, a sign-maker: 'I love my lads but I have begun to feel threatened at the thought of any more children. We have just had our fourth. I get the feeling that my wife would like to get her name into the *Guinnes Book of Records* for having the most kids!'

Keith, 33, a laboratory technician: 'I am fond of my son but I feel that he competes with me for my wife's attention, which I resent at times. I don't understand her desire to have children; I am interested in her alone. I must not be enough for her if she needs children as well. I would like to have sex with my wife in the privacy of my own home as and when we please, and this is not now always possible by any mean.'

Some men start off wary of the commitment and the disruption to their relationship with their partner which children might bring. Jonathan, 33, a garage owner: 'My wife is 27 and as yet not bothered about kids. We have two dogs and in a way they are our family. A lot less trouble and time-consuming than kids. I think I may be too selfish for children but time with tell.'

Owen, 27, a historian: 'I would not have got married had I not felt that there existed between my partner and myself a degree of understanding and mutual trust which I had not experienced in any other relationship. Neither of us feel that children would enhance our relationship in any way.'

Behind all these decisions to have or not to have children, or more children, there is another important factor – the choice about contraception. Bryan, 46, a teacher: 'In retrospect the relationship changes from coitus interrupus, to condoms, to cap, to pill, to children, to coil, to condoms.'

Most of the men, like Bryan, obviously feel they share the responsibility, as they share the consequences, of family planning. Similarly, husbands these days talk about the effects of their wife's pre-menstrual tension or menopause problems on their relationship. However, the idea that contraception is the woman's concern has not died out among younger, unmarried men.

Andrew, 20, a carpenter: 'When I met my girlfriend she was slim and sexually attractive. On her next visit to the family planning clinic she was told that because the pill she had been taking was associated with cancer risks, it could now only be prescribed for women over 25. The pill they put her on made her weight shoot up three stones in three months or so. The clinic put her on the mini-pill, as there were no known side-effects. She's still got the extra weight and has lost interest in sex.

'She had a talk with the doctor who more or less said, "It's this pill or nothing." They offered to fit a coil but she doesn't want this because she already has bad period pains. She just wants her original pill back, then we can have a happy fulfilling relationship again.'

If it really is Andrew's girlfriend rather than Andrew himself who wants her to go back on the higher risk pill, you would still hope *he* would put her safety first and talk her out of it. In spite of the Men Too campaign, it seems that too many GPs and family planning clinics do not make enough effort to encourage the partners of the single young women who consult them to become involved in the discussions. If modern methods of contraception are to be used wisely, then both partners need to understand the implications behind the choices and advice they are offered.

As it is, the time at which many men first feel responsibility for family planning devolving firmly on them is when both partners feel their family is complete. Malcom, 34, a lecturer: 'The children have had a marvellous effect, keep us active and interested in all sorts of things, but we don't want any more. Neither of us like condoms nor can my wife go back on the pill, so I am awaiting a vasectomy.'

Many men find this the trouble-free, perfect answer to contraception once they are sure they do not want any more children. Adrian, 36, a security officer: 'I've had the snip now which makes our love life that much better – less tense. My wife can forget about the pill and me the Durex.'

Terry, 36: 'Before we were married I used a sheath, but we found this messy as it came off occasionally. Then we took no serious precautions after our first child. Then my wife used the cap until three years ago when I had a vasectomy. We find our sex life a lot more spontaneous now. I had no worries about a vasectomy either before or after. I had always said I would rather be sterilised than my wife, when we decided our family was complete.'

To many men, however, the 'snip' is still very threatening. Geoff, 42, self-employed: 'My wife is on the pill but making waves about my being vasectomised. I have to admit that the idea scares me to death. I suppose it's the fear of castration. We are trying to come to terms with our divergent views on this sometimes vexed topic.'

It is crucial for a man to be sure that he has no obvious or hidden anxieties before deciding to have a vasectomy, which must be regarded as an irreversible step. While there is no medical reason why a vasectomy should in any way change a man's sex life, apart from stopping him being fertile, if he has not thoroughly checked out the possibility of any subconscious fear or resistance to the idea, it can have a disturbing psychological effect.

Stuart, 43, an electronics engineer: 'After the birth of our daughter our sex life deteriorated rapidly. My wife did not want any more children so I had a vasectomy. Instead of improving our sex life, it made it worse because I began to reject my wife. I am still at a loss to explain this to myself and my wife is unable to help.'

It certainly looks as though Stuart blames his wife for manipulating him (as his subconscious at least sees it) into an operation which he did not want at heart. Equally, it is important for the woman to explore her feelings, not only before considering sterilisation for herself but before her partner has a vasectomy.

Several men mentioned that their sex life was better than usual when pregnancy was at least a possibility, even if remote. Knowing that pregnancy is impossible beyond all reasonable doubt can have a very dampening effect on some women. Roy, 43, an accountant: 'My wife blamed me for our "mistake" – we have a boy of three – so I had a vasectomy. I think she preferred the risk factor.'

Perhaps saddest of all are the men who have a vasectomy thinking that it will rescue an ailing sex life and failing marriage, only to find that the marriage breaks up anyway. If they then remarry it's very likely they will want to have a child within that relationship, particularly if their second wife has not already had any children.

Laurence, 42, a telephone engineer; 'My reluctance to take precautions meant I "had" to get married at the age of 18 years one month. I had three children by the age of 22. I had a vasectomy during my first marriage but it broke up and I have now married again. My present wife is only 24 and I am so sad I had the vasectomy in view of my wife's obvious desire to bear my child.'

How children affect marriage

Many men spoke ruefully about the difficult start a marriage can get off to when a child is already on the way. Men who start their family later may feel that the children come between them and their partner, but at least they have had the time together first to establish their relationship. David, 32, in the Forces, pointed out: 'My wife and I had to get married and unfortunately we've rarely had the chance to spend any time without the children.'

Gareth, 23, a computer programmer: 'My wife was pregnant when we married. Consequently we did not have time to arrange accommodation and moved in with my parents. Everyone hated it. After a year we moved out into a council house, when my daughter was six months old. The only area of unhappiness and argument in our marriage is over the rest of my family, probably arising from friction when we lived with my parents.'

Generally, however, Gareth feels that having children has enhanced his relationship with his wife. 'I love my children deeply, although I still place my wife first among my affections. I very much enjoy time spent playing with them, and do not regard baby-sitting as a chore. I turned down the offer of a university place and went to a polytechnic instead, so I could spend time watching my daughter grow. It is a decision I have never regretted.

'Our children, although obviously reducing the opportunity for sex, have made us much more considerate and committed lovers. I feel that being a father enables me to take a much longer-term perspective in life. Colleagues at work are concerned with little further ahead than the next rock gig or night at the pub. I find myself considering areas in which to buy a house, send children to school and generally build a settled life together.'

Many men agree with Tim, 28, that children, for all their demands, add a new and important dimension to marriage. 'Without them,' he said, 'there was no way for the relationship to develop.'

Just over half (56 per cent) of fathers believe that having children has had a good effect on their marriage, in general.

Bob, 43, in local government: 'Our two boys are the joy of my life. Bringing them up gives me a great sense of fulfilment and pleasure. Undoubtedly, they are the major factor in giving our marriage a sense of purpose, making us both reasonably happy. Without them we may well have split up.'

If the children are the cement holding a marriage together and little else is, there can be a risk that once the children grow up and leave home, the marriage can fall apart, or at least leave two middle-aged people in an empty house wondering what they have in common.

Those sort of fears haunt Alex, 29, who owns a store. 'It has been seven years since my wife and I have been alone together for more than a few hours. With four children and a small business to run, we are not able to spend the time we ought to working at our relationship. The effort of looking after four children really drains the resources, but things are gradually improving as the children get older. They've got to improve a great deal more! Every now and again I get a vision of an embittered man aged 50 to 55 who, once the children have gone, is left with nothing.'

Russell, 34, a postman, believes that the pressure of raising a family can wreck a weak marriage. 'Children do stabilise a marriage. That doesn't mean a couple with problems should have a baby in the hope it will bring them together. It won't. The pressures of parenthood are hard enough for a happy couple, but for an unhappy couple it would be disastrous. What I mean is, children give a lot of meaning to life, they give you hope for the future.'

The sudden loss of a child can equally make the future seem

meaningless. It nearly ended the marriage of Don, a dairy worker, and his wife. 'Two years ago we had a son who died at eight weeks of cot death. This affected us both deeply, even to the point of nearly splitting us up.'

Cliff, a window cleaner, and his wife did break up after the death of their baby son when they were both 20. They are back together now but looking back he says: 'After our son died we were both so empty and full of "whys". We were both too young to cope with such a great loss. We just blamed ourselves and couldn't talk.'

Often it is not being able to talk to one another, loss of communication, that makes a minority of men say that having children has had a bad effect on their marriage.

While 35 per cent say that having children has not affected their relationship or they're not sure, 10 per cent of men say that having children has definitely had a bad effect on them.

Guy, 36, a manager: 'I think I am a caring, affectionate father but I believe having the children was a mistake. My wife became cut off from the outside world and lost her interest in me. We rarely argue but her idea of conversation is the weather or the price of vegetables.'

Bruce, 37, a work study officer: 'We have three children and most of our rows occur because of differences in our approach to discipline etc. We are aware of the problem but it still occurs.'

Len, 54, unemployed, 'I would say the children had a bad effect on our marriage. We have more arguments over the children than over anything else. Their constant presence makes it difficult to have any sex life at all and the stress of bringing them up made us much more bad-tempered. I am not implying that the children themselves were in any way responsible, just that their birth and their presence worked against our relationship.'

A joy for ever

Even Len wanted to add: 'Having said that, it is probably true that if we hadn't had children we would have regretted it.'

Most men take enormous pleasure in their children, and don't sound at all like stern, remote father figures.

Colin, 29, a window cleaner: 'I tell my children every day just how much I love them, as that is something I never heard from my mother's lips. Maybe that's why I now put so much into my family life myself.'

Alan, 46: 'It gives me a nice feeling of being loved when, upon opening the door after a day's work, my two sons rush to me for a kiss and a hug. I am extremely proud of my children. One of the reasons I became self-employed was to "buy" my sons a job. I don't like to think of them ever being at the beck and call of employers like I was.'

Mark, 34, a postman, 'The good points far outweigh the bad. Children can be devils but they can also bring a lot of joy. Dads are lucky because we see the best of our kids – when they're clean and angelic ready for bed, or playing with them at weekends or seeing their faces light up on Christmas morning. It's generally Mums who see the tantrums and who end up with headaches.'

Fathers show some confusion over just how much time they really want to spend with their children day-to-day.

More than four out of five (83 per cent) say that they spend a lot of time with their children – yet one in three (30 per cent) says he is not that closely involved with his children day-to-day and a further one in three (29 per cent) that he does not see enough of his children because of his work.

Barry, 48, 'I love all my children dearly and have tried to be a good father to them. We have all enjoyed a close family life but I must admit my wife has done more to foster that than I have, though I've loved and cuddled them. I've worked hard to give them a good education and standard of living.'

It looks as if some fathers feel they spend a lot of time with their children – for *fathers*. They see that role as different from a mother's and would not want to change it, while others experience a real conflict between their longing to be with their children and their role as breadwinner. Barry added: 'I sometimes wonder now if it wouldn't have been more valuable to spend more time with them.'

Gordon, 24, an electrician: 'I resent having to work long hours to earn a decent wage to give my family a good lifestyle, as this denies me time with the wife and kids.'

John, 28, a lathe turner: 'I love my little girl more than anything else. She is a handful (aren't they all?) and my wife doesn't believe me when I say she is lucky to be home with her all day. I miss her so much at work I would gladly swap places and stay home.'

Some men working shorter or more flexible hours willingly share in the day-to-day care. Peter, 32, a teacher: 'I feel totally fufilled as a father. I love the role and the responsibilities, even though it is very hard work. I have always shared in rearing them, changing nappies, feeding etc. My step-father was never demonstrative with his feelings and I was determined from the outset that I would be as loving and caring as possible. That is not to say it has all been plain-sailing, particularly with our first-born, but in the final analysis they know how deeply loved and wanted they are.'

Mitch, 25, a policeman, 'As often as possible I let my wife have time on her own and look after the kids. I always bath and put them to bed at night except when I'm working.'

Fewer than one in five fathers (18 per cent) believes that his children are mainly his wife's concern.

New fathers can lack confidence, of course. Angus, 22, a motor mechanic: 'I am very proud of my baby son, although I am not very good with him when he cries, so he goes back to his Mum. I like to show him off to my friends as none of them have children yet. I suppose I think I have proved my manhood!'

Jimmy, 25, a service station manager: 'I love my daughter and enjoy playing with her and watching her growing. I look forward to the time when I can take her to the park or zoo or seaside. She was born only nine weeks ago, so at the moment I don't understand her or her needs as much as my wife, but I'm learning.'

It's often thought to be men who cling to the traditional roles, but some women feel threatened by men showing more interest and affection towards their children.

Scott, 28, a van driver: 'I am very close to both my sons, who are aged seven months and five years. Both are very happy and loving children. I have shared the bottle-feeding, dressing, changing and looking after with my wife, about 50:50. However, my wife gets very upset when either cry or are sad that they want me to cuddle them. She thinks that it is not normal for boys to like their Dad and that they should go to her. Usually it causes a row and a few days of silence.'

If fathers are shut out from childcare – or choose to cut themselves off – so that they lose the emotional rewards of parenthood, they can start to feel very exploited. Noel, 32, a bus driver: 'My saddest times are when I feel unwanted, rejected or a stranger in my own home, someone whose job is solely to supply the money.'

A worryingly high one in four fathers say they find it difficult to relate to their children.

Contrary to what one might expect, it's not so much the fathers of young babies who find it difficult to relate to their offspring. The older the children, the more likely it is that, though their father may still love them, some barrier has grown up between them.

Probably this ties in with the fact that so many fathers say they feel cut off by the demands of work and so have too little day-to-day contact. *By the time their children have reached the ages of 17 to 25, one in three fathers says he finds it difficult to relate to them.* These fathers are also more likely to say their offspring are mainly their wife's concern, than fathers of new born babies and toddlers.

Obviously this gap is partly explained by the need teenagers feel as they grow older to establish their own identity and to rebel. Clive, 46, a driving instructor: 'Our three children are now aged 20, 18 and 17. I'm quite close to the 18-year-old girl but the other two – one boy, one girl – have distanced themselves and mix with the low life. However, they all know the old man is still "The Man" and they can call on me for support when needed – financial, transport, etc. or if they are in trouble.'

It ties in with our findings that so few young men can talk openly to their fathers, and reminds us again that they do need other adults they can talk to, who will discuss embarrassing subjects such as sex with them. It is too glib to say it should be left to the parents, when such a high proportion of young people have fathers who admit they cannot relate to them.

As their daughters grow up many fathers admit they find it hard to adjust to the idea of their having sexual relationships. 'I try to keep men like me away from my daughter,' said Nick, 56, a director.

Alan, 38, said: 'My biggest problem at the moment is the impending adulthood of my daughter. I was shocked and surprised when my wife told me that she had put her on the pill. I still can't get used to people seeing my daughter as a sexual object (or rather a sexual person). But I try. I am coming to terms with her as a woman, but I realise I envy and resent their sexual freedom.'

The teenage years can cause uncomfortable conflicts in a father, not sure whether he is trying to protect his children – or whether he envies them. Fathers of young children often find that their feelings about such subjects as rape and child abuse change radically.

Phil, 36, a bus driver: 'In the past I was certainly against rape as a general principle. Now I have a little girl I would castrate the lads at the very least. Similarly in the past stories about cruelty to children did not really affect me. Now I feel very strongly about such cases. I suppose the basic difference is that I am now more responsible – in the past I did not really know what that meant.'

Some fathers will always be extra conscious of such risks because they were abused or harassed when young. This is a far more common problem among boys and young men than is generally realised, as we explain in the next chapter.

10 Men get raped, too

Assault, harassment and incest

Rape, incestuous abuse, sexual assault and harassment are appalling experiences not only inflicted by men on women. A surprising number of men have also been subjected to them though usually, again, by men.

John, 23, an electrical salesman, was only 10 when a teenage neighbour forced him to submit to anal sex. 'He was 15 or 16 and promised me a model car. I refused, he persisted. In the end I gave in. It was unpleasant and I was frightened of someone finding us. In later years I told friends what he had done. It made me feel an outcast (kids I didn't know came running up and asked, "Is it true that. . .") but I felt I was getting my own back.'

Gary, 27, a groundsman, was repeatedly abused by his father. 'I was 12 and he explained away his advances as teaching me the facts of life. He said it was only natural for young boys to relieve themselves using each other's back passage. Then I was given repeated demonstrations. He said boys didn't tell their Mums about this.

'I am sorry that this is the first time I've ever said anything about this to anyone, though I still remember it as clear as the nights it happened. My girlfriend, without knowing, has helped me to establish that I am a normal, healthy young man and this is one of the reasons I love her so much.'

One in ten men says he has been sexually harassed and a further one in twenty sexually assaulted (in some cases including anal penetration).

Only 10 per cent of these men were assaulted or harassed by a female. These were generally under 10 at the time of the incident, and most of the cases seem to have been childish sex play which went too far, so that the boy became disturbed.

161

We made it clear when conducting the survey that we were asking about sexual attack or advances which were at the least upsetting. When sex play involves children of roughly the same age – within about three years usually seems to be the comfortable limit – both are likely to be at something like the same stage of interest, and neither finds it too hard to call a halt when they have gone as far as they want to go. The risk of bullying and exploitation seems to become a problem when there is a larger age gap.

Larry, 34, unemployed, explained: 'I was only 4 when a girl of about 11 told me the facts of life and attempted to have intercourse with me. She was experimenting as we all do, but it did confuse me for some years.'

Boys are at risk of far more serious assault and harassment from other men.

Ninety-four per cent of men who have suffered from some form of worrying sexual advance or assault say it was from another man.

Three-quarters of the approaches and attacks (76 per cent) took place when they were aged between 6 and 15.

Alan, 36, a civil servant: 'My friend and I, then aged 8 and 10, were playing on rough ground. A youth of about 16 threatened to beat us up if we did not accompany him. We went to a concealed place in the field, where he took out his penis, and we had to play with it until he was erect. Then we had to lick, stroke and suck his penis to his demands. My friend managed to escape and brought my father. He threatened to kill the boy (if he had known precisely what had happened I think he would have). In retrospect, we were lucky that nothing more serious happened to us.'

Geoff, 32, a salesman: 'I was 15 and staying at my girlfriend's house. I was asleep in bed and I woke up to find her father's friend trying to penetrate me. I thought I was having a nightmare. Once I realised it was for real I leapt out of bed. He pretended he didn't know where he was or what had happened. I told my girl's Mum, who spoke to her husband. He just laughed.'

Only half of children and teenagers assaulted tell their parents.

If they do say something has happened, even then, like Alan, they may not tell their parents just how serious the incident was often because they are not sure how much they will be held to blame for what has happened.

Douglas, 52, a clerk, remembers being assaulted when he was 13. 'I was riding my cycle alone on a main road in the country. A man on a cycle caught up with me and ordered me to go with him into a field out of sign of the road and masturbate him, which I did. He tried to do the same to me, but was unable because he could not induce an erection. It is no wonder because I was terrified. He warned me not to tell anyone and to wait before riding away, which I did.

'I did not tell my mother because, whenever there was any kind of problem in my life, it was *always my fault*. I believed this would have been the same – it would have been due to something I had done. In any event, sexual matters were something which were never mentioned.'

Clearly, if we want to help protect children (in that the molesters might more frequently be caught and prevented from molesting again) and help them recover from such an experience, we must try to make it easy for them to confide in us about sexual worries. They cannot always understand that we will feel differently about their being victims of an adult's misplaced sexuality if we seem to disapprove so strongly of their own that it has become a taboo subject.

One in four molested children and teenagers (26 per cent) tells no one what has happened and only 14 per cent of such incidents are reported to the police.

If the youngster is pressured into some form of sexual contact, such as masturbation, which brings him pleasure, he feels extra guilt. He knows there is something wrong about the relationship, but is too young to withstand this abuse of power by an adult who should be the one acting responsibly.

Chris, 32, and now a policeman himself, has always felt guilty about a relationship he was lured into when just 11 by a man of 30. 'He was the father of my "girlfriend" at school. One day when she and her mother were out, he took me into his bedroom, took down my shorts and touched my penis. I was too afraid to tell my parents, as he had told me never to tell anyone "our secret".

'I still saw my friend and on many more occasions her father would touch me while masturbating himself. When I reached puberty he taught me to masturbate. We would cycle into the country together, using the excuse of strawberry picking. He would than take me into a field, take my trousers off and masturbate me and make me do the same to him. I never told anybody about this and being able to write about it now, even at this late stage, has taken a weight off my mind.'

Another factor which inhibits youngsters, particularly the teenagers, from telling anyone what has happened, is that they think it must mean that they are homosexual – or look it. This worries them if they live in a society which regards homosexuality with suspicion.

Nick, 20, a student: 'I was 17 and the school chaplain asked me if I wanted a lift home after a school dinner-dance. He stopped in a deserted lay-by with my door close against a wall. He asked what was bothering me – I had been wandering around alone most of the evening – and said that what I needed was more love.

'He started holding me and hugging me, saying he could give me the love I needed. I asked if he was gay. He answered yes, and I asked if I could get out. After a while he decided to run me home. When we were about two miles from my house, I jumped out at a junction and ran off. I was fraught for a long time, thinking that if he thought I was gay, other people must, too. I didn't tell my mother or any of my friends at the time.'

Since most sexual assaults are by other men, it gives many of those assaulted a hatred and distrust of homosexuality.

Cliff, 24, also a student: 'My mother was in hospital and I was staying with another family with my brother. My father had had to stay elsewhere, as there wasn't room. One day I was having a bath and this married man came in and looked at me funnily. He came over, washed my penis, and then sucked it. I was too young to understand. I now cannot stand gays.'

Such incidents undoubtedly add to prejudice against homosexuality, but most homosexual men do not behave in this way any more than most heterosexual men do with girl children. In fact, specialists in the field of protecting children against sexual abuse say that most such abuse of children is by heterosexual men, even when the child is a boy. The abuse of young children is not generally the expression of sexual attraction, but of a frustrated need to have power over another individual.

A few homosexual men harass teenagers, but this does not mean that it is common behaviour. Far many more women complain of rape, assault or harassment. In our survey of unmarried women we found one in ten had been assaulted or raped and one in four harassed, but few of us hold all heterosexual men to blame.

Rape, assault and harassment are not sexual acts but acts of

164

violence and aggression. It is not the sexuality of the assailant which is the problem, but their disordered personality and behaviour.

One result of being molested or assaulted for some men was to feel a common bond with female victims of such attacks. Keith, 44, a salesman, remembered: 'When I was 16 I was attacked by a man with whom I used to work. His face went grey and he tried to drag me into a quiet area. He was not playing around, either. I pity any woman who is subjected to any attack like this. I managed to struggle free and then run for it. I did nothing through fear and embarrassment, and can understand why women sometimes do the same.'

Incest

One in eight men (12 per cent) says either that he has made sexual advances towards a member of his own family, or that a member of the family has made advances towards him.

These figures include grown men who have made passes at their sister-in-law, those who have enjoyed sex play or more with cousins much the same age, those who have played 'doctors' with their sisters, and other situations which would generally be regarded as neither sexual abuse nor psychologically damaging – though they might have caused uproar had the rest of the family learnt of them.

Roughly half the cases of sexual contact within the family involved an incident or relationship where one was under 16 – and often a great deal younger – and there was such an age gap as to suggest that the younger one could not be thought to be participating with full understanding and without undue pressure.

Boys are abused by parents, grandparents, aunts and uncles, older brothers, sisters and cousins, and rarely seem to confide in anyone.

Greg, 33, in the entertainments industry: 'My mother tried to sexually assault me when I was 14. I was in bed when she came into the room. She played with my penis but I pretended to be asleep.'

Rory, 17, a clerk: 'My grandfather used to sit me on his knee and feel my genitals. He once tried to get me to feel his, but I wouldn't. After that I wouldn't let him near me.'

Jerry, 36, a civil servant: 'I was 12 and my sister 16 or so. At first I wasn't forced into it. We mainly just touched and kissed a little. Towards the end she started bullying and teasing me. She became too rough with me, as if despising and demeaning me, making me do things I didn't want to do. On the last couple of occasions she tried to make me kiss and lick between her legs. I didn't want to. It just felt so wrong and bad.

'I was too frightened to tell anyone else of this. I think these experiences made it hard for me to approach women. I was a virgin until I was 21. I used to find it hard to get and maintain an erection. Although I went to bed with several women between the ages of 18 and 21 when I was at college, I failed to have intercourse.'

We tend to think that boys and young men are able to take care of themselves, but their hopes of future happiness can be damaged by such experiences, just as much as women's.

When the youngsters do tell someone what has happened, they may be kept away from them in future, but there is rarely any effective action taken against the abuser. Families find it very hard to acknowledge to the world what has been going on in their midst and there are all the conflicts of family loyalties and others who would be hurt by the disclosure to consider. The trouble is that it can leave the abuser free to trouble other children.

Guy, 32, unemployed: 'I was 5 years old when my uncle got into bed with me. He had a son the same age as myself and I had gone to stay the weekend with them. He was a widower. I'd stayed there loads of times and nothing like it ever happened before. He was always fun to be with, he took me and my cousin to the pictures and local fairs, and even the circus once – anyway the perfect uncle, until one night he came into the bedroom.

'I woke up as he was getting into bed with me. He went all the way with me. Next morning everything went on as if nothing had happened, but even though I was only 5, I knew what he had done, and I was still messy, dirty and my mind was in turmoil. I went home and told my mother. Things are blurred after that, but I never stayed there again. In later years he went to court for molesting other kids, but nothing seemed to happen to him. He lives near me now. I wonder how many kids he's molested in the last 30 years.'

If such an abuse seems almost to be countenanced by the family, and it is not made clear to the child that they have been a victim of very wrong behaviour by an adult, who is then clearly held responsible – as children expect to be blamed when they do something wrong – they can grow up with their own sexuality damaged and confused as to the safe and acceptable boundaries of sexual contact.

Luke, 27, a window cleaner: 'My mother was always touching me through my trousers and I never saw any wrong in it until my wife caught her at it one day. She told her she wasn't right in the head and that it's not natural for a mother to touch her sons in that way. As she'd done it for so long, I first of all sided with my mother. It wasn't until I thought later that I realised how wrong it all was.'

The risk is that the abused children become abusing adults. Abuse can become a grim pattern repeated down the generations.

Gordon, 34, a local government officer: 'When I was 12 my brother-in-law, who was 22, used to get me to masturbate him while he touched me. No one ever knew. I first made sexual advances to my step-daughter when she was 12 and I was 26. They took the form of mutual masturbation during bedtime cuddling, usually when my wife was away or working. I never used violence and it continued irregularly over four or five years.'

The few men who could bring themselves to talk about their abuse of children in their family felt very guilty.

David, 23, a salesman, 'When I was 15 I exposed myself, erection and all, to my six-year-old sister and her friend. I have felt bitterly ashamed of this ever since.'

Alex, 44, unemployed: 'My daughter is now 19 and I masturbated her from the age of 9 to 15 about 25 times. I also licked her clitoris when she was 10. At no time did she object, though she must have been confused. I pray to God every night to keep my hands off her, and for the last three years I have. Fortunately, she has not been affected by these dreadful happenings and is a terrific daughter.

'I once touched my other daughter who politely said, "Don't do that," and that's as far as it went. Because my youngest never asked me to stop I carried on. I try to please the three women in my life constantly and I thought I was pleasing her.

'I am regarded as having a very happy family. I am not an ogre, but in those days when I could not handle them, my sexual urges used to take control of me. My wife would no doubt murder me if she found out. I repeat I have not touched her for three years and I feel the longer this goes on the less likely I am to touch her.

'Please don't misunderstand these comments. I have had a normal upbringing. I have no real sexual problems apart from touching my daughter. I am happily married, I am a Christian and have high moral values, but I have been cursed with this problem.'

It is typical of this type of abuser that Alex almost seems to hold his daughter responsible. Because, when as young as nine or ten, she did not tell him to stop, he convinced himself that she wanted him to continue. It demonstrates just how important it is that we teach all our children to say no to any form of touching that makes them feel uncomfortable (see the Help Directory) – and also how important it is that children have the opportunity to discuss sexual matters outside the home.

If parents have the option to withdraw children from sex education classes, there will be those who do so because they intend giving them what they believe to be a better and more moral education for life at home. There will also be those who withdraw their children because they are regularly abusing them and want to be sure of minimising any opportunity the child may have of realising that their parent's behaviour would not be accepted as normal by other adults, and of getting help.

Alex clearly feels guilty, but he is almost certainly fooling himself if he thinks that it has all had no effect on his daughter. He is also taking a fearful risk by relying on his self-control.

It is crucial that such families seek help, not only to prevent further abuse, but also to help repair the damage to the abused child and the family's relationships generally. At least now there is more guidance available – all listed in the Help Directory.

11 *Men who love men too*

Homosexuality and bisexuality

Many gay men object to being defined by the sex they happen to find most attractive. They have a very good point. Sex may be an important subject to many, but it occupies comparatively little of our waking hours – even for the most enthusiastic. How would most heterosexual men and women feel about being defined by ther sexual preferences? To have it considered of relevance to their job prospects to be known as having a liking for oral sex, say, or to have their own parents disown them because they 'came out' with the news that they like intercourse with the woman on top?

These are not such a far-fetched comparisons. Under the guidance of their priests, Spanish *conquistadores* tortured and slaughtered South American Indians for just such 'perverted' practices. We now regard the attitudes, let alone the retribution, as barbaric, yet men and women in our culture who happen to prefer to share their sexual affection with others of the same sex still face great suspicion and prejudice.

Partly because of society's attitudes, men who are mostly attracted to other men tend to have different experiences of forming relationships than those who are attracted to women. While what heterosexual and homosexual couples actually enjoy doing in bed varies far less than is often supposed, other factors affecting their sexual happiness do tend to be very different. There are not many gay men who are too tired to make love because they have just had a baby, for example, or who have been raised with the conditioning against taking a lead sexually that many women have.

Particularly because much of the subject matter of our survey is not just what couples do in bed together, but how their relationship in general and family circumstances affect their sex lives, we needed to ask men who filled in our questionnaire what they considered to be their sexual orientation, so that those whose partner is another man did not distort our findings on those whose partner is a woman.

We were careful when wording the questionnaire not to exclude gay men who wanted to participate. For example, we used the word partner rather than talking about wives and girl-friends. Nonetheless, these questions about marriage and children inevitably meant the survey seemed to some to have a heterosexual bias. We did not receive a substantial enough number of replies from men who consider themselves gay to feel confident that we had a representative sample, to be able to analyse their responses in the same depth as we could those from men who consider themselves heterosexual. If we had, this would have had to have been another book, rather than one chapter.

However, the replies and comments we did receive from gay men were too valuable to be ignored, even if we cannot claim them to be statistically valid. We always intended that gay men should have a place in our survey. We whole-heartedly agree with Steve, 22, who wrote: 'I feel that such a survey needs to take into account the experiences of gays as well as straight men. We are still men, after all!'

Gay's problem is Society

Steve summed up the dilemma facing men who are, or who think they might be, gay. That it is often not forming loving, healthy relationships which is their problem, but others' attitudes towards them. 'I am currently having a relationship with another man who is the most important person in my life,' said Steve. 'I love him very much indeed. He is kind, gentle and loving, and we have become very close. This makes me very happy.

'What makes me sad is how society frowns upon gay relationships. They are viewed as abnormal, perverted and indecent. My parents are strongly homophobic. I told them three years ago that I am gay. They told me that if I want to live my life in such a manner I will have to leave home – which would be difficult from a financial point of view, since I am still a student. It upsets me that I have to deceive them in order to see my boyfriend. I wish they could see and understand how I feel about him – and that being gay is not dressing up in women's clothes, hanging around in public lavatories and other such incorrect, preconceived ideas.'

Since just being gay is so often seen as a problem, it seems important to stress that many wrote very happily about their relationships with other men. Simon, 21, working in his family business: 'I have found love and understanding with my boyfriend that I never knew existed. To be lonely and confused and then find someone who loves and understands my needs is heaven. My partner and I have never had intercourse, mainly because we are happy with our sexual relationship as it is. The only thing is that I can never show my love for him to anyone else. To be forced behind closed doors is really sad.'

Michael, 24, a musician: 'I live with my boyfriend and we filled in your questionnaire together. We were both a bit embarrassed and a lot of laughing and joking was done when we first read it through together. Then we settled down and completed it carefully. We try to be open with each other and I knew most of the time what his answers would be. My boyfriend answered honestly and when I later read through his answers I saw how close we really are and how strong our relationship is. At times we have our ups and downs like most couples, but I'm glad to say the majority of our relationship is very happy.'

These are the men who have won through. As Paul, 28, a printer, pointed out: 'The most difficult thing for me and for most gays is "coming out". From the time of leaving school and coming out to my parents at 21, was the most lonely and difficult period of my life.'

Since the age of consent for homosexual relationships is 21 – a fact which many object to – there are some very lonely teenagers who are sure that their feelings are not 'just a phase'.

Gary, 18, an insurance agent: 'I did not realise I was gay until I left school. I've fallen in love with quite a few normal men, but have not met any gay person at the moment. I'm desperate for a relationship, but I have never told anyone about my being gay. I want help to understand why I'm gay and to get in touch with others.'

Mark, 21, a student teacher, was so devastated he tried to kill himself. 'It amazes me how promotion prospects, style of dress, political and media clout and all of society's attitude towards you depend on who you take to bed. I've seen the thought of being gay destroy two people, three people try to cover and hide it, resulting in misery, heartbreak and, in one case, nervous breakdown.

171

'Every boy goes through a questioning phase and so did I. I fought the feelings that I had. It ripped my mind apart, so I fought harder, I hid it and looked over it. Eventually it drove me to a suicide attempt. Finally I decided to admit to myself what I was feeling. I hated it but accepted it. Since then I have felt so happy inside, so secure and calm.

'I've seen how beautiful, natural, secure and loving some pairs of men are together. Now I won't sleep or have sex with anyone whom I don't love or go out with.'

Some can never face coming out even though it means years of loneliness. Tim, 46, (who wrote in his job but then obliterated it, presumably through fear of being in any way identifiable): 'I enjoy the company of both sexes, but I have known for many years now that I am sexually attracted only to my own sex. I have never had the courage to "come out" for fear of ridicule and the embarrassment to the rest of my family.

'I would have loved to have been "normal" and to have had a wife and family. I feel very unhappy at the prospect of the lonely years ahead. I am a loving person and have no one to love, care for and share my life with. I do not know what I have done to deserve this fate but I try to "grin and bear it", if only because there is no alternative.'

Of course, there is an alternative, the one Tim is too frightened to take – to acknowledge his sexual preference. Perhaps this is easier these days for younger men. Many wrote to say that their parents have accepted their being gay and there are now various organisations who try to help the men and their familes see that being gay is no tragedy and need to be no problem at all.

Not a matter of choice

It is true that for gay men there is no real alternative to being gay. Attempts to 'treat' gay men with aversion therapy in order to encourage them to be attracted to women failed, and would now be regarded as insulting by most gay men. There always have been and always will be people who prefer their own sex. As Alan, 34, a solicitor's clerk, explained: 'Society neatly calls someone like myself a deviant, but no one chooses their sexuality. Since I got to 14 or 15 I have found that no matter how I try, women hold no sexual attraction. People make jokes about being homosexual without one thought of how a homosexual feels. They do not always want sex, they want a caring relationship as well. None of us want pity, but a little understanding would go a long way.'

Finding a caring relationship is not always easy. Paul commented: 'I think being gay makes it more difficult to meet partners. There are less places to go where you know you will meet gay people, and generally gays are not into long-standing partnerships.'

It is difficult to know whether it is true that gay men are generally not interested in lasting relationships, or whether the problem is that gay men without a partner are forced to go to known gay clubs and bars in order to find any acceptance. Like heterosexual singles bars, these can easily be dominated by those who want 'no-strings' sex – or at least seem to.

Mark explained: 'I've had a glimpse of what I want and what I don't want. In some pubs and discos there are umpteen single gay men, each night looking for someone different to make love to. Whatever the feelings of the other people, whatever the circumstances, they would make love to anything below 25 in trousers. The discos are like cattle markets. Why? On being asked to and included in such clubs, I discovered they hate the way they carry on but they have to. Their jobs, their environment, society won't let them settle down and live with someone. They have to creep around in secret, playing a dangerous game of bed and breakfast with men night after night. They cannot go out and be themselves, they cannot get an "affair" to live with, so they gallivant around with many men.'

Even if they eventually can manage to say 'I'm proud to be gay', in view of the pain and struggles these men have had just to accept their own sexuality, it's ironic that efforts merely to win some acceptance so often seem to be misinterpreted as their trying to 'convert' others to homosexuality. They, more than most men, know that sexuality is not a matter of choice.

Lewis, 25, a medical representative, seems to feel very threatened. 'I find the homosexual community OK as long as they keep it to themselves and don't try to preach to heterosexuals to try it, especially on a sexual level. The idea of anal intercourse makes my stomach turn and, if anyone tried to seduce me in that way, or preach homosexuality to me to try and convert me, I would probably give them a knuckle sandwich and more than just a small piece of my mind.'

Colin, 20, a student who considers himself heterosexual, suggested: 'People who show strong hatred or dislike of homosexuals probably have underlying homosexual tendencies themselves, which they attempt to conceal by a blanket of hysteria which they direct against those most likely to discover them.'

Blanket generalisations, like blanket hysteria, are suspect in this complicated area of human relationships, but it is true that very few people are 100 per cent heterosexual in their capacity for being attracted, even if they are in the response they choose to act on.

If a man is completely confident and secure in a heterosexual male identity, then a homosexual approach would probably be regarded as a case of mistaken identity rather than anxiety-provoking. Dean, 19, a student, realises: 'My masculinity feels threatened by overt displays of homosexual behaviour. I think I am worried that if a man finds me attractive there must be something wrong with me.'

Loving men and women

Many men who took part in our survey have been conscious of 'feelings' towards other men at different times in their lives. Many took part in mutual masturbation sessions with other boys while at school. Phil, 39, an area manager, wondered: 'I'd be interested to know how many admit it in the survey, but a good 30 per cent of our school was at it.'

Some, though they do not consider themselves homosexual, have had relationships with other boys or men.

Seven per cent of married men and a similar percentage of single men now in heterosexual relationships have had a romantic friendship with another male. For just over half of these (55 per cent) the relationship included sex.

Very nearly two out of three of these relationships took place when the men were under 19. James, 26, a student, remembers: 'When I was about 13, my friend and I played around with each other. Once or twice he entered me, but most of the time we just felt each other. I felt no guilt about this. We were just curious and playing around, rather than being conscious of being gay or whatever. I enjoyed it. I wouldn't do it again now, though he and I are still friends and see each other occasionally.'

Sometimes two young men make love together when what they at least believe they really want is to make love to a girl. Warren, 24, unemployed: 'The only homosexual experience I've had was with a friend whom I'd know since school. We both used to worry about our lack of girlfriends, until one night we both got drunk and slept together. Although oral sex turned me on I couldn't bring myself to have intercouse with him, which is what he wanted. I don't know if I would do it again, but I was glad at the time because I knew I wasn't homosexual. I suppose I could do it again if I was desperate enough.'

Men like James and Warren are likely to look back on these experiences and see them as 'just a phase' – the phrase which so maddens many gay people, since it seems to imply that their sexuality is immature, to be grown out of and renounced at will. Of course, this is not true.

While we are young it often seems as if we have a sexual compass which is spinning widly, not sure which way is north for us. However, once it has settled, usually by the early twenties, it is pretty unchangeable. Though suppressing true feelings can lead to an apparently wild swing in our behaviour, this is just our true sexual identity finally emerging, rather than a deep inner change.

There were one in three who had relationships with other men when they were between 19 and 25, and they were less likely to dismiss them as just experiment or substitute for the 'real thing.'

Dominic, 20, a student: 'A year ago I became very friendly with another student whom I knew was homosexual (or at least bisexual). We became very affectionate. The situation split due to external pressures (he being a medical student), but it has left me with a realisation that a meaningful relationship can be formed between any two people irrespective of gender, and that if those people are "sexual" in their outlook, physical relations are a natural progression. My girlfriends since then have all accepted my bisexuality and make no attempt to leave me feeling a "deviant".'

Four per cent of both single and married men taking part in our survey consider themselves bisexual.

It is not always affectionate caring relationships such as that enjoyed by Dominic which leave the men knowing that they are attracted to and/or enjoy sex with a man as well as a woman. Enjoyment of experiences which other men might have regarded as molestation seemed to have left some with a taste for anonymous or casual homosexual encounters.

Rex, 53, a telephonist who is separated from his wife, 'I was quite a late starter in sexual matters. My first experiences were being fondled in the cinema by men.' [Many men remembered being approached in the cinema as youths.] 'I enjoyed them, while being ashamed and feeling I had sinned (a result of my upbringing). At sixteen I was seduced by an older man and it was then I formed the belief that it could not be a sin when I felt so wonderful.'

Rex later married but not long afterwards 'I was impelled to seek sex with a man and visited a public toilet. I stood next to a man who was obviously there for that purpose. I let him reach for me and masturbate me.' All through his life Rex has felt continually drawn to such casual homosexual encounters.

Andrew, 25, married and a technician: 'I was assaulted when I was 10. This man made me masturbate him, perform oral sex and let him touch my penis and put fingers in my anus, but he didn't rape me. Instead of telling my parents about it, I found myself curious about the way this man ejaculated from what seemed to me then a huge penis. My cousin and I started masturbating to see who could ejaculate first. Since then I have been attracted to men but only for sex. I have never formed or wished to form any regular relationship with a man. I have never been in love with a man, but I have been in love several times with a woman and found this marvellous. Sex with women I find much better, but it's much more difficult to obtain. Gay men are very promiscuous and much more willing to have sex on the first night than women.'

Many husbands find their bisexuality a great strain, as of course do their wives if they learn of it. Malcolm, 38, a computer engineer: 'I realised I was bisexual at about the age of 14. My first real sexual experience was with a man at the age of 21. On being introduced to the "gay scene" I realised that if this was being gay then gay I am not. This, coupled with the fact that I was unknowingly the reason for the bust up of two guys. I married at the age of 23 to a 20-year-old girl. For a year before getting married and for two years after I had no inclination or desire to pursue men. It is true to say that my thoughts during this period were 100 per cent heterosexual.

'Then one day I was approached and, with my consent, turned back into the gay world. I lied to and cheated my wife for about seven years. Towards the end of last year I came clean and told my wife everything. After much upset and many rows, but above all complete frankness, we have both come to terms with my lifestyle. I am unable to promise not to go with men. She disapproves of the situation, but accepts my needs for these homosexual pursuits. Finally, I have no desire to have extra-marital sex with a woman. I am 100 per cent satisfied with my heterosexual sex-life. I also feel that I am not capable of homosexual "love", therefore there is no emotional strain on our marriage.

'I look forward to reading the results of your survey. I would estimate that of the homosexuals that I meet about 80 per cent of them are married.'

Few wives can accept their husbands continuing to have homosexual relationships. Quite apart from the emotional strain, these days the spread of the AIDS virus must make such a wife feel very vulnerable. (We look at the effect of the AIDS scare on sexual behaviour and at help available in Chapter Thirteen.) If the marriage is to survive, the husband usually has to promise to try to end all homosexual activity.

Francis, 36, a lecturer: 'I now consider that I have been bisexual from an early age. I first had sexual contact with another man at the age of 20. I met my wife soon after and told her of my problem. We were both virgins, but soon had an active sex life before we were married. I hoped that my problem would go away because of this.

'We married two years later and for the next two years I remained faithful. Then I started again, around the time of the birth of our first child; occasionally at first, but much more frequently as the years went by. These contacts took place in public conveniences and occasionally I went back to the man's house. These contacts were rarely with the same person. I used to feel guilty and dirty after each contact and would vow to myself not to do it again. But a week or so later, if the opportunity arose so did my excitement, and I would do it again.

'I never got emotionally involved with these other men until about three years ago. I met a man of my own age who lived locally. He was a homosexual but not in any obvious outward way. I became infatuated with him to the extent that I knew my home life and work were being affected. I knew that this situation could not continue. So during a row with my wife, I told her. This was about two years ago.

'My wife is a very special person and did not leave or throw me out. It was obviously in a way a terrific relief to tell her, but it placed a tremendous burden on her. Since that time I have remained completely faithful to my wife, which is a very nice feeling. We do not kid ourselves that it has gone away forever; so we talk about it sometimes, which is unpleasant for me now, but I know is good for her and us. I try very hard now to show my love for my wife who has shown so much love for me. I think that we will make it. Thank you for the opportunity of telling someone else.'

Emotional escape route?

Only one in four of men who consider themselves bisexual are currently having homosexual relationships.

Most have had at least one sexual relationship with a man in the past but are determined not to risk their marriage. Pete, 24, unemployed: 'In the past I have had a few affairs with men. The first was with a teacher when I was 18 and at college. My affairs with men gradually tailed off after making love with a girl. I now consider myself bisexual, although I would not jeopardise my marriage by having an affair with a man or a woman.'

Ian, 28, a catering manager and now married: 'I once had a special relationship with another boy of the same age as myself – this was at the age of 19 to 21. I have never had any other homosexual experience but I know I still have these feelings. I find men as well as women sexually attractive. I believe my homosexual feelings are wrong and try to hide them, even from myself, but I know they are still there.'

If a man is not so much bisexual – enjoying making love to a woman as much as to a man – but homosexual and suppressing this preference because of all the pressure to conform, then it is obviously very hard for either of the couple to enjoy a fulfilled sex life, no matter how loyal and determined not to risk his marriage the man may be.

Ray, 51, a quality controller: 'For many years I have had to keep any desires I had to myself. I did not marry until I was 25, my wife was 20. I had a very brief homosexual encounter in the army when I was 23, almost a one-night stand. I was a virgin soldier until then, but it did include intercourse. I think I was a bit of a latent homosexual, but have not repeated the episode since, though hardly a day goes by without me thinking "That's where my desires really lie."

'I almost amazed myself when we married, but I needed sex like a drunkard needs booze and did not care how I got it. Unbelievably we had six marvellous children, four girls and two boys. I love them all dearly but find it hard to relate to them. They, I feel, are really their mother's children.

'Although I have written I am mainly bisexual, for almost 30 years I have only been heterosexual, even if my desires have been the opposite. I have never been sexually unfaithful. My wife is the only woman I have had sex with. I have never had even a minor interest in other women. I look at other men with lust, but just looking can never satisfy the craving I have.

'I am now too set in my ways to pursue the path I know I should have taken without ruining the life of the wonderful woman I married. I have ruined every chance of a sexually fulfilled marriage for her. I love her like a dear friend but she deserves much better.'

The temptation is for the man to pretend, even to himself, that it is not homosexual yearnings that are causing problems in his sex life but more workaday, 'normal' pressures.

Eddie, 32, a youth worker, blamed tiredness. 'I regard myself as bisexual mainly because from time to time I have been attracted to other males and have felt a sexual desire. This has never been fulfilled and only once did the other person know about it. This was when I was in my late teens and feeling very alone. I got friendly with a young artist who offered me warmth, love and affection. However, my mother got very suspicious and split us up before any sexual activity could take place. We never even kissed, cuddled or held hands. I have always since wondered what I would be now if my first sexual experience had been with a man.

'At this moment I am suffering from pangs of thinking about a young man who is a friend. He again has shown warmth and tenderness towards me when I have felt a bit down. In fact the other evening I was feeling fed up and he came and put his arm around me and I went weak at the knees. I still love my wife very much and would not want to hurt her, but on the other hand, I would like to respond to this other person in a way that might lead to sex.

'Usually I am so involved that I don't think. However, once or twice for some reason, I have imagined having sex with another man – there has been no one in particular and I couldn't describe him. It's just a feeling of being in close, intimate contact with someone of the same sex.

'Over the last 18 months our frequency of love-making has dropped so much so that it troubles my wife. It is mainly due to my lack of interest. I put the cause down to being tired through work and work-related problems. If I am not really tuned in to sex then my wife is dissatisfied and that makes me feel depressed, so unless I know or feel I can perform well I don't bother, as I can't stand my wife being upset about it.'

However, what some men seem to be expressing by calling themselves bisexual, is not a real longing to have any sexual relationship with a man at all, but a discomfort with and rejection of the stereotyped male identity, the demand that they always be strong and in command.

Jake, 20, an office worker: 'Although I have never had a proper sexual experience with a man I do wonder what it would be like. Perhaps because I was always teased at school I like the idea of having a protector-like figure, a strong man to hold me and make me feel safe.'

Edwin, 29, a scientist: 'This is the most difficult area for me. I have not ever had close physical intimacy with any other male. However, since a boy of twelve, I have had "romantic" ideas about first other boys and steadily men and boys, a few years either side of my own age. I am not in the least interested in most males, but now and then I make friends and find myself highly curious about that person's sexuality, sometimes female but sometimes male.

'With the men it is a semi-hero worship at times. I feel less male with them and find myself admiring their physique and especially interested in their "sexyness", by which I mean sexual power, prowess, attraction, purely physical.

'I dislike intensely the actual aspect of relationships between men but find myself kind of "flirting" in a way that places me in the power of their maleness. I could imagine oral sex with another male mutually, or as a service I might perform to reinforce the dominance of a male over me. Yet I am a dominant type and very "macho" in most respects, though sensitive intellectually and emotionally.

'Fortunately no male friend has ever responded except in jest. I feel safe that I shall probably never realise any of my imaginings. My favourite male friends just observe an affectionate and attentive buddy.'

Women now have legislation on their side to help them escape the stereotype. It may only proclaim that women should have equal access to jobs, pay, and opportunities, rather than put much muscle into seeing that they get them, but it puts an offical stamp on an attitude. It is more acceptable now for women to appear tough, capable and unemotional. A man who finds the conventional expectations put on him a strain, finds precious little backing for the idea that it is OK for him to feel weak, tearful and helpless occasionally.

12 A question of identity

Men who enjoy dressing as women

More than a century has passed since Mrs Bloomer was attacked in the street for her revolutionary garb, yet today a man who goes out dressed in a skirt runs the risk of being arrested for causing a breach of the peace. Although a liking for wearing women's clothes causes others no hurt or injury, transvestites are despised by almost all other men. Gay men, who might have been expected to have some understanding of people's varying sexual needs, were quick to point out angrily that they were 'normal' in comparison. Grant, 21, a student: 'The idea that men who dress up in women's clothes are all gay is one of the stereotypes least deserved by gays. We have enough to contend with without people implying anything other than that gays are normal people.'

Which seems to leave transvestites firmly in the camp of the abnormal or perverted, yet many men have found it intriguing to dress up in women's clothes. *One quarter of all men have dressed up as a woman at some time.*

Fourteen per cent dressed up as a woman for a party, performance, or a joke. Playing pantomime dames in amateur dramatics, drag parties and even hen nights were all mentioned as giving an enjoyable chance to try a different role for a night – though most hurriedly added that they had no desire to cross-dress often. Lewis, 25, a medical representative, pointed out: 'On the rare occasions that I wear women's clothes as a joke, or go to a party, it is *only* because it's a drag party and I *always* take a female with me just to harder enforce that it is only a joke.'

However, it is a joke that persists over the centuries and that many people, men and women, find at least a little challenging and exciting. Richard, 42, 'I believe that there is in every man, apart from a homosexual element, a secret desire to experiment

182

in cross-dressing, as is evidenced by the current trend in young men in gender-bending. I think that a lot of young men would like to see what they look like in their girlfriend's clothes and make-up. I also believe that women enjoy seeing men dressed up as women, which is a popular feature of hen nights.'

One in twelve (8 per cent) of men, both married and single, said they have regularly enjoyed cross-dressing.

'I find it exciting and sexually arousing to shed my maleness temporarily,' said Richard, 'and transform myself into an attractive female. I wish that transvestism did not have to be carried out in such a secretive way.'

The hidden woman

More than half (62 per cent) of self-declared transvestites say they have now given up cross-dressing.

Transvestism often starts very young. Dale, 25, unemployed, could remember 'wanting to wear a dress from the age of 3. At about 9 I often put on a sister's dress when people at home were out. By 14 or 15 years it was happening more often. I liked wearing my sister's school uniform. I didn't then realise that I always had an erection while doing this, but I did enjoy a fantastic feeling all over my body.'

However, what may be unselfconscious dressing up to a boy starts seeming strange and wrong when he reaches the teenage years, puberty and greater sexual knowledge. Gary, 19, a student, is very worried. 'I have never had a girlfriend so felt lonely. Once while baby-sitting for my sister I went to my sister's room and dressed completely in her clothes. I wore a dress, bra, panties, suspenders, stockings, shoes and stayed like this two hours while masturbating.

'I only intended to dress like this when baby-sitting but I realised that I enjoyed the feeling of the silk and nylon of my sister's underwear against my skin very much. Since then I have worn only women's underwear. It then began to get a hold on me and I have regularly bought different items of underwear. Of a week day I wear tights and panties under my jeans. Of a weekend or night out, I wear my favourites – camisole top and French knickers.

'I know this is not right and believe me it does worry me. In fact, I am desperate to talk to someone and get advice on this problem. I live with my parents and they do not know of my secret side. I just cannot help myself. I love to wear women's clothes and enjoy it.'

Advice and support available for men and their families worried by cross-dressing is detailed in the Help Directory, but for some young men this does prove to be just a stage in their development.

Morris, 28, a soldier, explained: 'I joined the army at 15 so was subjected to heavy pornography at an early age. I found I could neither physically nor mentally cope with these new urges I was experiencing. No girl wanted to know me, naturally enough, so I sought relief in other ways.

'Masturbation was one way but I needed constantly new "highs" to assist my masturbating. This took on new forms, the most popular being to dress up in women's clothing.

'After six or nine months, when I was 16, I became distressed. I thought of having a sex-change operation – maybe I was a woman in a man's body. I was about to see the army psychiatrist when I took a chance on a captain instructor instead. When I told him my problem, he laughed. He said, "If I told you the things I do you'd probably die of fright." He assured me it was just a stage, but cautioned me not to be seen dressed this way. Sure enough, less than a year later (and since then) I never needed that form of "high" again.'

It seems more likely to be 'just a stage' when the young man has taken to wearing women's clothes after puberty, and almost to create out of himself the girlfriend he longs for. Like the young men – and women – who kiss, cuddle and made love to one another, imagining each as a partner of the opposite sex, once they can find a 'real' partner, the substitute slips away without regret.

If anything, the fact that it is a passing phase for some confuses our understanding of those for whom it is not. They resent it being talked of as something they will grow out of or can voluntarily give up, when it is an integral part of their sexual identity, not chosen and not to be relinquished at will either.

Terry, 29, a civil servant. 'Transvestism can cause problems for a man who does not understand or cannot come to terms with it. It is a feeling quite separate from that which attracts a man to a woman. It can cause acute anxiety and depression for a young man who is growing up and feels deeply ashamed of this so-called unnatural feeling. It is only when he discovers that it affects thousands of men, from effeminate hairdressers to butch lorry drivers, that he will understand that nothing can be done to suppress his feelings, in fact they get stronger as he gets older.'

It is estimated that one in ten transvestites is gay. Scott, 21, unemployed: 'I have had plenty of affairs with other men. I know teenagers go through a phase where they fancy their own sex, but this is not a phase. I feel I need a man sometimes, a strong man at that, with me being quite small. I sometimes like to act like a female, and that's why I find it rewarding to dress up in women's clothes. It makes me feel more feminine.'

A very, very small percentage of men who start by dressing as women gradually come to feel that they are not a man with a feminine part of their nature needing expression, but a woman in a man's body. These transsexuals usually have a long struggle to have their belief in their female identity accepted by others and possibly to have surgery. Pat, 53, a draughtsperson: 'It was a problem to me being biologically male, but three years ago I decided to change my gender to feminine, after many years of transvestism. I studied womanhood carefully, I have had hormones and hypnotherapy, and now consider myself almost a full woman. I will be in a few months, due to surgery. I have both men and women friends who accept me, but I am concerned about my family's attitude. I hope one day to marry, but in any case to be a wife in every way.'

The vast majority of men who enjoy cross-dressing are heterosexual and find female partners. The most common reasons they say they are not cross-dressing now, though they may have started when they were very young, is either that they have never told their partner or that she disapproves.

Lester, 37, doing scientific research work: 'I first began to fantasise about wearing women's clothes and being taken for a woman when I was about 11 or 12. I did not wear women's clothes until I was 29, living alone. Since beginning to live with my fiancée, I have not revealed this side of my nature, although I have come very close to it on occasions. I think she possibly suspects it and may be sympathetic, but I fear very much that on occasions when we are at odds she might use it as ammunition.

'What I have is a perversion, I suppose, but it does little harm to anyone except myself, and I didn't ask for it. I have kept the tendency out of sight for a long time, out of necessity, but it doesn't diminish with time. I'll have to admit it soon, I'm sure. I'm likely to have to see a psychiatrist to see if I can find a way round my difficulty. I feel as if I have a strongly female other side of my personality that I have to keep well out of sight.'

Dressing the part

Many transvestite men try to suppress their need to cross-dress when they get engaged or are first married. Murdoch, 24, an electronics engineer: 'I used to cross-dress, but now with the possibility of a permanent partner I have stopped doing this. (Being overweight and hirsute I always looked ridiculous, but loved the sexual thrill.)'

Most find cross-dressing impossible to give up entirely, and some wives find the revelation traumatic. Derrick, 56, a clerk, had 'tremendous guilt feelings' about his cross-dressing, but was unable to stop. 'Sometime after I married the compulsion returned with renewed force and I used to dress in my wife's clothes unknown to her. After three years of marriage I confessed to my wife, who did not leave me but went through what I suppose was a nervous breakdown. Despite our problems we managed to soldier on, because our feelings for one another are very strong and my wife is a most kind and caring lady. However, sexual difficulties have arisen. My wife consulted a GP and a psychiatrist who were no help. They just said, "Why don't you leave?", "I don't want to", "Well, I can't help." Finally she saw a sex therapist who said you must both compromise, which is in fact what we try to do, but my wife finds the image of me as a woman is strong.'

Barry, 43, foreman of a television repair workshop, has not told his wife he cross-dresses yet is taking tremendous risks of discovery, venturing into their town centre dressed as a woman.

'During my teens I started dressing in absurd ways in my own clothes,' he remembered, 'but I suppose I eventually exhausted all possibilities and turned to female clothes. However, this did not take the form of absurd ways of dressing. As I was now some 15 years old and had only my mother as a source of clothing, I was very restricted. After I had been married a while, my wife was working and I frequently had a day off while she was out for the day. This gave me the opportunity I had needed. I had no wig, but fully dressed as a woman at home, including make-up, and with a headscarf on ventured out for rides in a car.

'More recently, with the coming of children, I have been very restricted as to opportunities and frequently have had to rely on dressing in the car for the short journey home. I have obtained a wig and shoes, and am striving to become as female as possible in my appearance. I think I am succeeding fairly well, as twice I have ventured into the local town centre, I believe undetected.

'When away from home on work (not often) I take clothes to travel in, and a nightdress. If I had the ability to dress or live as a woman for a prolonged period, I think I would soon tire of the idea. It is the lack of opportunity which excites my need for being a transvestite. I believe my wife is quite unaware of my activities. We are very content as a married couple.'

Barry is probably mistaken in thinking that if he had more opportunity to cross-dress the urge would die down. It seems to be a characteristic of transvestites that they long to go further and further in their attempts to become transformed into a woman, if only for limited periods.

Most of those who are going as far as Barry, dressing completely as a woman and going out, have taken their partner into their confidence. Otherwise the repercussions of discovery are enormous. The rest of us may remember Mother's warning that it is the day we go out wearing grubby underwear that we will meet with an accident but Pete, 24, manager of a garage, shudders at the possibilities. 'I don't know if it is normal, but I enjoy wearing my wife's underwear – she has some very sexy underwear. I have often been tempted to go out to work or in the evening wearing them, but I am worried about having some sort of accident and being carted off to hospital with them on.

'I would like to be able to make love to my wife while wearing some of her underwear. We did do it once, but I wasn't sure of her reaction so I didn't try it again. She does know about me wearing her underwear, though, and says she doesn't mind.'

Many wives and girlfriends seem able to tolerate their partner cross-dressing, as long as they are not asked to be involved or present.

Bernard, 46, an architect: 'I confessed my problem to my wife over a period of time. After the initial disbelief her reaction was to decide that she would accept it, providing that she was not involved – in other words was out of the house – and I had assured her that I would ensure that our children would not in any way become aware of the situation.'

Some wives and girlfriends seem completely unrattled by varying degrees of cross-dressing and even to welcome it as an added stimulus to the relationship and perhaps a shared interest.

Alistair, 25, a motor mechanic: 'I occasionally enjoy putting on my wife's sexy underwear when we have sex and I think she quite likes it, too. I wouldn't enjoy wearing proper women's clothes, though, such as normal dresses and shoes.'

Dale told his girlfriend he is a transvestite after just two weeks together. 'She thought she had a problem so I told her mine to balance it out. She doesn't mind at all. When I sleep with her we both wear sexy nighties.'

Leigh's wife shares her wardrobe with him. Leigh, 38, a manager, explains: 'My wife is fully aware of my tendencies. I told her before we married. She is very understanding and helps me with clothes, make-up, wigs and so on. We talk about it openly and she doesn't appear to feel threatened by it. I "dress" on average about once every six weeks or so, and occasionally go out as a woman. I seem to be able to pass in public as I am slim and dress conservatively. My wife and I take the same size (12/14) so we often share clothes and choose them together.

'I am completely heterosexual. I don't dress to attract men. My best explanation of my reasons for doing so is that it gives me great emotional satisfaction and helps me relax in a way that nothing else can.'

Rest from the role

It is relaxation from the role of Superman, rather than sexual satisfaction, that the men who cross-dress for years mostly seem to obtain from putting on women's clothes. Bernard explained: 'My sexual appetite and performance has never been affected. Initially a degree of sexual arousal was achieved by the "dressing up", but this has now been replaced by a state of feeling comfortable and accepted when dressed as a woman, though for the majority of time I think, act and dress as a normal heterosexual male.'

Dressing as a woman lets a man 'off the hook' of the traditional masculine identity for a while. Even very small boys can feel these pressures as they, perhaps subconsciously, realise they get less kissing and cuddling from their parents than their sisters, are expected to hold back their tears and show how tough they are. Even the longing to have soft fabrics next to their skin becomes more understandable when we remember it has been found that babies who have to start life in incubators thrive better if laid on soft and cuddly lambswool, rather than a crisply folded sheet.

Jeff, 33, a labourer, 'I've always enjoyed wearing women's clothes. The earliest age I can remember doing it was at infant school. At that time I remember I liked the feel of silky materials (boys had to wear thick cotton flannels and wool in those days). During teenage years it gave me a real sexual thrill.

'On the very rare opportunities I get to indulge these days I find it gives me the most relaxing feeling possible. Like a sort of escapism. I work in a dirty, noisy, smelly, factory doing a hard dirty job. I feel I have to keep a manly front up for the kids' sake and my wife's sake, even for my own sake. As a husband and father a man has a lot of responsibilities and is under a lot of pressure and, as far as I am concerned, giving way to the feminine urges I have inside me acts like a safety valve. My wife knows but she doesn't approve.

'Incidentally, I really think I would have been a better woman than I am a man. Most of you women don't realise how lucky you are – you can have the best of both worlds. Anyway, that's my opinion.'

Many men spoke of 'release from the male hunter-gatherer stereotype, removing the demands of the male role,' seeing it as a strait-jacket of convention. Neil, 27, a civil servant: 'It allows me to escape from the macho, very conventional image that goes with being a man, and to express the more artistic/feminine side of my nature.'

Dale believed that if we could revolutionise men's attire they would not be driven to wear women's. 'We must encourage men to be more inventive and orginal. No wonder men aren't interested in fashion. Who wants to know whether a lapel is long and thin this summer, short and fat the next? If you could encourage men to think that a kilt is a man's garment, that would be a start. Skirts may not be as practical as trousers, but there is more freedom and would be great for the office and at home for men, especially in summer.'

Fashion designers have tried such innovations, but they never catch on with the majority. It is not just men who exert the pressure to conform on each other. Most women, too, have very conventional ideas of what makes a man. Women can wear almost every item of men's wear, from jeans to dress suits these days, but imagine their reaction to the man who turned up to the club dinner in a cocktail dress!

189

David, 36, a civil servant envies – and resents – women. 'Women are allowed to show both feminine and masculine sides. I feel I should have the right to express both masculine and feminine sides of myself. Clothing is an important aspect of sexual expression and provides for a development of sensuality and erotic experiences.

'As a transvestite, with a wife and child, I suffer from tension over maintaining a masculine identity on occasions. Unlike women I am not free to dress in trousers *and* skirts. My wife is understanding and occasionally makes me a skirt. I wear one approximately once a fortnight, yet I am at all other times ''manly'' and masculine. (Incidentally I enjoy cooking and helping with housework, etc., whether I am dressed as a man or a woman.) I feel a more complete person when dressing or after dressing as a woman, but suffer tension as I am aware this is not socially acceptable (as yet!)'

'I get depressed with the media's and women's continual criticisms of men in general. We are criticised when we are macho and we are criticised for being weak and gentle. We can't win. Women continually claim they are more intelligent and stronger (both mentally and physically) and never miss an opportunity to put a man down. This leaves us men confused, and causes a loss of confidence and libido.

'Surely both sexes should be looking for the good parts in each other? Women's continual criticism of men only seems to make harmony more difficult to achieve. Are women so faultless that they feel they have the right to make men so unhappy? Surely we should all be bolstering each other up to improve the self-esteem of both sexes, and to achieve equal respect and equality generally? The alternative is to increase men's fear and possibly dislike of the female sex, when we should be working towards a greater understanding and harmony.'

Lois never really accepted that when Superman hung up his cloak he reverted to fallible and near-sighted Clark Kent. Will she ever fancy him in a skirt?

13 *Want to do something about it?*

Problems and the help available

If a couple are having trouble with their car, a parent, a teenager and even with money, friends are likely to hear about it, to have chats about how to cope, a chance to offer sympathy and perhaps to come up with the answer. However, your closest friends might have a sexual problem for years and never talk about it. In fact, sexual problems are far more common than we might think.

Half of married couples (49 per cent) have had specific sexual difficulties and one in five couples (21 per cent) are troubled by them now.

In this chapter we will look not only at the problems pinpointed in our survey, but also at how to try to resolve them. They can cause great unhappiness. Brian, 43, a technical supervisor: 'I cannot interest my wife in sex or even kissing, in spite of trying everything. I wish she'd respond even by telling me to kiss off, or something. Any reaction beats none.

'My marriage works well as a partnership, there are few disagreements about most things, but there's no love shown. I've given up after five years. This problem only occurred after she became pregnant and she says it's her fault. There's no pain worse than wanting to give and no one wants what you have.

'I couldn't have an affair. I love my wife and kids so much. I didn't think one could feel such love as I feel for my kids. I suppose one has to swap one pleasure for another. My wife rarely refuses sex, but I feel as if I'm raping her. She lies there not even putting her arms round me.'

Two out of five single men (39 per cent) in sexual relationships

191

say they or their partner have experienced difficulties and 15 per cent are currently troubled.

One problem may interlock with another. If a couple would like the woman to reach orgasm during intercourse, it is going to be harder for her to do so if the man suffers from premature ejaculation. Damian, 20, a student: 'I tend to ejaculate fairly quickly after we have started having intercourse. My girlfriend becomes very excited yet has never climaxed. It doesn't seem to bother her, but she admits she is curious as to what an orgasm feels like. Many a time I wish she would have an orgasm. It may be daft, but at the back of my mind I will always feel I am not doing something quite right as well as feeling guilty that I can climax yet my girlfriend can't. I suggested my girlfriend try masturbation, but she is not keen on the idea.'

Married couples are more likely to be bitter and desperate. Usually, if an unmarried couple have a serious problem which they cannot sort out it will break up the relationship. A married couple may feel bound by children, home, loyalty, yet one or both feel frantic with frustration. Obviously, it can lead to one or both looking for satisfaction outside the marriage.

John, 28, self-employed: 'I met my wife shortly after five years in the Royal Navy during which I led a very active sex life. During four years of courtship I respected her views, so we only had intercourse three times during this period. I didn't mind the situation, as I understood her feelings and guilt about sex before marriage. I was led to assume that everything would be all right once we were married.

'This was true for the first six months, after which my wife's interest deteriorated, first with semi-polite refusals, then blatant hurtful coldness, and finally physical attacks if I so much as touched her.

'I explained to her the effect this was having on me, that for a sexually oriented person such rejection undermined my self-confidence and led to problems in other areas of my life. This fell upon deaf ears. She offered no reasons. I was still faithful up to that time but not since then.'

Couples who have loved one another deeply can be forced into anger and bitterness by the very aspect of their relationship which should be a pleasurable and satisfying expression of their affection for one another. They can see it poisoning their whole relationship, what they often cannot work out for themselves is what is poisoning their sex life.

Jack, 46, a lecturer, believed: 'If we could have talked about our problems, I probably would not have been unfaithful to my wife. However, I didn't understand her reasons and she did not appreciate my needs.'

Women are often affected by inhibitions resulting from a 'nice girls don't' attitude instilled into them during childhood; having been molested as a child; not enjoying the way their husband makes love but not liking to tell him or ask for changes; resentments about other parts of their life together which they have not managed to bring into the open; finding it hard to reconcile the roles of wife and mother with being a lover.

Men can have 'performance' worries – not lasting as long as they would like during intercourse, erection problems – which actually lead to them avoiding sex rather than risk another 'failure'. Phil 24, joiner, said, 'My hair-trigger problem really bothers me and so does my wife's lack of interest in wanting to cure or do anything about it. At one time I got really depressed because whenever we went to bed I always seemed to end up apologising.'

No one *wants* to have an unhappy sex life but because so few of us have been given any example while we were young of how to talk about sexual matters really frankly, in detail and without embarrassment or need to blame, the whole subject can become blanketed with anxiety and guilt. The couples who talk least openly to one another are most likely to have lasting sexual problems and the least likely to feel able to seek help. Harry, 43, a civil servant: 'I am very troubled by my wife's low sex drive. She can't relax and has no wish to try different things. We have not tried help. My wife is too shy, says it's all my fault anyway, and I feel that I've just got to put up with it all.'

Only two out of five of those with sexual difficulties have sought help.

Half of these saw their GP and half read books and/or magazines. Comparatively few also tried marriage guidance counselling or sex therapy.

Yet assuming that the whole relationship has not broken down entirely and that there is some willingness on both sides to try to understand one another better and bring each other comfort and pleasure, most couple's sex lives could be greatly improved. Even the anxiety that cuts so many off from communicating with each other openly and seeking help could be relieved, and so many unnecessary fears laid to rest, if they can just manage to take that first step.

How to improve your sex life

There are self-help ways for couples to improve their sex life and you might like to try this before seeking expert help. Among the basic 'tools' of a sex therapist's work are sensate focus exercises. There are usually the first steps for treating most sexual problems and even people who reckon they have a pretty good sex life often find that doing sensate focus exercises helps their loving become more sensitive, tender and deeply satisfying. Sex therapists evolved sensate focus exercises as a way of helping people get back in touch with their bodily feelings and 'the pleasure of the flesh' in the very best of senses.

They are one of the few true aphodisiacs. These exercises actually raise the levels in the blood of the hormones which make us feel sexual desire – which tend to decrease if we do not make love very often.

Stage one: If you are going to help someone else give you pleasure, then first you need to discover for yourself what gives you pleasure. Do not think you know it all. Many men and women are quite surprised to find how sexy it feels to have certain parts of their body, which they have never thought of as remotely erotic, caressed. Both partners should do this exercise separately. A pleasant place to do this is in a warm bath or bed, having made sure that you will not be disturbed, even by your partner.

Stroke yourself all over. Experiment with soft stroking or firmer massage. It is important that you do not chafe your skin, so use soap – in the bath – or cream or body lotion, so that your hands can glide smoothly. If you are tired or tense, it can be good to start by massaging the face, ears and back of the neck. If you have been standing all day, start with a firm massage of the feet and legs. Try touching all the parts of your body that you may not previously have thought of as sexually sensitive. Try using a light and a firm touch. Just see how it feels.

Stage two: Repeat the exercise this way until you feel at home with your body and able to relax enjoyably. Then you can move on to the more obviously sexual areas of your body. Women should caress their breasts, their nipples, explore the genital area. So many women were brought up to feel ashamed of what is 'down there'. Now, the first thing many sex therapists try to do when treating a couple is to help a woman get to know her own sexual parts – the vagina and particularly the clitoris, which is the little sensitive peak of tissue in front of the vagina. It is stimulation of the clitoris which causes most women to reach orgasm, and not penetration of the vagina, though this may be happening at the same time.

A woman doing this sensate focus exercise should feel that it is perfectly all right to bring herself to climax through rhythmically touching and caressing the clitoris, or area around it, in the way that feels best to her. There is absolutely nothing wrong with masturbation, and it is a positive help in getting back in touch with your own sexuality.

Men should do these first exercises in much the same way as women. Nearly all men are well aware of how to bring themselves to climax, but what men often find they need more help with is in learning how to stroke and caress gently all the less obviously sexual parts of their, and their partner's, body so they should not be tempted to skip over these stages. Practise until you can unselfconsciously touch and stroke tenderly, sensitively – lose that bull-at-a-gate feeling which can wreck love-making for women.

Stage three: After you have each spent a week getting in touch daily with your own feelings – longer if you are not comfortable by the end of a week – then you can start doing the sensate focus exercises together. Again, you should do them every day.

With your partner, choose a time when you will not be interrupted. Start it early enough so that you both have some energy left. Get the room warm; have a drink or some background music – whatever helps you to relax. Leave a soft light on so that you can see each other. Choose one of you to start – you take it in turns to lead. Using a little cream or oil, you massage and stroke one another all over. Do not be afraid to show your pleasure at what you enjoy. Say whether light stroking or firm massage feels good, and where. Keep your thoughts on how your body feels. Do not worry about looking funny, or whether your partner is getting tired – their turn will come.

The first time you do this sensate focus exercise, do not touch one another's sexual areas. Do not move on to touch these until you are both comfortable doing the exercise. *The important thing is not to hurry the stages*. Do not give up thinking: 'This is not getting me the intercourse I'm after.' In time you will begin to see – or rather, feel – the benefits. In the meantime, this massage will be deeply pleasurable if you concentrate on what is happening *now* or the good feelings *now*, rather than wondering where this is all going to lead in the future.

195

This is what the exercises are about – focussing your mind, your attention, on what your body *is* feeling rather than on the possible outcome. You should just enjoy the pleasure of the massage, rather than worry whether you are going to feel like intercourse.

Stage four: When you *both* feel ready (and you must be honest – there must be no pressure to agree before one of you is ready or the exercises will fail) then you can move on to touch the more sexually sensitive parts of one another's bodies. You can begin showing one another how to give the most pleasure by stroking and massaging the penis, the breasts, around the anus, if you enjoy that, the clitoris and vagina. Lick one another all over, if that feels good. Experiment with kissing and licking one another's sexual parts. The only rule is that you should *both* enjoy it. Though it is important to pay attention to hygiene. You should always wash between touching the anus and the vagina.

Again, talk. Tell one another what is feeling good. Being able to communicate about sex is an important part of this therapy. Just use the words that come most naturally to you. Do not feel you must use the 'proper' names. Try to concentrate on the positive – not 'That doesn't do anything for me', but, 'Do more of that wonderful thing you were doing before.'

If one of you becomes very eager to climax before the other is honestly ready for intercourse, then the other can help by caressing him or her in the right way to climax. You should feel free to show one another what feels good, what works for you. It is important that neither of you feels pressured into intercourse before you really want it.

That is something to remember for the future, too. Even if these exercises do stimulate your sexual appetite, do not feel that from then on sex must always mean intercourse, that you must always have that as the goal. As I have mentioned, many couples with differing sex drives work out a happy compromise. If there are times when one is longing for sex and the other does not feel like it, the less eager partner may well be willing to join in some massage like this, and manually bring their partner to climax, even though they do not feel like intercourse themselves. This is far better than pressurising an unwilling partner into intercourse they do not want, which is likely to make them find ways – consciously or unconsciously – of avoiding sexual contact in future.

This sort of massage and caressing is loving, comforting and gives the partner with greater sexual tension release, while not putting too much pressure on the other. However, doing these exercises will often stimulate the appetite for intercourse, as long as you give them enough time and do keep practising them. It is no good just trying them for a couple of nights. Give them at least a month.

Older couples who may find intercourse uncomfortable or impossible can get a lot of enjoyment from stroking and caressing each other like this. It may well be rather like the days when they were petting before they married. Thinking about the sensate focus exercises as 'petting' may help other couples who feel rather self-conscious about setting out solemnly to do 'homework' on their sex life. If you call it 'petting' and 'erotic massage' to yourselves, it sounds more light-hearted.

If one of you is disabled, these exercises can also bring a lot of pleasure and a new richness to your love-making. You might also be helped to extend your sex life with advice and aids via your doctor, or from specialists listed in the Help Directory.

Relaxation and massage

Sensate focus exercises are in themselves relaxing and can be a great help in relieving what is probably among the most common causes of an unnaturally low sex drive – tension and chronic anxiety. This is the sort of nagging worry – about work, tasks to be done, family responsibilities – that is always with you, preventing you from relaxing and enjoying life . . . or sex.

Circumstances are not always conducive to you and your partner sharing a session of sensate focus exercises, but you give yourselves a much better chance of sharing some good loving if you both learn how to relax. Our sexual responses have little chance of reacting if we are tired, tense and snappy.

Become conscious of your breathing. When you are getting wound up your breath starts to come in short, panicky pants. Learning how to control such physical symptoms of stress helps you feel calmer and more able to tackle whatever is upsetting you.

Aim for slow, steady breathing. When you feel tense, breathe in through your nose to a count of four, hold for a count of four and breathe out through your mouth to a count of six. Repeat six or eight times.

197

Once or twice a day, wearing loose clothes, lie down or sit in a comfortable chair, do the breathing as described above, and then work your way through your body, first clenching then relaxing each set of muscles. The point of clenching them first is that you can then feel the contrast when they are relaxed. This helps you learn to keep a mental eye on the tension levels in your own body. It is easiest to start at the toes and then work up the body to the face. These techniques are simple – but do not underestimate them.

Such exercises do actually affect body chemistry and safeguard your health as well as your sex life.

Giving one another a massage is also a wonderful way to relax together, as well as sharing some very pleasurable touching. This should not be seen as only a prelude to sex. A lot of men need to learn to share tender touching and caresses, apart from when they want sex. Many women need to learn to relax into their physical sensations, but will resist the idea of massage if they feel sexually pressured whenever it is suggested. Take it in turns to massage one another – both roles are enjoyable. As with the sensate focus exercises, enjoy what is happening at the time, to your body *now*. You can decide afterwards whether you both feel sexy – which is more likely if your whole body feels wonderfully soothed and alive.

Fully explaining how to give an all-over body massage is a book in itself – and some are listed in the Help Directory. If you want to start now you can do so very simply using baby oil. Make sure the room is very warm and you are lying on something soft but firm. A sleeping bag covered with a towel on the floor is better than a yielding mattress. Lightly massaging the face eases tension and then you can massage all over the body, using both firm and gentle strokes. The important rules are: always use firm strokes towards the heart, and avoid any direct pressure on the spine.

If it does put both of you in the mood for love, use light feathery strokes at the end to caress the breasts and nipples and brush over the genitals – until the massage merges into lovemaking. If this happens, you will almost certainly find that it is extra-pleasurable because your whole body has already enjoyed so much attention.

If you and your partner are at such loggerheads that you cannot face trying some of these techniques together, or one of you resists the idea, or they do not seem to work for you, then you need expert help. This is explained under the headings of the various specific problems.

Loss of sex drive

Husbands say that by far and away the most common problem bothering married couples is the wife's low sex drive.

More than two out of five (42 per cent) of married men with difficulties say that the problem is their wife's lack of interest in sex. (See Figure 17, page 200).

Laurence, 35, a musician: 'I love my wife very much but I cannot show it to her. I like her sexually but she thinks that's all I want her for, even though our love life is nil. If there is any help you could give to my wife I would be obliged. I have tried everything I know and it is now starting to affect my marriage.

'I would like to be a happily married Christian man, but my wife being like she is making me feel more inclined to go off with another woman (which is not a Christian thing to do). I am not bad-looking bloke and I have got plenty of tempting opportunities with some very attractive women. If you can advise anything to help my wife or help me understand I would be over the moon. I'm just a normal red-blooded male that happens to like sex very much and would prefer to have it only with my wife. Is it possible?'

It is not just that men are pressuring their wife to a level of sexual activity which she does not want. In our survey on women, wives also agreed that this is by far their most common worry.

It is not only a women's problem either. One in ten husbands (11 per cent) with sexual difficulties says the problem is *his* lack of interest in sex.

A relationship in which both partners want to have and enjoy a lot of sex is not necessarily any better than one in which neither is very keen on making love often. As long as both partners are happy with the frequency of love-making, it does not matter a jot whether it is twice a day or once a month. Especially as the years go by, some couples are quite happy to stop having intercourse, but continue to have a very successful marriage based on love, respect, companionship, tolerance.

When a couple can have a very real problem is if one wants to make love more often than the other. There are some marriages in which the couple will *never* be able neatly to 'match' their sex

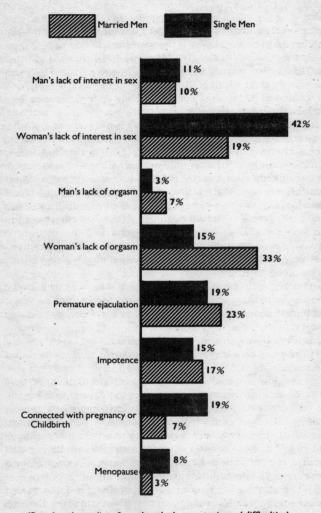

Figure 17

What are the most common sexual problems?

///// Married Men   ■■■■ Single Men

Man's lack of interest in sex — 11% / 10%

Woman's lack of interest in sex — 42% / 19%

Man's lack of orgasm — 3% / 7%

Woman's lack of orgasm — 15% / 33%

Premature ejaculation — 19% / 23%

Impotence — 15% / 17%

Connected with pregnancy or Childbirth — 19% / 7%

Menopause — 8% / 3%

(Based on the replies of couples who have experienced difficulties)

drive. We are all individuals, so it is unlikely that we should be able to. However, in a happy relationship in which both partners feel relaxed, open and confident about the sexual side of their life together, this need not cause any problems. They manage to work out a genuine compromise, understanding that the quality of the sex they share is more important than clocking up a lot of notches in the bedhead. The partner who might want intercourse every night accepts this will happen less often, while the other may make a special effort to share in loving caresses, and perhaps bring their partner to climax in other ways apart from intercourse, even though they themselves do not feel the need for sexual release.

It is when the difference in sex drive is exaggerated by other factors that it is much more likely to cause real difficulties within the relationship. In many of these cases, the partner who is said to have no interest in sex is not happy about it, either – though they may keep their anxiety hidden. They would like to show more affection, to get and give more sexual pleasure, but for a variety of reasons their sexual feelings have got locked away and they cannot find the key. Sometimes this may have happened as a result of the way they were brought up, and they will never have managed to establish a really successful and satisfying sexual relationship. Sometimes, after years of enjoying a very active and flourishing sex life, their sex drive just seems to have died away. They do not really understand why, and they do not know what to do about it, or whether anything *can* be done.

Almost anyone who feels that their sex life is not as satisfying as it might be, for whatever basic reason, will be helped by trying the sensate focus exercises explained on page 194.

If there are problems deep within the marriage, if there is a medical condition which needs investigating, or if there is a particular sexual problem apart from a general loss of interest in sex, then this will obviously need sorting out for libido to return.

First of all, a husband or wife may have lost his or her sex drive because they are unhappy about something else in the marriage. For example, a wife may actually always have enjoyed and responded enthusiastically to her husband's loving but, because she is disappointed in the way he is not making much progress in his career, finds that she loses interest in him sexually. She may not like to admit to herself that she is so bothered about worldly values, feeling she should love him for himself, and may be genuinely puzzled why she should have gone off sex.

If she can come to terms with her feelings about her husband's career, her desire for him can return.

Many wives, tired after caring for small children or being at work all day, feel resentful when their husband comes home and puts his feet up for the entire evening while she cleans, cooks, puts the children to bed, washes up, all completely unaided. By the time they go to bed, she feels that he is so selfish and has so little real consideration for her that she does not have the slightest desire to make love to him – and may genuinely be too tired. If she could learn how to ask effectively for more help, she might find her sex drive miraculously revive.

If one of you seems to have lost your sex drive, do both think hard about whether you have any hidden worries or resentments you have not liked to talk about. Try to talk over your deepest feelings, hopes and fears about the state of your marriage with one another. If you seem to run up against problems, make an appointment with your local Marriage Guidance Council (details in the Help Directory).

Many Marriage Guidance Councils have special clinics for treating sexual problems and in the Help Directory I have listed other sources of sex therapy.

Medical Problems

Some GPs are very helpful with sexual difficulties and underlying the loss of sex drive of both men and women can be a medical problem, which they should certainly take to their doctor.

Many women find they lose interest in sex when they have a baby.

One in five husbands (19 per cent) said that their difficulties had been connected with pregnancy and/or childbirth.

Nathan, 33, said, 'Our only problems have occurred during pregnancy. My wife couldn't even stand me putting my arms around her. Any kind of physical contact was repulsive to her. She was very upset.'

Sometimes it is not pregnancy or childbirth itself which has caused the problems, but the extra stress has brought a long-standing problem to light which needs discussing honestly. However, pregnancy does involve massive changes in hormone levels which affect different women in different ways. A slight hormone imbalance after childbirth can be aggravated by

202

discomfort from stitches, tiredness and post-natal depression. Not making love for a while can lead to a dropping in the levels of the hormones which make us feel sexually responsive, so it seems hard to get back to making love again. All that may be needed on the husband's part is patience, and literally staying in touch with kissing, cuddling, and sensate focus and massage, even if they do not have intercourse. However, the woman should check with her doctor in case any symptom does need treatment.

While some women feel more sexy during pregnancy, others go right off it, and the same applies during the menopause. Some women find that the change in hormone levels at the menopause makes them more eager for sex, others seem to lose their sex drive. These women should consult their doctor in case their hormone imbalance is such that they need treatment. The menopause is also often accompanied by some lessening of lubrication in the vagina and thinning of the vaginal walls, which can make sex uncomfortable for a woman and so turn her off the idea. This will not stop sensate focus exercises giving her and her partner a great deal of pleasure and helping to restore her interest. KY Jelly or Senselle from chemists help lubrication – assuming, of course, that there has been lots of loving foreplay to maximise natural lubrication first.

Some women suffer from extreme mood swings connected with their menstrual cycle which can also affect their sex life. Tim, 34, a work study officer, explained: 'My wife feels in the mood for sex at particular times of the month according to what stage she is at in her menstrual cycle. For a few days, usually towards the end and immediately after her period, she is extremely randy and enjoys our making love immensely. At other times of the month she is less interested and our love-making is not as intense. At these times she enjoys kissing and cuddling and a longer time spent making love before we have intercourse.'

An understanding husband like Tim helps a lot but if the mood swings are troublesome, her GP may suggest treatment.

The Family Planning Association can advise where a woman can get specialist help with the premenstrual syndrome and particular problems following the menopause or a hysterectomy which their doctor has not been able to solve. While a woman's hormone balance will be seriously affected if she has the type of hysterectomy (removal of the uterus) which includes removal of the ovaries, these days the lost hormones which this involves can be replaced in pill form, and the woman should be able to regain her old responses in time.

Illnesses which you might not expect to affect sex drive can cause loss of libido, because they cause a change in hormone levels. These include diabetes, various forms of anaemia, and long-term depression. Drugs prescribed for some conditions, such as heart complaints, high blood pressure, and depression, can cause a loss of sex drive as can the conditions themselves.

Ray, 38, a radiographic assistant: 'I have been taking anti-depressant tablets for five years as a result of depression which completely put me off sex for a long time. My wife tried to encourage me but I always refused.'

If you are suffering from any problem try the sensate focus exercises described, but also tell your doctor about the effect your illness or treatment prescribed is having on your sex life, since he may be able to help. Depression, of course, can be very difficult to clear up. You may need not only the doctor's help but also that of a skilled counsellor, and your local Marriage Guidance Council, referred to earlier, will be able to help you here.

Drinking too much alcohol lessens sexual responsiveness. Three pints of beer or six single measures of spirits or glasses of wine are as much as a man's body can cope with healthily in a day, much less than that for women. If you are regularly drinking more than that, then this may be one cause of your difficulties.

It has now been realised that smoking is an important cause of loss of sex drive in men and women. Smoking and unhealthy diet both can cause circulation problems, which affect the blood supply to the sexual areas. The first thing many top specialists now recommend to people with sexual problems, especially if they are 40 or more, is to stop smoking and to follow a healthy high-fibre, low-fat diet. Changing your habits can transform your sex life – for the better.

Being overweight often lowers sex drive. Partly this can be because you feel too sluggish if you feel too fat, and you do not feel desirable.

Ray was one of several husbands who complained about his wife putting on a lot of weight. 'Because I wouldn't make love to my wife this made her think that I didn't love her any more so she took to eating for comfort. Now that I am feeling better, she is quite fat through compulsive eating habits, and I refuse to have sex with her until she has tried to lose weight. She thinks I am being unfair, but she has tried hard to lose weight (although it has not been very successful).

'Although I would never consider an extra-marital affair, I cannot bring myself to have full sex with her. We usually kiss and cuddle a lot, but we are both dissatisfied with the sexual side of our marriage. Her argument is that lots of people are fat but that shouldn't make any difference, if you really love someone. They are still the same people deep down.'

Marked changes in body weight can affect hormone levels, and this can apply whether you put on a lot of weight or suddenly lose it. Talk to the doctor about how to achieve a steady, healthy, weightloss – if he agrees that the weight is excessive, and it is not that the husband expects his wife to live up to unnatural standards of thinness based on models and pin-ups. Has *he* looked in the mirror lately?

People who have problems with their eating habits usually need plenty of reassurance that they are loved and lovable. Food is often a substitute for affection or a cover for a deeper problem. If that is the case, talking to a marriage guidance counsellor will help pinpoint the root of the problem – and how the partner may be contributing to it.

Female orgasm

One in three (33 per cent) of single men with sexual difficulties said the problem is their partner's lack of orgasm.

William, 19, a student: 'My girlfriend has never experienced orgasm during intercourse. Although she has assured me that she hasn't with any of her other lovers it has left me feeling inadequate.'

As long as no one is being hurt or pressured into things they do not enjoy, there are no rules for good sex. It is not compulsory to have an orgasm. If a woman is left feeling satisfied, neither she nor her partner should feel that they have in any way failed because she has not experienced 'orgasm'. Sex is for *your* pleasure, not to pass some test or keep up with the Joneses. If you are happy, that is what matters.

You can get the impression that for a woman to experience orgasm, to climax, is a bit like a cash register being rung up. Bells ring, the right numbers flash up, and it is the same every time. In fact, the experience can vary so widely, both from woman to woman, and for one woman at different times, that some women do not realise that the gentle feeling of satisfaction that they may reach during intercourse goes by the same name as the peaks of wild ecstasy they have heard about.

During a course on sexuality for doctors and other advisers I attended, we were shown a film of a woman experiencing orgasm. Afterwards one commented that the woman overacted terribly, another that she underacted the experience of climaxing. The woman was not acting at all. She was really experiencing an orgasm – her orgasm. One knew it as much more extreme than the girl on the film, the other as much quieter.

Neither one is better than the other. What matters is that *you* enjoy *your* sex life and that you are left feeling satisfied. For a woman to hanker after an explosive climax when her orgasm is peaceful and brings a feeling of quiet content, and to let this become a problem, is as sensible as spending her life worrying because her hair is straight rather than curly. If a woman is satisfied after one orgasm, and feel no wish to seek more, it is silly to become unhappy because she does not experience multiple orgasms. Her one might be more satisfying than the many experienced by others. You are how you are, so enjoy yourself as you are.

Many women, however, while they enjoy intercourse with their partner, never manage to climax, never have an orgasm, and are left feeling dissatisfied as a result. They may get very excited during foreplay and intercourse, but they cannot peak, they cannot let go. Their partner may go on to have his orgasm, ejaculate, lose his erection and intercourse may end, but the woman is left feeling worked up, sexually excited and longing for the release of the tension. This can be very upsetting for her, and also for her partner, who can feel that he is failing to satisfy her. She may feel she is failing as a woman, and he feels he is failing as a man.

Women's problems over orgasm vary. Some women have never experienced an orgasm at all. This is usually because they were brought up to think of sex as something not quite nice or even positively dirty. Girls should not show they enjoy it, they are told. They learn from very small children that they should not touch themselves 'down there'. Parents, worried about daughters getting pregnant, keep impressing on them that they must not get carried away. It is small wonder that when they

206

have a partner, they cannot suddenly undo all those lessons to their subconscious. Their thinking mind may say to them, 'Women can enjoy sex. It would be good to let go and have an orgasm', but deep down their subconscious is saying, 'Keep control. Do not let on how good this feels. Who knows what terrible things might happen if you let go?'

Before a woman who has never experienced an orgasm can help her partner to stimulate her to climax, she has to learn for herself what pleases her. She has to learn that sex is a positive pleasure, and there is nothing wrong with enjoying it, even when she is alone. Having given herself permission to enjoy her sexuality, she has to find out what turns her on, and then show her partner. The sensate focus exercises explained on page 194 should be followed and extra care taken not to rush the stages.

Some women find a vibrator helps them achieve orgasms when all other ways have failed, and this can be incorporated as part of love-making. If they find it difficult to get into the mood, fantasies of whatever seems most sexually exciting are helpful and nothing to feel guilty about.

Many women can climax when masturbating or when stimulated in some way by their partner, but cannot reach orgasm during the intercourse – only a minority do, in fact.

However, it really does not matter how or when they reach their climax, as long as they enjoy it. They should not worry about reaching their climaxes at the same moment as the man. The old myth that a woman could become pregnant only if she reached orgasm is absolute baloney, and many couples have perfectly happy ways of making love which involve the man stroking or licking the clitoris until the woman climaxes, either before or after intercourse. If a couple feel that they very much would like the woman to climax while the man is inside her – some women find this more satisfying, and the man can feel the waves of contractions of the vaginal wall, which can give him extra pleasure – they may find that a change in the position in which they have intercourse will help.

The vagina has comparatively few nerve endings, and the clitoris has many. The man can make sure his thrusting movements press on the clitoris – she will be able to help guide him as to how and where it feels best. Or he can enter her from an angle which leaves him free to caress her clitoris at the same time as having intercourse – from behind for example. Some women find this position gives increased stimulation in the vagina, too.

The woman can caress her own clitoris during intercourse, if that heightens the pleasure. It often helps if the woman takes the upper position during intercourse, so that she is freer to move into the most stimulating position – and, of course, the man has his hands free.

Improving the tone of the pelvic muscles which surround the vagina can increase pleasure and sensation during intercourse. A woman can work on this herself, if she imagines she has a string looped round the vagina and running up through the top of her head. If she mentally pulls upwards on this string, she will feel the muscles round the vagina tightening – but she should try not to tense the muscles around the back passage at the same time. Hold and repeat as often as possible.

It is important for the man to be sure that his partner is really ready for intercourse before he attempts to enter her. Women lubricate, and the vagina feels moist, at a very early stage of sexual arousal, and it does not necessarily mean that they are ready for intercourse. Also some men do not realise that, unlike men, it is important to keep stimulating a woman right up to and during orgasm, and any break or change in rhythm immediately beforehand will prevent her climax.

As long as a couple feel free to experiment with what feels good to them, then they have a good chance of discovering how the woman can reach orgasm – fairly frequently, if not every time. However, there will be some couples who try the exercises and experiment with different positions and techniques, and still find that the woman cannot climax. If this is true of you, then seek expert help. She should have a check-up with her doctor, explaining why she is worried. GPs are not always the best people at solving sexual difficulties, but they certainly are not shocked by anything you tell them. Depression, for example, can severely damp down sexual feeling, and the doctor could help you cope with this. Family planning clinic doctors are often very helpful over sexual difficulties. The pill can be associated with orgasm problems.

If the doctor is not very helpful or well informed ask to be referred for specialist help, and see the Help Directory. Do explore the possibilities with those who can help.

It could be that anxiety about sex, or some problem in your relationship with your partner, is buried deep, and unaided she cannot stop it getting in the way. The best way to find out what is really bothering you and how to cope with it, is to go for Marriage Guidance Counselling.

Alan, 27, an electrical contractor, did not know for years of marriage that his wife was faking orgasm, which she could not reach during intercourse as a result of being abused by her brother. 'Since we've been married – six years – my wife has climaxed just once during intercourse, though she always orgasms through oral sex. She used to fake orgasm but didn't tell me until a year ago. It turned out she was sexually abused as a child, and once after we were married, by her older brother. Now everything is out in the open and we're much happier and trying to start again.'

Premature ejaculation

Nearly one in four single men (23 per cent) with difficulties is bothered by premature ejaculation, as is one in five (19 per cent) of married men.

Chris, 36, a TV repair engineer: 'I always climaxed too quickly as a teenager. I could ejaculate from petting even without masturbation, I am not now as bad as I was, but I would dearly love to have more control over the timing of my climax.'

It is a problem which obviously makes it harder for the woman to reach orgasm during intercourse, if this is something they both want. Premature ejaculation in its turn is aggravated by infrequent love-making.

Eric, 25, a research officer: 'My girlfriend started to lose interest in sex after we had been going out together for about a year. I was demanding sex when she was not interested. This came to a head when I was unemployed and fairly depressed. I was trying to use sex as a sort of therapy. We made love less and less and my premature ejaculation got worse and worse. Happily we thrashed it all out over a couple of weeks, now I'm employed again and we are enjoying a happy sex life.'

There is no rule about how long a time a man should be able to carry on making love, but if the man climaxes before he has even entered his partner or very soon afterwards, and the couple are distressed by it and do not know how to cope, then the man can be said to be suffering from premature ejaculation.

It is very common, especially among young men. Making love is so new and exciting for them. Young people tend to have sex in a rather hurried, anxious way, and men can develop a habit of climaxing quickly. This can then be difficult to unlearn once they have a more settled sex life with a regular partner with whom they want to share richer love-making. They are stuck with 'Wham, bam, thank you, ma'am'. Time alone often cures the problem. But sometimes the very natural experiences of the early days set up a chain reaction that makes premature ejaculation a long-term difficulty. The man feels a failure and fears it will happen again. He steers clear of sex until his feelings get too strong for him and then, of course, the same thing does happen again.

A man suffering from premature ejaculation is obviously not going to be helped by rushed sex with a casual partner. He needs to be able to feel relaxed. He needs a woman he feels close to, can trust to go on loving him in spite of the problem, and who is prepared to do all she can to help. With a loving partner there are many helpful approaches to try, though a man who has no regular partner can still do quite a lot alone to begin to learn to control his ejaculation.

If, when you are making love, you find you climax before you want to, the first essential is that you and your partner feel able to talk about it rather than try in an embarrassed silence to pretend that nothing is wrong. Discuss it, even laugh about it, and then try making love again. If she is unsure, a man can show his partner how to caress him, how to fondle his penis, so that he can manage another erection very soon after he has ejaculated. The second time around he will almost certainly find that it takes him longer to climax.

Repeating this pattern of love-making often enough can end the difficulty. It may take some time, but with frequent intercourse the problem will resolve itself, and the man will eventually be able to control his orgasm for a long enough time to give himself and his partner satisfaction. However, it is important to remember that *many* women find that intercourse is not what leads to climax for them. If the man can maintain intercourse for several minutes, but this does not result in orgasm for his partner, they should probably be exploring other ways.

Two crucial factors in solving most sexual problems, including premature ejaculation, are reducing tension and becoming more comfortable with your body's sexual responsiveness. Follow the relaxation and sensate focus exercises explained in How To Improve Your Sex Life (page 194).

When you want to, masturbate to orgasm. As you masturbate, pay close attention to the feelings in and around your penis. Concentrate particularly on the feeling leading up to the point of no return before climax. When you feel that moment approaching, stop stroking your very sensitive areas, but do not stop caressing yourself in less sensitive spots. When you feel it is safe, resume stroking the penis. Vary fast and slow strokes, firm and gentle. In time, you should be able to work up to lasting around 15 minutes, but do not worry if you make a few mistakes and misjudge it while you are learning about your reactions. Gradually you will learn to control your ejaculation.

The process is greatly helped if you get into the habit of deep, regular breathing, and make sure you keep that up whenever you near the point of no return.

You should aim to repeat these exercises in self-touching and masturbation at least three times a week for an hour. You can share them with your partner. Once you have each learned your own reactions, you can take it in turns to caress and explore one another's bodies.

When you move on to intercourse with a partner, you can again apply the stop-start technique you have learnt during masturbation. If you feel yourself approaching that point of no return, you should both stop moving until the urge to ejaculate subsides. With a regular partner, you can work out a signal, but in any case it is easy to say 'hold it a minute', or just hold the woman's hips tightly for a minute. Most men find it best to stop in the vagina by pressing in as far as they can. Do let your partner know why you may want to stop moving for a few seconds every now and then. Secrecy just adds to tensions – and adds to your problem. While you may stop movement in the pelvic area, do not forget all those other pleasurable caresses you have learnt during the sensate focus exercises, and continue to stroke and pleasure other parts of the body. Many women find the variety a great bonus during love-making.

An exercise which may help more serious cases of premature ejaculation not solved by the measures I have mentioned so far is this one evolved by the American researchers Masters and Johnson. It has helped many couples.

It may seem a very clinical approach to those used to thinking of sex as something secret yet magical – close your eyes, hold your breath and wait for the bells to ring! Well, it can take an effort to start with – but isn't that worthwhile if your love life stands a good chance of dramatic improvement? And though it looks cold typed out on a sheet of paper, that does not mean you cannot have the lights turned down low and soft music playing.

First, the couple have to resolve not to have intercourse at all until the man has been able to develop control. No protests! The ban on intercourse is a very important aspect of the treatment, but there is going to be lots of kissing, cuddling and caressing.

The couple sit undressed against a backrest – the bedhead or wall behind the bed. The woman sits behind with her legs spread wide apart. The man sits between her legs, with his back to her and his legs parallel to hers. She reaches round the man and takes hold of his penis, with her index finger and middle finger just above and below the ridge where the 'cap' on the top of the penis meets the shaft. She rubs gently, arousing him to the point where he feels that he is about to ejaculate. He must tell her or signal, and then she squeezes the head and shaft of the penis really tightly for about six seconds. She should not worry or be too afraid of hurting the penis, which can take quite firm handling when erect. Once she has got the timing right – which will take some practice – then the man will not ejaculate and will lose some of his erection.

With short pauses in between, she should carry on stimulating and squeezing him in this way several times, for a thirty-five or forty-minute period. As long as she squeezes firmly, preventing him from ejaculating and making him lose some of his erection each time, he will find that the time he can last before climaxing is gradually but markedly increased.

Of course, his partner may get very frustrated in the meantime, but he can relieve this by caressing her to orgasm. She should be able to show or tell him what feels best.

After about three weeks of daily practice of this technique the man should find that he can control his ejaculation during this type of stimulation. Now the couple can try intercourse.

At first it is best if the man lies on his back with a pillow under his head and the woman straddles him. After several minutes of the stimulation and squeeze technique the woman should gently insert his penis into her vagina and then the couple should lie absolutely still together, making no movement. If he feels he is losing control then he should tell his partner in time for her to lift away from him and use the squeeze technique again quickly. When he feels stable again, they can gently resume intercourse. Gradually, the man should find that he can extend the time he can last before ejaculation and increase the movement until his partner may also be ready to climax.

If trying these techniques for a few months does not clear up

212

the problem, then you should seek professional help as previously explained.

You may also need to seek expert help if your partner does not feel able to help you with the techniques described. Inhibitions, or other tensions between you which may be nothing directly to do with sex, can make a woman unwilling to take part in touching exercises or to use the squeeze technique. If that is the case, then I do stress that you will both need to seek help if the problem is to be cured. Your local Marriage Guidance Council would probably be the best place to start. You can go alone in the first instance if necessary.

Erection problems

One in six men with sexual problems says he has had difficulty getting or maintaining an erection.

Gil, 36, unemployed: 'I think the reason was guilt although it was largely subconscious guilt. Of course, once I had failed the problem multiplied as I worried about failing again. My lover was wonderful and understanding over this period, but despite this I felt an utter and abject failure. It was a very unhappy and desperate time for me.'

Often, the first reaction of a man who one day finds that he cannot get or maintain a firm erection is panic. He thinks it is going to be a permanent condition – like losing a hand in an accident – rather than a passing phase, like tiredness or anxiety. However, in the overwhelming majority of cases, the *cause* of erection problems is psychological rather than physical – one of the mind and emotions, rather than the body. If a man experiences erection difficulties lasting longer than, say, three months he should certainly seek medical advice. The understanding of the physical factors which can be linked with impotence has dramatically increased with modern methods of surgery and research. However, for most men who have experienced an erection problem when making love, self-help should be enough to resolve the problem. It is often *worry* following an illness rather than the illness itself which causes erection failure. It may be due to tiredness, work problems, money worries, anxiety about performance after a long period during which the man has not had intercourse, or he may be particularly worried about pleasing his partner. Often it can be simply cleared up as long as the man does *not* panic.

Worrying about whether he is going to be able to achieve and maintain a firm enough erection for intercourse is precisely the way to make sure he does not. With each failure, the worry builds up, until a couple may stop even attempting to kiss and caress, in case it is seen as an opening to another sexual failure.

The first important step is for the man to *talk* about his worry. If a husband does not tell his wife why he is not making love to her as he used to, she may get the impression that he no longer loves her, does not desire her, is having an affair. All manner of dreadful ideas come to her mind as she stews around wondering what is wrong. That can make her bitter, and the whole relationship can be wrecked through mutual misunderstanding.

There is no shame in not being able to keep an erection. It happens at some time to most men. A loving woman is going to be very sympathetic if only she knows what the problem is, and the man will feel much better for having shared his worry. That said, it is important that they do not end up panicking together. Many cases of impotence are simply cleared up by the couple agreeing that they will not try to have intercourse for a while. That absolutely does not mean that they have to give up making love – kissing, cuddling, caressing, doing absolutely everything loving they feel like doing, except attempting intercourse itself. After a few days, or weeks, they find that one time they have intercourse easily just because they were not thinking of it.

If they find it difficult to alter their patterns of love-making they can try sensate focus exercises on page 194.

When they, together, move on to the sexual areas, the man may well be able to achieve an erection. Have the confidence to let it die down again. If the woman gets very excited caressing her man to erection, he can bring her to climax with caresses of fingers or tongue. Only after giving one another a lot of pleasure for some time, and when erections are coming easily and frequently, should a couple attempt to move on to intercourse.

Using all you have learnt about how to please one another, bring yourselves to the point where the woman is fully aroused and the man erect. This is the first time you are going to attempt penetration, *but* the man is going to leave the responsibility for intercourse to the woman. She takes the upper position, she places the penis in her vagina, she begins the movements. If his penis goes softer, then she knows how to caress it back to firmness. Gradually, the man can begin to move with her.

If you are a man without a regular partner you may wonder

how you can help yourself in this predicament. It is very common for a man to end up avoiding sex, even when the opportunity arises, for fear of experiencing failure. The answer is to concentrate on Stage One of the sensate focus exercises – in other words, enjoy as much masturbation as you feel like. Do not force yourself to masturbate to a timetable, because you think you *ought* to try it frequently. Just follow your fancy. As well as masturbating directly to climax, sometimes prolong the experience. Try allowing your erection to subside and then build up again. Gain confidence in the fact that your erection can disappear and then return. When you do meet a partner with whom sex seems likely, confide in her. Most women will be very sympathetic about this problem as long as you explain, and there is plenty of sexual pleasure to be discovered by an affectionate couple without needing a rock-hard erection.

Although most cases of temporary impotence are psychologically based, it is increasingly being realised that keeping the body in reasonably good working order helps keep us ticking over well sexually, too. Alcohol causes the notorious brewer's droop, but also can increase a tendency towards impotence. It is now estimated that one in ten men who smoke will suffer from impotence. Specialists now recommend that men suffering from impotence, particularly if they are 40 or more, stop smoking, follow a healthy, high-fibre, low-fat diet and take regular exercise.

It can happen that, in spite of taking the emphasis off intercourse, and in spite of lots of loving and caressing, a man still cannot maintain an erection. If this continues for three months or more, then he should see his GP. One group of illnesses, affecting nerve tissue, such as in some (not all) cases of diabetes, can permanently damage the nerves involved in causing erection – though this need not always prevent orgasm. Circulation problems, some drugs, such as diuretics and those used to treat blood pressure problems, can make a firm erection difficult. Pain and infections can obviously damp down the sex drive. Depression, and some of the drugs used for treating it, can be linked with sexual problems. Even if he cannot achieve an erection, the loving and sensate focus exercises described should bring a man worried about impotence, and his partner, much pleasure.

If the GP seems at a loss, do ask for referral for specialist help. There have been considerable developments in the treatment of impotence over the last few years, but they are usually only available through specialist clinics.

Delayed ejaculation

Some men are able to get and maintain a firm erection, but suffer from what some sex experts regard as a variation on impotence – they can ejaculate while masturbating but cannot climax during intercourse. Iain, 54, a clerk: 'When beginning a sexual involvement with both my second and third wives, I found it difficult to reach an orgasm for some weeks, possibly because I was too anxious to please.'

There can be a variety of reasons for this problem. Tensions or anxiety may be blocking their sexual responsiveness. In this case the sensate focus exercises as described should help.

It may be that they simply cannot 'let go' enough with this partner – or any woman – to reach their climax. It may be that they have a deep down feeling that sex is dirty, and if they love their partner they should not 'soil' her. As with problems over getting an erection, it helps enormously simply to talk about your worry with your partner. Start with the sensate focus exercises mentioned above. Assuming that you can climax through masturbation, let the sensate focus exercises gradually lead into your partner – or you and your partner – masturbating you, on each occasion bringing the penis closer and closer to the entrance of the vagina at the time of climax. After some time, you should be climaxing in the entrance of the vagina, and it should not be too difficult to manage to climax an inch or so inside next time, and the barrier will be broken.

If this practical approach does not help, then you will need to talk through your feelings with a counsellor or sex therapist, who may be able to help you discover the cause, and so start to clear up the problem. Certainly a man who cannot climax at all, even when masturbating, may well have a severe psychological barrier or medical problem, and should get expert help immediately.

Older men need not despair if they have problems. Like other parts of the body as you get on in years, an erection may need more care and encouragement as you get older, but generally there is no reason why an older man should expect to become permanently impotent. Often it is the worry that the passing years or an illness will mean impotence that causes the erection failure, rather than any physical problem or deeper psychological anxiety. Concentrating on giving and receiving loving pleasure apart from intercourse for a while, as explained in the section on How To Improve Your Sex Life, should help.

It is natural that an older man should find his erection not as hard as when he was young, nor so frequent, that he takes longer to climax, may find that he does not always reach orgasm when having sex, nor feel the need to. The important thing is to concentrate on enjoying what you have got, rather than on missing what you have not. An older couple can give one another a lot of physical pleasure even if intercourse is less frequent, or does not lead to climax.

Sexual infections

One in ten men (11 per cent) has suffered from a sexually transmitted disease or infection.

The highest rates (16 and 15 per cent) were among men in their late twenties and thirties, compared with only 7 per cent of men in their fifties.

By far the most common were non-specific urethritis, a diagnosis which can cover a multitude of infections, and thrush, which is not strictly speaking a sexually transmitted disease at all, followed by gonorrhoea, which can be very dangerous if left untreated.

The list shows how common are the various problems among those who have suffered from an infection.

Non-specific urethritis	33%
Thrush	28%
Gonorrhoea	19%
Pubic lice	11%
Herpes	6%
Genital warts	5%
Others	4%
Syphilis	1%

Urethritis is the inflammation of the tube running from the bladder to the tip of the penis, and 'non-specific' means the germ causing the infection has not been discovered by laboratory tests. It is usually spread by sexual intercourse but it is possible for a man to suffer from NSU even though he and his partner have intercourse only with each other. Some get NSU many times and then it is especially important for their partner to be checked as well and treated if necessary.

Thrush is an irritation (literally) rather than a danger. It usually arises because of a disturbance in the balance of the woman's vagina, due to pregnancy, illness, taking antibiotics, stress, tiredness and so on. She then passes it on to her partner, who may in turn reinfect her.

It is easier for men to clear this problem up than women, though it is always best to get treatment from the doctor for both partners. To guard against this and other infections, men should always roll back the foreskin and wash their penis thoroughly at least once a day and before making love.

Gonorrhoea can cause serious problems to both men and women if left untreated, but this happens more frequently in women because up to half of women with the disease experience no symptoms, so may not know they have it unless informed by their partner. It can leave them infertile if not treated quickly enough.

Anyone experiencing any worrying symptoms should always go immediately to their GP or – and probably even better – to their local clinic for genito-urinary infections or 'special clinic'. They will get the most expert and confidential help there, and it does not even go on your medical record.

Apart from hygiene, men can, of cause, guard against both catching and transmitting sexual infections and cervical cancer by wearing a sheath. You may feel it lessens sensation a little, but that is probably preferable to catching or passing on a disease.

Of course, the really sure way to guard against catching infections is to stay celibate – not a very acceptable solution to most – or to limit your sexual contacts, at best to one faithful partner.

The fear of catching or transmitting AIDS has led gay and bisexual men actively to restrict their relationships.

Jonathan, 32, in catering: 'My best friend died from AIDS, I helped nurse him through his illness and gave him my support when many of his friends were deserting him. We were not lovers, just friends. It upset me to see him dying. It affected me badly. I used to have casual sex at least once or twice a week. I have now stopped this as I feel I owe it to my partner to be faithful. AIDS is very frightening and I would certainly do anything I could to avoid contacting it.'

Of the bisexual men who took part in our survey only one in four said he was not bothered by the reports about AIDS.

The rest were either already staying faithful to their partner or had decided as a result to restrict their relationships.

Ken, 40, a sub-postmaster: 'My wife did not know and still does not know the degree of male sex which took place. Up to the AIDS scare I continued with my bisexual life, meeting casually for sex or after contact in my car or his house/flat. (I still had and have normal sex with my wife three times a week.) I stopped a year ago and have no intention of repeating it. I know this will be difficult but (if I have not already got AIDS) there is no way I will expose my wife to this danger.'

AIDS can take years to develop and it should not be regarded as a risk only to gay men and their partners. It is feared it will spread into the heterosexual population and everyone should be aware of the risks, how you can catch AIDS and how to guard against it.

Since there has been so much panic, it is important to stress that normal everyday contact with an infected person is perfectly safe. The virus has not been passed on through touching or shaking hands, or through saliva or tears. You cannot catch the virus by touching objects used by an infected person, such as cups, cutlery, glasses, food, clothes, towels, toilet seats and door knobs. Swimming pools are also safe. The virus itself is not very strong. It does not survive for long in the open and it cannot withstand heat or household bleach.

You should avoid sharing any device that punctures the skin, unless it has been properly sterilised. This includes hypodermic needles, syringes, ear-piercing equipment, tattooing and acupuncture needles (needles or syringes used by medical staff are completely sterilised every time).

The Health Education Council's advice is that, to reduce the risk of AIDS, the fewer sexual partners you have, the less risk you have of coming into contact with someone who has the virus. The fewer partners your partner has, the less risk of you getting the virus.

Though you will only catch the virus if you have sex with an infected partner, if you are unsure of your partner, some ways of having sex are much more risky than others. Anal intercourse is particularly dangerous. This may be because the walls of the rectum are much more delicate and more likely to tear than those of the vagina, making it easier for the virus to pass from one person to another. Vaginal intercourse is also risky. Oral sex carries some risk because there is always a chance that the virus could pass from the man's semen into the other person's body. Any practice that breaks the skin or draws blood, either inside the vagina or anus or on the skin, could increase the risk of getting the virus. Sharing sex toys, such as vibrators, could be risky as they can carry the infection from one person to another.

Using a sheath during sex will reduce the risk of getting the virus and other sexually transmitted diseases, too. If you use a lubricant with the sheath make sure the lubricant is water-based rather than oil-based. Oil-based ones tend to weaken the rubber. Researchers are currently investigating whether some spermicides kill the AIDS virus but they are no safe substitute for a sheath properly used.

The good news is there is no risk involved in masturbation or in partners caressing each other.

The Help Directory lists sources of more advice and books for those worried about AIDS and any other problems.

Help Directory

W hen writing to any of the organisations listed, please remember to enclose a stamped addressed envelope. Many, particularly those which are charitably funded, are often short of funds as well as of helpers. Some organisations and practitioners have to charge for their help, so always check about fees before making any appointments or arrangements.

Great Britain

I am sorry that, because of lack of space, I have rarely been able to give contact addresses for Scotland, Wales, Northern Ireland and Eire. Usually, however, the head office given here will be able to refer you where necessary. Books mentioned on pages 238 to 240 can be ordered from good bookshops if not in stock. If it is hard for you to reach a bookshop you could phone your nearest and see if they will supply you by mail order. The Family Planning Association and National Marriage Guidance Council both supply advice books by mail order.

Your GP can refer you for specialist help with relationship and sexual problems to a psychotherapist, or clinic for psycho-sexual problems, and with problems connected with fertility, to a fertility clinic.

Family Planning Information Service. A very comprehensive source of further information and advice, not only about family planning but also about sexual and related health problems. They can often refer you to your nearest source of specialised help – psycho-sexual and fertility clinics, for example. You can write or phone, and at the same address the Family Planning Association Book Centre runs a mail order service supplying a wide range of guidance books. They will send you their booklist but will also supply other books on request. Family Planning Association, 27/35 Mortimer Street, London W1N 7RJ (01-636-7866).

National Marriage Guidance Council can give you details of your nearest MGC if you want counselling for any relationship problem. Some MGCs provide specialist sex therapy. They help people of all ages, single as well as couples – and couples don't have to be married. Fees if any are modest. You may have to wait a few weeks for an appointment but don't let this put you off. Most couples have lived with their problems for years before seeking help and can manage to last another few weeks, and once your appointment is made at least you know you have taken a positive step towards improvement. The NMGC bookshop will supply books on relationships and sexuality on their mail order list and supply special requests in this field. National Marriage Guidance Council, Little Church Street, Rugby, CV21 3AP (0788 73241).

Scottish Marriage Guidance Council, 26 Frederick Street, Edinburgh EH2 2JR (031-225-5006).

Northern Ireland Marriage Guidance Council, 76 Dublin Road, Belfast BT2 7HP (Belfast 323454).

Catholic Marriage Advisory Council, 15 Lansdowne Road, London W11 3AJ (01-727-0141). Counselling, education for relationships and natural family planning advice.

Jewish Marriage Council, 23 Ravenshurst Avenue, London NW4 (01-203-6311).

British Association for Counselling, 37a Sheep Street, Rugby, CV21 3BX (0788 78328), can put you in touch with a counsellor near you if you feel strongly that a MGC counsellor would not be suitable.

Brook Advisory Centres for Young People, 153A East Street, London SE17 2SD (01-708-1234), specialise in helping the under-25s in confidence on all problems connected with sex and relationships, including contraception and pregnancy. Head office will put you in touch with your nearest branch.

National Association of Young People's Counselling and Advisory Services, 17–23 Albion Street, Leicester LE1 6GD (0533-554775), also specialise in helping the under-25s by acting as a referral service. They will find you help to work through any relationship problems, including those with your parents. If there is no young people's centre near you – and there are far from enough – they may be able to suggest an alternative source of help.

Samaritans, 17 Uxbridge Road, Slough SL1 1SN (0753-32713). Local numbers are listed in the directory and the operator will put you through if you don't know the number. No matter what your worry, the Samaritans will always provide a sympathetic listener and are particularly helpful in an emergency.

Institute of Psychosexual Medicine, 11 Chandos Street, Cavendish Square, London W1M 9DE (01-580-0631), will advise patients of doctors in their area who have completed their comprehensive training. Write for details enclosing a s.a.e.

Association of Sexual and Marital Therapists, PO Box 62, Sheffield, S10 3TS, can put you in touch with your nearest practitioner. Please enclose a s.a.e.

The Association to Aid the Sexual and Personal Relationships of People with a Disability, (SPOD), 286 Camden Road, London, N7 OBJ (01-607-8851).

British Pregnancy Advisory Service, Austy Manor, Wootton Wawen, Solihull, West Midlands B95 6BX (05642-3225). For problems connected with fertility, including counselling for abortion, vasectomy and female sterilisation and artificial insemination.

National Association for the Childless, 318 Summer Lane, Birmingham B19 3RL (021-359-4887). For those with fertility problems.

The Miscarriage Association, 18 Stoneybrook Close, West Bretton, Wakefield, Yorks WF4 4TP (0924-85515). Newsletter, information and support for those who have suffered a miscarriage. Send a s.a.e. for reply.

The Foundation for the Study of Infant Deaths, 5th Floor, 4 Grosvenor Place London SW1X 7HD (01-235-1721 and 01-245-9421).

Compassionate Friends, 6 Denmark Street, Bristol BS1 5DQ (0272-292778). Help and support for bereaved parents of young children.

Sexually transmitted diseases and infections: Phone your local hospital and ask for the nearest special clinic or clinic for genito-urinary infections. Treatment is confidential; it doesn't even go on your medical record. They are experts at treating infections such as thrush, as well as sexually transmitted diseases.

Terrence Higgins Trust, BM Aids, London WC1N 3XX. Helpline 01-833-2971. Advises those who are suffering from AIDS (auto-immune deficiency syndrome).

Body Positive, BM Aids, London WC1N 3XX. Support group for all those who have been identified as HTLV3 Positive.

Albany Trust, (01-730-5871), helps with psycho-sexual problems in all relationships, especially those of sexual minorities or those worried about their sexual orientation.

Identity, Beauchamp Lodge, 2 Warwick Crescent, London W2 6NE (01-289-6175). For those worried about their sexual orientation.

Friend, 274 Upper Street, Islington, London N1 2UA (01-359-7371), provides counselling and contact for homosexuals.

Gay Switchboard, (01-837-7324). 24 hour helpline for advice, social contact and referrals.

Parents Inquiry, 16 Honley Road, Catford, London SE6 2HZ. Counselling and support for the families of gay people.

Sigma, BM, Sigma, London, WC1N 3XX is for the 'straight' partners of homosexual men and women.

Gay Christian Movement, BM 6914, London WC1N 3XX (01-283-5165).

Beaumont Society, BMWOBS, London WC1N 3XX, for the families of transvestites. Beaumont Trustline: 01-730-7453 (Tues 7–11 p.m.). Wives and partners: 061-256-2521 (Wed 7–10 p.m.).

GRAIN, (Gay Rural Advice and Information Network), 107 Cambrian Drive, Colwyn Bay, Clwyd, LL28 45Y. Write enclosing a s.a.e. for quarterly newsletter for gay men living in isolated places.

SHAFT, (Self Help for Transexuals) c/o Miss Antonia Allen, 195 Battersea Bridge Road, London, SW11 3AR.

TV/TS, (Support group helps all transvestites and transexuals), 2/4 French Place (Off Batemans Row) Shoreditch, London E1 6JB. Helpline: 01-729-1466.

Victims Support Scheme, c/o The Women's Therapy Centre,

Manor Garden, London N7. Can offer psychological help to men suffering as a result of a sexual assault.

National Council for Civil Liberties, 21 Tabard Street, London SE1 4LA. (01-403-3888), can advise on cases of harassment.

Life-line, PO Box 251, Marlborough, Wilts SN8 1EA (079–373–286) helps abused and abusers in violent relationships.

Incest Crisis Line, (01-890-4732) and (01-422-5100) for anyone who has suffered as a result of incest, either recently or in the past.

Childline, (0800-1111) free helpline for abused children.

Alcoholics Anonymous, PO Box 1, Stone bow, York YO1 2NY (0904-644026/7/8/9).

Al-Anon, 61 Great Dover Street, London SE1 4YF (01-403-0888) for families of people who have a drink problem.

Drinkwatchers, 200, Seagrave Road, London SW6 1RQ (01-381-3157). For people who wish to develop healthy drinking habits.

ASH, (Action on Smoking and Health) 27/35 Mortimer Street, London W1N 7RJ. Advises those who wish to give up smoking.

Relaxation for Living, 29 Burwood Park Road, Walton on Thames, Surrey KT12 5LH, provide information and run classes in various parts of the country. Please send large s.a.e. when writing for leaflets.

The Stress Syndrome Foundation, Cedar House, Yalding, Kent, ME18 6JD. Can send leaflets about particular stress-related problems. Send a s.a.e. for details when writing.

Fellowship of Depressives Anonymous, 36 Chestnut Avenue, Beverley, North Humberside, HU17 9QU provide a newsletter, some local groups, postal contacts and national open meetings.

Outsiders Club, PO Box 4ZB London W1A 4ZB (01-499-0900), for those who feel that some physical or social handicap makes it difficult for them to make friends and find someone to love.

National Association of Youth Clubs, Keswick House, 30 Peacock Lane, Leicester, LE1 5NY (0533-29514).

National Federation of 18+ Groups, Nicholson House, Old Court Road, Newent, Gloucestershire, GL18 1AG (0531-821210), for 18 to 30 year olds.

Families Need Fathers, BM Families, London WC1N 3XX, a society for equal rights for parents after separation and divorce.

National Federation of Solo Clubs, Room 8, Ruskin Chambers, 191 Corporation Street, Birmingham B4 6RY (021-236-2879), for singles under 65, separated, widowed and divorced.

National Council for the Divorced and Separated, 13 High Street, Lt. Shelford, Cambridge, CB2 5ES.

Scottish Single, Widowed, Divorced and Separated Clubs, c/o Celia Donnelly, 12 Wardie Road, Glasgow, G33, (041-773-2295).

Gingerbread, 35 Wellington Street, London WC2E 7BN (01-240-0953), runs local groups as well as provides advice for lone parents.

CRUSE, 126 Sheen Road, Richmond, Surrey, TW9 1UR (01-940-4818/9047), for the widowed, and their children.

Men's Anti-Sexist Newsletter, 60 Rhumney Street, Cathays, Cardiff. Gives details of men's anti-sexist groups.

Achilles Heel, 79 Pembroke Road, London E17 9BB. Articles, poems etc of interest to anti-sexist men.

National Federation of Retirement Pension Associations, (Pensioners Voice) 91 Preston New Road, Blackburn, Lancs, BB2 6BD (0254-52606), for the retired.

National Council for Carers and Their Elderly Dependents, 29 Chilworth Mews, London W2 3RG (01-724-7776). For those looking after elderly relatives.

Association of Carers, 21/23 New Road, Chatham, Kent, ME4 4QJ, for all those caring for a disabled or infirm spouse, child or other relative.

Australia

Do not despair if you cannot find an organisation for your specific problem – the list is not exhaustive.

Talk to your GP. Contact your local Community Health Centre or Municipal Council. Many of the teaching/public hospitals have social workers, support groups, counselling for specific problems and may be able to help you. Women's hospitals in particular are a good source of help for infertility, sexually transmitted diseases, and AIDS.

Look in your local papers and major daily newspapers for details of support groups (e.g. for single parents), courses for self-awareness and personal growth etc. TAFE Colleges and CAE also offer courses.

Contact your local Municipal Council for details of youth refuges, youth counselling, youth support schemes, emergency accommodation etc.

Your local Citizens' Advice Bureau may be able to help with your problem or refer you to someone who can.

Look at the Help Reference Page in your White Page Telephone Directory for telephone numbers of organisations which may be able to help you.

Victoria

Marriage Guidance Council of Victoria, 46 Princess Street, Kew (861 8512).

Family Planning Association of Victoria, 270 Church Street, Richmond (428 1414, 429 1177/1868) – contraception, pregnancy advice, counselling, abortion, sex education for the intellectually handicapped.

Family Planning Association of Victoria Action Centre, 35 Elizabeth Street, Melbourne (61 3445) – adolescent counselling and referral service.

Family Life Movement of Australia, 475 Collins Street, Melbourne (62 4251) – education in human sexuality.

Catholic Family Welfare Bureaux, 491 Nicholdson Street, Carlton (342 0866).

Concern (Victoria), P.O.Box 125, Vermont – support, counselling for infertile couples.

Lifeline, (662 1000).

VD Clinic, 364 Little Lonsdale Street, Melbourne (602 4900).

AIDS Line 7–10 pm daily (419 3166) – telephone counselling, support information and referral.

AIDS Hotline, 24 hours – (347 3000).

227

AIDS Resource Centre, (The Peter Knight Centre) and the *Aids Council of Victoria*, 61 Rupert Street, Collingwood (417 1759), (also details of the Support Group for Antibody Positive People on same phone number).

Gayline Telephone Advisory Service, 126 Franklin Street, Melbourne (329 5555) – also Direction, social support group for young gays.

Homosexuality Task Force, 130 Little Collins Street, Melbourne (654 2488).

Parents Without Partners Inc (Vic), 200 Canterbury Road, Canterbury (836 3211).

Birthright (Victoria), 238 Flinders Street, Melbourne, (63 2364) and 422 Collins Street, Melbourne (67 2415). Supports single parents.

Paulian Catholic Association, P.O.Box 188, Glen Waverley (366 2014) – Catholic support for solo parents.

Youth Affairs Council of Australia, 179 Barkly Street, St. Kilda (537 1833).

GROW (Vic), 316 Queen Street, Melbourne (67 7595) – run self-awareness and growth courses, often advertised in local papers.

The Cairnmillar Institute, 993 Burke Road, Camberwell (882 1361) – courses in personal growth and self-awareness.

New South Wales

Marriage Guidance Council of New South Wales, 226 Liverpool Street, Enfield (745 4411).

Family Planning Association of New South Wales, 161 Broadway, Sydney (211 0244).

Centacare, Catholic Family Welfare Bureau, Catholic Family Planning, 176 Pitt Street, Sydney (264 7211).

Family Life Movement of Australia, 47 Brays Road, Concord (736 2838) and 41 The Boulevarde, Lewisham (560 3377).

Concern (NSW) 61 Undercliff Street, Neutral Bay – support, counselling for the infertile couple.

Lifeline: Sydney (264 2222),
Hornsby Northside (477 4440),
Manly – Warringah (949 6699),
Parramatta (635 9000).

VD Clinic, 93 Macquarie Street, Sydney (Female: 27 4851; Male: 273634).

AIDS Council of New South Wales, (332 441).

AIDS Enquiries, 150 Albion Street, Surrey Hills (332 4000).

Gay Counselling Service and *Gayline*, 51 Holt Street, Surrey Hills (211 1177).

Acceptance, Catholic Gay Community, 57 Holt Street, Surrey Hills (212 5247).

Parents without Partners (NSW), 48 Railway Parade, Granville, (682 6677) and 316 Pitt Street, Sydney (267 5177).

Solo Parents of Australia, 267 Pitt Street, Sydney (264 8133) – operates within Catholic Church to provide support to single parents.

One Parent Family Resource Centre, 4 Ingram Road, Wahroonga (48 5390).

Birthright, 121, Pitt Street, Sydney, (232 6455). Supports single parents.

Family Access and Support Programme, 411 Liverpool Street, Darlinghurst (331 3291).

Youthline, 153 George Street, Parramatta (663 3666), and 210 Pitt Street, Sydney (264 1177).

A.C.T. (Australian Capital Territory)

Marriage Counselling Service Inc., Canberra Savings House, Petrie Plaza, Canberra (480 0530, 47 0603).

Family Planning Association ACT Inc., Childers Street, Canberra (47 3077).

Catholic Family Planning Centre, Canberra Avenue, Manuka (95 2484).

Concern in ACT, 44 Mackay Crescemt Kambah – support, counselling for the infertile couple.

Lifeline, (82 2222).

Sexually Transmitted Diseases, Telephone Information Service (45 4316).

AIDS Reference Centre, (84 2184).

AIDS Task Force, (89 8433, 89 1555).

ACT AIDS Council, (47 4153, 51 6213).

Youth Advice Line, 2 Mort Street, Braddon (49 7668).

Birthright (ACT), Griffin Centre, Canberra (47 4282).

Parents Without Partners (ACT) Inc., 72 Anthill Street, Dickson (48 6333).

Paulian Solo Parents, Canberra, Avenue, Manuka (95 3832) operates within Catholic Church and supports solo parents.

Queensland

Marriage Guidance Council, 159 St. Paul's Terrace, Brisbane (831 2005).

Family Planning Association of Queensland, 100 Alfred Street, Fortitude Valley (52 8096).

Family Life Movement of Australia, 120 Rode Road, Wavell Heights, (266 6933) – education in human sexuality.

Sexual Problems and Relationship Counselling Service, Fionaven Street, Kenmore (378 0590).

Lifeline: Bowen Hills (52 7527),
          Ipswich (261 9555).

VD Clinics, 484 Adelaide Street, Brisbane (Male: 227 7091; Female: 227 7095).

Queensland AIDS Committee, (832 3679).

Homosexual Counselling & Welfare Service, Brunswick Street, Fortitude Valley (852 1414).

Homosexual Information & Advice Service, 379 George Street, Brisbane (221 9373) (and Gayline).

Youth Care and Counselling, 4 Tully Street, Keperra (355 4073).

Centacare, Catholic Family Welfare Bureau, Catholic Solo Parents, Morgan Street, Fortitude Valley (52 4371).

Birthright, 174 Queen Street, Brisbane (229 4186), supports single parents.

Parents Without Partners, 19 Clarence Street, South Brisbane (44 8567).

Lone Fathers Association of Queensland (Inc), 344 Queen Street, Brisbane (229 7095).

Lone Parent Self-Action Group of Australia, 21 Thuruna Street, Stafford (359 3700).

South Australia

Marriage Guidance Council of South Australia, 55 Hutt Street, Adelaide (223 4566).

Family Planning Association, 17 Phillips Street, Kensington (31 5177).

Family Life Movement of Australia, 220 Wattle Street, Unley (271 0259).

Lifeline, (212 3444).

VD Clinic, 275 North Terrace, Adelaide (218 3557).

Sexually Transmitted Diseases Services, 275 North Terrace, Adelaide, (218 3666).

South Australian AIDS Action Committee, (223 6944).

Gay Counselling Service Association and *Gayline*, Kilkenny (268 5577).

COPE (Centre of Personal Encounter) 114 Hutt Street, Adelaide (223 3433) – courses in all areas of personal growth and development.

Crisis Care, (272 1222).

Self Help at Salisbury Inc., Ann Street, Salisbury (258 7380).

Cresco Self Help Centre Inc., 109 Woodville Road, Woodville (268 7000).

Catholic Family Welfare Bureau, 33 Wakefield Street, Adelaide (223 6313).

Birthright, 88 Currie Street, Adelaide (51 6660), supports single parents.

Parents Without Partners, 17 Currie Street, Adelaide (212 6280).

Child Youth & Family Service (Para District), 100 Philip Highway, Elizabeth South (252 0133).

Western Australia

Marriage Guidance Council of Western Australia Inc., 32 Richardson Street, West Perth (322 4755).

Family Planning Association of Western Australia Inc., 104 Colin Street, West Perth (321 2701, 321 3144).

Sexual Counselling and Research Centre, 9 Hampden Road, Nedlands (386 3057).

Concern for the Infertile Couple, Bagot Road, Subiaco (381 9313).

Centacare, Catholic Marriage Guidance Council, Catholic Family Welfare Bureau, 27 Victoria Square, Perth (325 6644).

Samaritans, 60 Bagot Road, Subiaco 6009 (381 5555).

Crisis Care, (321 4144).

Youthline Samaritan, 60 Bagot Road, Subiaco (381 2500).

Western Australian AIDS Council, (227 8355).

Homosexual Counselling & Information Service and *Gayline*, 329 Pier Street, East Perth (328 9044).

Parents Without Partners (WA) Inc., 504 Hay Street, Perth (325 4575).

Lone Fathers Home Support Service, 146 Beaufort Street. Perth (328 4344).

Birthright, 504 Hay Street, Perth (325 7343) – supports single parents.

TLC Emergency Welfare Foundation of WA Inc., 84 Beaufort Street, Perth, (328 1751, 328 6982) – all social welfare problems.

Tasmania

Marriage Guidance Council, 192 Charles Street, Launceston (31 9157) and 22 Main Road, Penguin (37 2334).

Family Planning Association of Tasmania Inc., 73 Federal Street, North Hobart, (34 7200) and 77 Cameron Street, Launceston (31 9662, 31 9100).

Centacare Family Services, Catholic Family Welfare Bureau, 19 Canning Street, Launceston (31 6811) and 44 Sandy Bay Road, Sandy Bay (23 1000).

GROW, Launceston, (39 1992).

Samaritans, PO Box 228 7250, 3355 Macquarie Road, Launceston.

Youthline, Launceston, (31 4477) Hobart, (23 2525).

Lifelink Centre (Launceston 31 3355).

Parents Without Partners, 12 Bank Arcade, Hobart (34 7172).

Northern Territory

Marriage Counselling Centre, Centrepoint Mall, Darwin (81 6676).

Family Planning Association (NT) Inc., 133 Mitchell Street, Laykyah (81 5335) and Shop 4 Turner Arcade, Alice Springs (52 5571).

Crisis Line: Darwin 7 pm to 7 am (81 2040),
Alice Springs 7 pm to 7 am (50 2266).

VD Clinic, Alice Springs Hospital (50 2639).

VD Information, Darwin (81 5460).

AIDS Information: Darwin (81 2951),
Alice Springs (50 2639),
Nhulunbuy (Cove) (87 0211),
Katherine (72 1733),
Tennant Greek (62 3166).

Gay Society of Darwin, (85 5880).

Parents Without Partners (N.T.) Inc., Anula, Darwin, (27 2261).

Disabled Persons Bureau, The Mall, Darwin (80 2753), and Todd Street, Alice Springs (52 6499).

New Zealand

Mental Health Foundation of New Zealand, The Secretary, PO Box 37-438 Parnell, Auckland 1, NZ. Information on nearest Parents Centre/Parentline/Marriage Guidance/Citizens Advice/Family Planning/Lifeline.

National Marriage Guidance Council of New Zealand, Box 6236 Auckland, Box 9295 Hamilton; Box 9309 Wellington; Box 13003 Christchurch; Box 603 George St. Dunedin.

New Zealand Family Planning Association Inc. 218 Karangahape Road, Auckland 1 or write to Box 68-200 Newton, Auckland 1.

Samaritans, 44, Laings Road, Lower Hutt and PO Box 30388 (644 591/664 252); YMCA Premises, Church Street, North Masterton (81259); 15 Amesbury Street, North Palmerston and PO Box 1963 (74400); Hakiaha Street, North Taumaranui (6664); PO Box Brooklyn 6309, North Tauranga (81001); 120 Guyton Street and PO Box 4116 Mid-Av. PO North Wanganui (55090); Cathedral Building, Molesworth Street and PO Box 12044, North Wellington (739739); Contact House, Corner Fenton and Arawa Street, Rotorua, PO Box 1682 (80567).

National Lifeline Association of New Zealand Inc., PO Box 5104, Wellesley Street, Auckland 1.

Lifelink/Youthline, PO Box 1682, Rotorua.

New Zealand Council for Civil Liberties, PO Box 337, Wellington.

Federation of New Zealand Parents Centres Inc., PO Box 11310, Wellington. Fifty-two centres across New Zealand.

CRUSE, for the widowed; Mrs M Wallace, 8 White Street, Taradale, Hawkes Bay; Mrs A E Blanchard, 13 Riverbend Road, Onekawa, Napier; Mrs M Drown, 303 Sylvan Road, Hastings.

Widows' & Widowers' Association of New Zealand Inc., Mrs Joy Black, PO Box 11-595 Wellington. Help and advice – branches throughout New Zealand.

60s-Up Movement of New Zealand Inc., PO Box 3143, Auckland 1.

Cancer Society of New Zealand Inc., PO Box 12/45, Wellington.

National Society on Alcohol and Drug Dependence, New Zealand, Head Office, PO Box 54-146 Plimmerton, New Zealand.

Canada

Canadian Guidance & Counselling Association, c/o University of Ottawa Faculty of Education, 651 Cumberland Street, Suite 212, Ottawa, Ontario K1N 6N5 (613 836 5354).

Canadian Association of Marriage & Family Life, 271 Russell Hill Road, Toronto, Ontario M4V 2T5 (416 968 7779).

Marriage Encounter, 129 Hannaford Street, Toronto, Ontario M4E 3G9 (416 694 8700), for marriage guidance and counselling.

Sex Information and Education Council of Canada, 423 Castlefield Avenue, Toronto, Ontario M4N 1L4 (416 691 3499).

Planned Parenthood of Toronto, 58 Shaftesbury Avenue, Toronto, Ontario, M4T 1A3 (414 961 8290), operate a phone-in for teenagers with sexuality problems. (10 a.m. to 1 p.m. Mon-Sat).

Canadian Mental Health Association, National Office, 2160 Yonge Street, Toronto M4S 2Z3 (416 484 7750).

Manic Depressive Association, (416 773 6184).

Survivor Support Program, (416 595 1716) dealing with a suicide in the family.

Bereaved Families of Ontario, (416 440 0290).

YMCA, 20 Grosvenor, Toronto, Ontario. (416 922 7765).

Canadian Association of Sexual Assault Centres, c/o 4-45 Kingsway, Vancouver BC V5T 3H7 (604 872 8212).

Queens Birth Control, VD and Abortion Information and Referral Service, 51 Queens Crescent, Kingston, Ontario K7L 3N6 (613 545 2959).

AIDS Committee of Toronto, 66 Wellesley East, Toronto. (416 926 1626).

TAG, (Toronto Area Gays), (416 964 6600), Mon–Fri 7 p.m. to 10 p.m.

Coming Out & After Your Out, two groups helping Gays deal with their problems (416 923 4297).

Gay Liberation, Bookstore (416 961 4161).

ADDICS (Alcohol and Drug Dependency Information and Counselling Service), No 209, 818 Pórtage Avenue, Winnipeg, Manitoba R3G ON4 (204 775 1233).

Addiction Research Foundation, 33 Russell Street, Toronto (416 595 6000).

Porter Place Mens Hospital & Support Service, for men 16 years and up. Emergency housing for men, bed and meals for up to 6 weeks. Counselling and support. Staff on duty 24 hrs., 475 Yonge Street, Toronto (416 898 1658).

Scott Mission meals etc. for homeless men, 502 Spadina Avenue (416 924 4437).

Canadian Cancer Society, 130 Bloor Street W, No 1001, Toronto, Ontario M5S 2V7 (416 961 7223), and 1118 St Catherine Street, No 700, Montreal H3B 1H5 (514 842 3424).

Canadian Rehabilitation Council for the Disabled, Suite 2110, 1 Yonge Street, Toronto, Ontario M5E 1E5.

Parents Experiencing Perinatal Death Association, c/o Gael Gilbert, 47 Alberta Avenue, Toronto, Ontario M6H 247.

One Parent Families Association, 218 Kent Street, Charlotte-town, Prince Edward Island (902 8923790).

Carrefour des Association de familles monoparentales du Quebec, 890 rue Dorchester est, Suite 2320, Montreal, Quebec H2L 2L4 (514 288 5224/5225).

Singles Association of Stoufville, (416 640 2123).

Community Contacts for the Widowed, 1643 Yonge Street, Toronto, Ontario M4T 2A1 (416 486 9945).

South Africa

Famsa – Pietermaritzburg Society for Marriage & Family Life, PO Box 928 Pietermaritzburg 3200.

Family & Marriage Society, Suite 525, Fifth Floor, 320 West Street, Durban (304 8991), will also advise young people on contraception, pregnancy and abortion and give general counselling.

Family Planning Association of South Africa, 412 York House, 46 Kerk Street, Johannesburg 2001.

Family Planning Clinic, 43 Werdmuller Centre, Main Road, Claremont (64 4330).

Institute for Child and Adult Guidance, Rand Afrikaans University, PO Box 524 Johannesburg 2000.

Indian Youth Advisory Centre, 263 Road 240, Chatsworth (031 431425).

Durban African Child & Family Welfare Society, Old Fort Road, Durban. (031 325506).

South African National Council for Mental Health, PO Box 2587, Johannesburg 2000.

Durban Indian Child and Family Welfare Society, PO Box 128, Durban 4000.

Samaritans, PO Box 2201, Bloemfontein, Orange Free State (83000) and Red Cross House, Stockdale Street, Kimberley 8301.

Lifeline, Head Office, PO Box 13454, Northmead 1511 RSA. (011 849 2747) can also put you in touch with local Rape Crisis Centres, and offer counselling and referral for sexual minorities and the disabled.

GASA, (Gay Association of South Africa), Box 3330 Johannesburg 2000.

Independent Living Centre, 1st Floor, Happiness House, corner of Loveday and Wolmarans Street, Braamfontein, Johannesburg, and PO Box 32099, Braam 2017. Help for the disabled.

Further reading

Growing Up by Dr James Docherty (Modus Books in association with the Royal Society of Medicine), a well illustrated guide for children and parents.

Boys and Sex and *Girls and Sex* by Wardell B. Pomeroy (Pelican) are informative and reassuring for young people and their parents.

First Love, First Sex by Kaye Wellings (Thorsons), a practical guide to relationships.

Men and Sex by Bernie Zilbergeld (Fontana), a guide to sexual fulfilment.

Making Love by Michael Castleman (Penguin) is written especially for men.

Women's Experience of Sex by Sheila Kitzinger (Penguin), an illuminating and liberating book for men and women to read.

How to Improve your Sex Life by Dr David Delvin (New English Library) a cheerfully written guide to sexual technique.

The Joy of Sex by Alex Comfort (Quartet), a gourmet guide to love-making.

Men In Love by Nancy Friday (Arrow), man's sexual fantasies.

My Secret Garden by Nancy Friday (Quartet), women's sexual fantasies.

Treat Yourself to Sex by Paul Brown and Carolyn Faulder (Penguin), a self-help guide to treating common problems.

A Common-sense Guide to Sex by Dr Sandra Pertot (Angus Robertson), particularly helpful for couples bothered by differences in sex drive.

How to Make Love to the Same Person For the Rest of Your Life – And Still Love It by Dagmar O'Connor (Columbus Books), American style but often hits the button.

Enjoy Sex in the Middle Years by Dr Christine Sandford (Martin Dunitz).

The Massage Book by George Downing (Penguin) is clear and straight-forward.

The Art of Sensual Massage by Gordon Inkeles and Murray Todris (Allen and Unwin), beautifully illustrated.

Stress and Relaxation by Jane Madders (Martin Dunitz), self-help ways to cope with stress and relieve nervous tension.

Physical Fitness (Penguin), the Canadian Airforce exercises taking just 12 minutes a day but building up from totally unfit to the peak level for your age.

How To Stop Smoking by George Target (Sheldon Press), no preaching.

How To say No to Alcohol by Keith McNeill (Sheldon Press), encouraging and understanding.

Depression by Dr Paul Hauck (Sheldon Press), why it happens and how to overcome it.

Herpes, Aids and Other Sexually Transmitted Diseases by Derek Llewellyn-Jones (Faber & Faber).

Stop Herpes Now – A Self-Help Guide to understanding and controlling Herpes by Barbara B. Morth PhD. MD and Penelope P. Crittenden (Thorsons).

AIDS Concerns You: What every man and every woman should know about AIDS by Dr Jonathan Weber and Annabel Ferriman (Pagoda Books).

So You Think You're Attracted to The Same Sex by John Hart (Penguin).

How To be A Happy Homosexual by Terry Sanderson (Other Way).

The Married Homosexual Man by Michael W. Ross (Routledge & Kegan Paul).

Infertility: A Sympathetic Approach by Robert Winston (Martin Dunitz).

You're a Father! Editor Dr Eric A. Turner (Pagoda Books), a man's guide to new parenthood.

Fathering for Men by Martin Francis (Generation Books, Haverstock Road, Bristol). A down to earth journey from maternity classes through to first days at primary school.

Help! I've Got a Teenager by Robert and Jean Bayard (Exley), a survivors' guide for desperate parents.

No More Secrets For Me by Oralee Wachter (Penguin), helping to guard your child against sexual abuse.

Incest: A Family Pattern, by Jean Renvoize (Routledge & Kegan Paul).

Making Marriage Work by Dr Paul Hauck (Sheldon Press).

Surviving Divorce: A handbook for men by Gay Search (New English Library).

Divorce and Separation by Angela Willans (Sheldon Press).

How To Start a Conversation and Make Friends by Don Gabor (Sheldon Press).

Note on Methodology and Sample

Before we had completed our survey of women's feelings about love and their sexual activity we decided that we must complete the picture by repeating the survey for men.

The decisions about the research design were thoroughly worked through for the earlier survey. For the sake of completeness we repeat what we wrote then as it applies to men.

Our objective was to obtain reliable and honest data about the sexual activity and experience of men and their feelings and opinions about them. We knew from our own research experience, and believed it to be generally understood, that people overclaim their levels of sexual activity and satisfaction in the same way as they underclaim the number of cigarettes they smoke and pints of beer they consume.

We considered several options.

1. *Face-to-face interviews with a representative sample of men.* We decided against this method because previous surveys on similar subjects carried out in this way had, we understood, proved to be rather unsatisfactory. We also knew from our own previous experience that, faced with an interviewer, people do not always feel able to answer honestly questions about very sensitive, perhaps painful, areas of their lives.

When, for example, we (Deidre Sanders and Anne Rigg) once conducted a survey through interviews of a representative sample on the problem of working women, which included questions as to whether and how often working mothers left children alone at home, we were faced with almost 100 per cent denial that interviewees ever did so – even though this is known to be a significant problem in many areas, and despite the fact that the intention of the survey was not to blame but to highlight the need for help. A bound-in self-completion questionnaire on the same subject carried out earlier had revealed that significant numbers of mothers were leaving young children unattended at home for some time after school.

241

In the case of a survey on sex, we felt that using interviewees would have made the findings extremely liable to bias, resulting from the interviewers' own feelings and anxieties about different areas of sexual experience, and how comfortable they felt in asking questions about this very private side of our lives. It would have also biased the results towards those interviewees who were most readily able to discuss sex.

2. *Random sample self-completion questionnaire by post.* We decided against this method because it would have presented enormous problems in ensuring that respondents took the survey seriously and that we received an adequate response. There is no doubt, either, that some people would have found it extremely offensive to have an unsolicited questionnaire about their sex lives dropping through their letterbox. You do, after all, exercise choice in buying a magazine and bringing it into your home which would not have applied if we had mailed out the questionnaire to a random sample.

3. *A questionnaire bound in* Woman *magazine and subsequently sampled in proportion with the population statistics for age and region.* We chose this method because we were sure we could present the study honestly and without bias. As explained in the introduction, we were careful to encourage responses from those who were content as well as the disillusioned, from different age groups, from those who thought sex important and those who thought there had been a great deal of fuss about very little. We could monitor the response thoroughly ourselves, and a consideration of the statistics of the readership profile of *Woman* led us to conclude that there is no reason to believe that the readers of *Woman* are biased in any way that might affect our results, given that we sampled from the response.

Why did we chose Woman *magazine as the media for a survey of men?*

We wanted obviously to do a survey of men comparable to our survey of women. Before we decided on *Woman* we considered all kinds of other magazines and newspapers which had a male readership higher than that known for *Woman*. At that time there were no suitable magazine alternatives and the newspapers we considered would, we thought, present either difficulties with response rates or undesirable biases as to the intention and purpose of our study.

We knew from marketing data and general reader responses that considerable numbers of men read *Woman*. We also know that *Woman* readers pass relevant articles to their husbands and partners to read.

It was decided therefore to put the survey in *Woman* and see what response was achieved.

The total number of completed questionnaires returned was 5,000, which was more than sufficient for us to carry out subsequent random sampling from that total.

The results in this book are therefore based on a sample of men reflecting the national population of men in the right proportions for age, region and marital status.

As with the earlier surveys we undertook a number of precautions to ensure that all the questionnaires included in the computer analysis were honest and genuine replies:

1. The questionnaires were screened on receipt for the obvious 'jokers' – the type who say they're under 18 and married for more than thirty years, have sex every day and are keen on gang-bangs. There were, in fact, very few of these.

2. Each questionnaire was then individually coded by a psychologist who read all the accompanying material (many men enclosed letters with their questionnaires), and who could ensure that the questionnaires were consistent records. Any whose stories could not be reconciled with their answers were dropped from the analysis.

3. We conducted a 10 per cent quality-control check of the coding.

4. Before computer analysis the questionnaires were edit-checked by the computer for simple inconsistencies missed in coding. All queried questionnaires were checked again.

Love & Sex –
The Man's View

The Questionnaire as
printed in Woman *magazine*

Men are supposed to think it's a waste of time to talk about their feelings – but is this because no one really asks them or stops to listen? In fact, we know remarkably little about how men feel – we just rely on myths and assumptions. Here we've given this space to men. Please will you take the time to answer our questions so we can begin to learn?

- Do you find it difficult to stay faithful?
- Do you feel you have to keep your real desires secret?
- How many men feel their marriage has lost its excitement?
- How many men enjoy pornography?

These are some of the issues men raised during our initial research. There were some surprises for us, and we have tried to ensure that this questionnaire covers the subjects which men said interested them. It's been printed on the special pull-out section so you can take it away and complete it in privacy. And we have arranged for FREEPOST so it costs nothing to send it off. Of course, it's important to be honest, or its conclusions will be worthless. It's your chance to say what you really feel, with no fear of come-back – the survey is completely anonymous. The questionnaire may look on the long side but we have had to allow for the fact that men, married and unmarried, of all ages, are going to complete it. Just follow the "signposts" and fill in the sections which apply to you. We will welcome any extra views or experiences you would like to tell us about on extra sheets of paper. Please attach these firmly to your questionnaire. *Note to women WOMAN readers*: Greater understanding between the sexes can only help towards happier, more harmonious relationships and we're sure you'll be interested to see the results of our survey on Men and Love. You can help by passing these pages to a man in your life, be he husband, boyfriend, lover, son, brother, or simply a friend. We know it's going to be tempting to ask to see what he has filled in, but please resist it. No truthful survey can be conducted without guarantees of privacy and confidentiality and, of course, we won't obtain reliable answers unless this starts at home.

● *We're aiming to collect facts and views from all kinds of men – single, married, divorced, widowed – so please skip questions which don't fit your life, and just ring the number next to your answer.*

Setting the scene

1 Are you:

Married	1
Single	2
Separated	3
Divorced	4
Widowed	5

2 Do you:

Live with your wife	1
Live with your girlfriend	2
Live singly with your parents	3
Live singly with others	4
Live alone	5
Other	X

3 Are you happy with your current sex life?

Very happy	5
Most of the time	4
Sometimes	3
Hardly ever	2
Never happy	1

4 How important to you is a good sex life?

Very important	4
Fairly important	3
Not very important	2
Not at all important	1

5a Which of the following do you think most important for a rela- tionship to last successfully? Ring column a. **(b) Which least important? Ring columb b.**

	(a) Most important	(b) Least important
Partner looking attractive	1	1
My looking attractive	2	2
Love	3	3
Few money worries	4	4
Showing affection	5	5
Agreement over household responsibilities	6	6
Satisfying sex life	7	7
Talking openly about feelings	8	8
Shared sense of humour	9	9
My fidelity	10	10
My partner's fidelity	11	11
Other (write in)	X	X

. . . .

● **Please write on a separate sheet more about your current or most recent relationship, what makes/-made you happiest and saddest.**

245

(Married men – please think back where necessary!)

6 How easy do you/did you find it to meet partners?

Very easy	4
Fairly easy	3
Not very easy	2
Not at all easy	1

7 Which of these characteristics are:
(a) important for you to feel attracted towards a partner?
(b) not important?

	(a) important	(b) Not important
Beautiful hair	1	1
Sense of humour	2	2
Nice breasts	3	3
Intelligence	4	4
Lovely face	5	5
Warmth and kindness	6	6
Good figure	7	7
Shapely legs	8	8
Nice bottom	9	9
Other (write in)	X	X

....

8 Are you happy that it's men who are usually expected to make the first move to start a relationship?

Yes, I like feeling I can choose	1
Yes, I don't like pushy women	2
No, I find it a strain	3
No, it's an out-of-date attitude	4
I don't agree men are usually expected to make the first move	5

9 Who made the first move in your most important steady relationship?

I did	1
My partner did	2

I haven't had a steady relationship (i.e. one lasting six months or more)
GO TO Q11a   3

10 Where did this relationship start?

At a disco/dance	1
Through friends	2
At work	3
At school/college	4
Through hobbies/interests	5
Through a social club	6
A friendship/marriage agency	7
Other	X

• Please tell us, on a separate sheet, more about your experiences of meeting partners.

• **Married men please go to Q15**

11a Do you have a current special relationship?

Yes, lasting more than six months	1
Yes, lasting less than six months	2
No	3

11b If NO, would you like one?

Yes, very much	1
Quite like one	2
No	3

NOW GO TO Q12

11c If YES, do you think you're in love?

We're both in love	1
I'm in love	2
My partner's in love	3
Neither of us is in love	4

12 Do you go out with just one partner?

Yes	1

No, I go out with more than one 2
I'm not going out with anyone 3

13 Have you ever had sexual intercourse?

Yes 1
No (NOW GO TO Q19) 2

14 Are you having sex with anyone at present?

Yes, with one special partner only 1
Yes, with my one regular partner and others 2
Yes, with more than one regular partner 3
Yes, on a casual basis 4
No 5

The first time

● For all men with sexual experience

15 How old were you the first time you had intercourse?

Under 16 1
16 to 18 2
19 to 21 3
22 to 25 4
26 to 30 5
Over 30 6

16 What was the main reason you had sex on that occasion?

I was in love 1
I really liked that particular girl 2
I wanted to know what sex was like 3
All my friends had had sex 4
I'd had a lot to drink 5
Other (write in) X

....

17 Did you enjoy the first time?

A great deal 4

Reasonably well 3
Not very much 2
Not at all 1

18 Did you use, or *make sure* the girl was using, contraception?

Yes 1
No 2

The facts of life

19a Do you feel your parents had talked openly enough with you about sex?

	Mother	Father
Very openly	4	4
Fairly openly	3	3
Not very openly	2	2
Never talked about it	1	1

19b Used you to feel guilty about sex?

Yes 1 No 2

20 Do you feel your school had given you enough information about sex, contraception, etc?

Yes 1 No 2

21 Have you ever worried that your penis isn't large enough?

Yes, did in the past 1
Yes, still do 2
No, happy as I am 3
No, worried it's too large 4

22 Has a partner ever complained your penis is too small?

Yes 1 No 2

23a Have you ever visited a prostitute?

Yes 1 No 2

23b Is YES, how old were you when you last did so?

Please write in ....

....

24 If NO, have you ever considered going to a prostitute?

Yes, I would like to go   1

I have wondered what it would be like   2

No, I would never dream of it   3

• **All men**

25 What do you feel prostitutes can/could provide?

Extra sex without risking a relationship   1

A particular type of sex a man cannot get in his relationship   2

Sex when away from home   3

A prostitute is a more responsive sexual partner   4

Other (please write in)   X

....

Nothing   5

• **Please tell us more about your youthful and other experiences on this matter on a separate sheet.**

Your life now

• **For all men, married or not, with a current sexual relationship.**

• These questions should be answered about the sex you have with your wife, woman you live with, or regular partner.

26 How long has this relationship lasted?

Please write in years ....

....

27 How happy is this relationship generally?

Very happy   4

Fairly happy   3

Not very happy   2

Not at all happy   1

28 How often do you and your partner usually make love?

Less than once a month   1

Less than once a week   2

About once a week   3

2 to 3 times a week   4

4 to 5 times a week   5

Every day   6

We never make love now   7

29 Would you and do you think your partner would like to make love:

	You	Partner
More often	1	1
Less often	2	2
Happy as you are	3	3

30 If you wish you made love *more often*, what gets in the way?
RING ALL THAT APPLY

Lack of privacy from parents, others   1

Lack of opportunity because of children   2

You are often too tired   3

Your partner is often too tired   4

You don't feel like it that often   5

Your partner doesn't feel like it that often   6

Your partner is married to someone else   7

Other, please write in   X

....

31 How do you rate your partner as a lover?

Excellent   5

Good   4

Average   3

Passable   2

Poor   1

32 How do you rate yourself and how do you think your partner rates *you* as a lover?

	You	Partner
Excellent	5	5
Good	4	4
Average	3	3
Passable	2	2
Poor	1	1

In the mood

33 How often do you tell each other "I love you"?

	You tell her	She tells you
Every day	1	1
Frequently	2	2
Rarely	3	3
Never	4	4

34a Do you and your partner often kiss and cuddle *apart* from before having sex?

Very often	4
Fairly often	3
Not very often	2
Not at all	1

34b Is this often enough for you and your partner?

	For you	For partner
Yes	1	1
No	2	2

34c Is kissing and cuddling as important to you both as sexual intercourse?

	To you	To partner
More important	3	3
Equally important	2	2
Not as important	1	1

35 Do you ever have difficulty becoming sexually aroused?

Often	3
Sometimes	2
Never	1

36 Who makes the first move towards making love?

Always/usually me	1
About 50:50	2
Always/usually my partner	3

37 Do you wish your partner made the first move more often?

Yes, much more often	4
Yes, occasionally	3
No, it's about right	2
No, less often	1

38 Do you ever refuse to make love?

Never	1
Occasionally	2
Often	3
Always	4

39 Does your partner ever turn you down?

Always	4
Often	3
Occasionally	2
Never	1

40 What do you usually do to help you or your partner feel in the mood for sex? Please write in.

Partner . . . .

. . . .

You

. . . .

41a Do/would you like your partner to dress (undress) in a special way for sex?

Naked	1
Stockings and suspenders	2

Sexy nightie 3
Special outfits – uniform etc 4
Other (please write in) X
....
....
No 5

41b Does your partner ever dress like this for sex?
Yes 1
No 2

42 Do you fantasise while making love (such as imagine yourself somewhere else or with someone different)
Always 3
Sometimes 2
Never 1

• If you do fantasise please write your favourite one on a separate sheet.

Making changes

43 If you could change things about you and your partner's love-making would you want to/want her to:

	You to:	Partner to:
Kiss, cuddle, take more time in the beginning	1	1
Be more responsive	2	2
Be more skilful	3	3
Be less demanding	4	4
Talk more about how it feels	5	5
Be more experimental	6	6
Be keener to make love more often	7	7
Other	8	8
I wouldn't want to change my partner	X	X

44 Do you and your partner talk about sex or your sexual feelings?
Completely frankly 4
Fairly openly 3
With embarrassment 2
Never 1

45 Do you ever refuse your partner's requests to try a new position or technique?
Yes 1
No 2

46 If so, what is it usually?
Please write in
....
....

47 Do you ever make requests your partner refuses?
Yes 1
No 2

48 If so, what is it usually?
Please write in
....
....

• If you care to tell us more about anything mentioned in this section, please write on a separate sheet.

49a Do you climax when you make love?
Always 4
Usually 3
Occasionally 2
Never 1

49b Do you ever have difficulty keeping an erection?
Usually 3
Occasionally 2
Never 1

49c Do you climax before your partner?
Never 1

250

Occasionally		2
Often		3
Always		4

49d Do you have any difficulties with reaching climax when you want to?

Usually climax too quickly	1
Sometimes climax too quickly	2
Sometimes have difficulty reaching climax	3
Usually have difficulty reaching climax	4
Other (write in)	V
No difficulties	X

49e Are you and is your partner happy with the frequency with which she climaxes?

	You	Partner
Yes	1	1
No	2	2

49f Does your partner reach orgasm when you make love?

Usually	3
Occasionally	2
Never	1
Don't know	X

49g What usually causes a climax for you and partner? RING ONE ONLY IN EACH COLUMN

	For you	For partner
Intercourse	1	1
Manual stimulation	2	2
Oral sex	3	3
Vibrator	4	4
Other	5	5

49h Does your partner ever fake orgasm?

Usually	3
Sometimes	2
Never	1
Suspect she does	0
Don't know	X

50 Do you or your partner masturbate?

	You	Partner
Often	3	3
Occasionally	2	2
Never	1	1
Don't know	X	X
No partner	–	V

51 Do/would you object to your partner masturbating?

A great deal	4
A little	3
Not very much	2
Not at all	1

Erotica

52a Do you read/see erotic/girlie magazines/films

Often	3
Occasionally	2
Never (Go to Q53)	1

52b Is the material you see/read pornographic?

Not really	1
Soft porn	2
Hard porn	3
A mixture of both	4

52c Does your partner mind?

Yes, hates it	1
Yes, minds a bit	2
No	3
She doesn't know about it	4
Don't know	X
No partner	V

52d Does partner read/watch this material too?

Yes, frequently	3
Yes, occasionally	2
Never	1
Don't know	X

• If you can say more about your feelings about erotic material please write on separate sheet.

53 Do you use sex aids to increase sexual pleasure? If so, please write in which ones you use

---

Other lovers

54 Did you and your partner have other lovers before you met?

	You	Partner
No	1	1
Yes, please write in how many		
Don't know	–	X

• (Unmarried men, go to Q56a)

55a Did you have sex with your wife before marriage?

Yes	1
No	2

55b Have you or your wife had any other sexual relationships since marriage (including one-night stands)?

	You	Wife
No (Go to Q.55h)	1	1
Yes, please write in how many		
Don't know	–	X

55c What is the longest time such a relationship has continued?

	Your affair	Your wife's affair
A day/night	1	1
A few weeks	2	2
Up to a year	3	3
More than a year (write in how long)		
. . . .		
Don't know	X	X

55d Did the affair(s) have an effect on your marriage?

	Your affair	Wife's affair
No	1	1
Improved the sexual relationship	2	2
Worsened the sexual relationship	3	3
Improved the emotional relationship	4	4
Worsened the emotional relationship	5	5
Other	6	6
(Please write in)		

. . . .

55e How did this sexual experience of yours compare with your marriage?
RING ALL THAT APPLY

More satisfying	1	1
Less satisfying	2	2
More exciting	3	3
Less exciting	4	4
More emotionally rewarding	5	5
Less emotionally rewarding	6	6
Same as marriage	7	7
It was just for extra sex	8	8
Don't know	X	X
Other	V	V
(please write in)		

. . . .

55f What do you think led to your having an affair?

Poor sexual relationship with wife	1
Poor emotional relationship with wife	2
Boredom	3
Being away from home	4

Her having an affair 5

Opportunity presented itself 6

Other (please write in) X

....

55g Are you or your wife (as far as you know) having an affair now?

	You	Your wife
Yes	1	1
Off and on	2	2
No	3	3
Don't know/I'm suspicious	–	X

55h If you have never had an affair, do you rather wish you had?

Yes 1

No 2

Don't know 3

55i Why would/do you wish you had had an affair?

Just for a change 1

To see if I am good in bed with someone else 2

To find a more satisfying emotional relationship 3

To find a more satisfying sexual relationship 4

To prove I'm not too old 5

To prove I'm still attractive 6

Other X

• If you can tell us more about your feelings or experiences, please write on a separate sheet.

Problems

• For all men in a sexual relationship

56a Have you or your partner ever been troubled by sexual difficulties?

Yes, we are now 1

Yes, in the past 2

No 3

56b If YES, what was or is this difficulty?

Your lack of interest in sex 1

Partner's lack of interest 2

Your lack of orgasm 3

Your partner's lack of orgasm 4

Premature ejaculation 5

Impotence (loss of erection) 6

Connected with pregnancy, childbirth 7

Connected with menopause 8

Your infidelity 9

Partner's infidelity 10

Other (please write in) X

....

56c If YES, from whom did you seek help? RING ALL THAT APPLY in (a). Of those which *one* source gave most help (b)?

	(a) All sources	(b) Most help
GP, doctor	1	1
Marrige Guidance	2	2
Sex therapist	3	3
Books/Magazines	4	4
Family/friends	5	5
Other	X	X
No one	6	6

56d How well did this one main source help with solving the problem?

Very well, solved the problem 4

Reasonably well 3

Not very well 2

Not at all well 1

Sexual identity

57a Do you consider yourself mainly:

Heterosexual 1

| Bi-sexual | 2 |
| Homosexual | 3 |

57b Have you ever had a "romantic" friendship with another male?

| Yes | 1 |
| No (NOW GO TO Q59) | 2 |

If yes, how old were/are you?
Please write in age

57c Did/does this relationship include making love?

| Yes | 1 |
| No | 2 |

57d Are you having such a relationship now?

| Yes | 1 |
| No | 2 |

58 Have you been affected by the news about AIDS?

Yes, I've restricted my relationships	1
Yes, I've had a medical check-up	2
No, it doesn't bother me	3
No, I wasn't active/have only one partner anyway	4

59 Have you ever enjoyed dressing in women's clothes?

Yes, for a party/joke	1
Yes, in the past	2
Yes, I do now	3
No	4

• If either of these last two sections applies to you, please tell us more about your feelings on a separate sheet.

Infections

60a Have you ever had a sexually transmitted disease or infection?

| Yes | 1 |
| No GO TO Q61a | 2 |

60b If YES, what did you have?
Write in

. . . .

Losing a partner

• **For widowed, separated and divorced men**
61a How did you lose your partner?

She died	1
She left me	2
I left her	3
We decided to finish	4
Other	X

61b How easy has it been to find a new relationship?

Left to live with someone else	1
Fairly easy	2
Not very easy	3
Do not want a new relationship	4
Have not tried yet	5

• **For divorced/separated men only**
61c Have you seriously regretted parting?

Yes	1
Sometimes	2
No	3

61d If you had children do you still see them regularly?

Live with me	1
See them regularly	2
See them sometimes	3
No	4
No children	X

• If you can tell us more about your feelings and experiences of being widowed, divorced or separated, please write on a separate sheet.
• For all men

Family problems

62a Did any member of your family ever make sexual advances towards you?

Yes, a female	1
Yes, a male	2
No (NOW GO TO Q62e)	3

62b How old were you at the time?

Write in age ....

62c How old were they?

Write in age ....

62d What relation were they to you?

Write in

62e Have you ever made a sexual advance towards a member of your family?

Yes, a female	1
Yes, a male	2
(NOW GO TO Q63a)	

62f How old were you at the time?

Write in ....

62g How old were they?

Write in ....

62h What relation were they to you?

Write in ....

• If you feel able, please write on a separate sheet about these experiences.

63a Were you ever sexually assaulted or harassed in a way that could have upset you?

Yes, assaulted	1
Yes, harassed	2
No (NOW GO TO Q64	3

63b If YES, was the person who assaulted or harassed you male or female?

Male	1
Female	2

63c How old were you at the time?

Write in ....

63d How old were they (approximately)?

Write in ....

63e Did you tell anyone about your experience?

No	1
Yes	2

63f If YES, who did you tell?

Please write in ....

• If you feel able, please write on a separate sheet saying what happened to you.

Men and marriage

• **Unmarried Men**

64 How do you feel about marriage?

Expected to marry one day	1
Have definite plans to marry within two years	2
Want to live with partner but not bothered about marriage	3
My partner wants to but I do not want to get married	4
Not bothered about living with a partner or marriage	5
Never want to get married	6
Other	X
NOW GO TO Q66	

• **Married Men**

255

65a Does your wife understand you?

Yes, completely	1
Yes, reasonably well	2
Not very well	3
Not at all	4

65b Do you understand your wife?

Yes, completely	1
Yes, reasonably well	2
Not very well	3
Not at all	4

• Fathers/Children

66 If you have children, do you feel close to them?

Yes, I spend a lot of time with them	1
Yes, but I don't see enough of them because of my work	2
Yes, though I'm not that closely involved day-to-day	3
No, I find it difficult to relate to them	4
No, they're mainly my wife's concern	5
No, I'm separated from them now	6
Other (please write in)	
....	X
....	
I have no children (GO TO Q68)	7

67 Has having children had a good effect on your marriage?

Good effect	3
No change	2
Bad effect	1

• **Please tell us, on a separate sheet of paper, more about your marriage, your feelings as a father and how your children have affected your marriage and sex life.**

68 Here are some things people have said. PLEASE RING ALL THOSE YOU AGREE WITH.

Girls who have sex with several boys get a bad reputation	1
Boys who have sex with several girls are admired	2
Sex is best when you're young	3
Sex gets better as you get older	4
Sex isn't as important to women as it is to men	5
These days women are too demanding sexually	6
Sex is best with one partner you love	7
One-night stands are okay when the opportunity arises	8
You can have a happy marriage without an active sex life	9
Press, TV make too much of sex	10
Understanding each other's sexual needs is important in marriage	11
Sex isn't something men discuss with their friends	12
Women are more inhibited than men	13
Affairs are okay as long as they don't hurt anyone	14
Men don't know where they stand with women these days	15

General facts

69 How old are you?

Under 16	1
16 to 18	2
19 to 21	3
22 to 25	4
26 to 30	5
31 to 40	6
41 to 50	7
51 to 60	8
60 +	9

70 If married, how long have you been married?

Less than 5 years	1
5 to 10	2
11 to 20	3
21 to 30	4

More than 30   5
Not married   6

71 Have you been married before?

No   1
Yes   2

72 Do you have children living with you (excluding brothers and sisters)? RING ALL THAT APPLY

Child/children under 5   1
Child/children 6 to 16   2
Child/children 17 to 25   3
No children at home   4
I have no children   5

73 What job do you do?
(Write in) . . . .

74 What is your religion?
(Write in) . . . .

75 Does your wife/partner work?

Yes, full time   1
Yes, part time   2
No   3
No wife/partner   4

76 Where do you live?

North of England   1
Midlands, Wales   2
South of England   3
Scotland   4
Northern Ireland   5

■ **Please send questionnaire and attached notes to Men Survey, WOMAN Magazine, IPC Magazines Ltd, King's Reach Tower, London SE1 6BP.**

Index

innovations 8; frequency of affairs 10–11; and stresses of living up to their macho roles 11–12; and sexual harrassment in childhood 12; and conflicts resulting from image projection on to partner 24; and adolescent interest in penis size 26–7; search for sexual experience 29–39; motives which lead to loss of virginity 36–8; and their responsibility for the couple's sex life 46–7; and starting relationships 42–4; and frequency of love-making 51; views on partners' orgasms 86–7; and cross dressing 182–3; *see also*: fatherhood, homosexuality

Menopause, and frequency of sexual problems 200; and loss of female libido 203–4

Menstrual cycle, and loss of female libido 203

Men Too campaign 39, 152

Mixed schooling, asset for forming relationships 45

Non-specific urethritis 217

Obesity, and loss of libido 204
'Open Marriage' 132
Oral sex as means of reaching orgasm in women 84–5; female refusal of 93–4; and male fantasies 102, 105; and AIDS 219

Orgasm, percentage of women who fake 7–8, 86–7, 209; men's views on partners' orgasms 87; and sexual difficulties 200, 204–5

Partners, men's problems with meeting 44–5

Pelvic muscles, improving the tone of 208

Penis, as symbol of boy's maturity 27; worries about size of 27; women's refusal to touch 93; as ingredient in male fantasies 102, 110

Personality, as source of attraction to men 49–50

Petting, its role in helping to discover sexual responses 34–5; and sensate focus exercises 197

Physical attributes, as source of sexual attraction for men 49–50; and women's attraction to men 50

Pill, the, and orgasm problems in women 208

Pornography, the role of magazines in sex education 26–8; and male sexual lives 112–17; and feelings of inadequacy thrown up by 117

Post-natal depression, and loss of female sex drive 203

Pregnancy, and decline of love-making 147–8; and sexual problems between couples 191, 202–3

Premature ejaculation, adolescent experiences of 27–8, 83–4; and female orgasm 192; and sexual difficulties which arise 200; aggravated by infrequent love-making 209; common occurrence among young men 209; the need for a loving partner in curing 210; masturbation and control of orgasm for 210–11; exercises which help to prevent 211–12

Premenstrual syndrome 203

Promiscuity 41; nostalgic yearning for in faithful husbands 41; seen as useful experience 41–2

Prostitutes, men's interest in 2, 118; their role in fulfilling male fantasies 117–18; visited away from home by men 118–19; as a shortcut to gaining sexual experience 120

Puberty, fears thrown up by

and old age 216–17

Sexual skill, men's worries about lack of 90–2; orgasm as a sign of 90; women's expectations of men 92; in male fantasies 102–3; learnt through visiting prostitutes 120

Sexually transmitted diseases and infections 217–20

Sexual triggers, differences between men and women 74; visual 109; and fetishes 111–12

Sheath, the, and AIDS 220

Single sex schooling, as handicap to forming relationships 45

Smoking, and loss of libido 204

Soft porn, its useful function 114–15

Special clinics 218

Spontaneity, in love-making 76–7; teenagers as obstacle to 150–1

Stress, its effects on sexuality 75–6; and children 156–7; breathing exercises for 197–8

Syphilis, percentage of men who suffer from 217

Tension, as contributory factor to premature ejaculation 210; and delayed ejaculation 216

Thrush 217–18

Transsexuals 185

Transvestism 12; in male fantasy 102; and fetish clothing 112

Transvestites 182–9; and gays 185; and married relationships 186–9; relaxation from traditional male identity and 188–90

Tricomoniasis, percentage of men who suffer from 217

Trust, and infidelity 123–4

Under-age sex 31–2; and curiosity 36; contraceptive precautions taken 39

Understanding, how spouses assess each other 69

Unemployment, as strain on relationships 68

Vagina, thinning of walls leading to loss of female sex drive 203; and sexual intercourse 207; lubrication of 208

Vaginal intercourse from the rear 93; women's aversion to 96

Vasectomy, on completing family unit 152–3; resistance of male to 153; and remarriage 154

Venereal diseases, as obstacle to visiting prostitutes 118; most common 217; treatment of 217–20

Vibrators, as erotic sex aids 79; and orgasm 85, 207; and AIDS 219

Virginity, female expectations of losing 35–6; and marriage 125–6, 127

Virgins, as objects of fantasy 101

Women, their unwillingness to improve their sexual relationships 6; faking of orgasms by 7–8; and reactions to the first time they have intercourse 36–7; and men's approaches 42–4; and men's attractive qualities 50; resentment of being viewed as sex objects 50; decline of sex drive of 52–6; and making love when they do not feel loving 58–9; and erotica 79–81; and masturbation 87–8; and the role of sex within their relationships 89; and men's sexual skills 92; experimentation with sexual techniques by 94–7; reluctance to face up to their own sexual desires 97–8, 107; in sexual fantasies 106–7; and pornography 115–17; and men's self-confidence 190; and loss of libido 199–202